POPULAR

Finding Happiness and Success in a World
That Cares Too Much About the
Wrong Kinds of Relationships

MITCH PRINSTEIN

PENGUIN BOOKS

PENGUIN BOOKS
An imprint of Penguin Random House LLC
375 Hudson Street
New York, New York 10014
penguinrandomhouse.com

First published in the United States of America by Viking Penguin,
an imprint of Penguin Random House LLC, 2017
Published in Penguin Books 2018

ISBN 9780399563737 (hardcover)
ISBN 9780399563751 (paperback)
ISBN 9780399563744 (ebook)

Printed in the United States of America
1 3 5 7 9 10 8 6 4 2

Set in Adobe Garamond Pro
Designed by Cassandra Garruzzo

PENGUIN BOOKS

POPULAR

Mitch Prinstein is the John Van Seters Distinguished Professor of Psychology and Neuroscience and the director of clinical psychology at the University of North Carolina at Chapel Hill. He and his research have been featured in the *New York Times*, the *Wall Street Journal*, the *Los Angeles Times*, *U.S. News & World Report*, *Time*, *New York*, *Newsweek*, Reuters, *Family Circle*, *Real Simple*, National Public Radio, on CNN, and elsewhere.

www.mitchprinstein.com
@ mitchprinstein

Praise for *Popular*

"What makes *Popular* fascinating [is] the depth with which Prinstein explains the world in its perma-*Mean Girls* ways. . . . His book reads as a cheerful overview: an exploration of popularity as both a sociological phenomenon and a physiological one. Prinstein is a lively writer, and he illustrates his arguments with personal anecdotes [and] with evocative turns of phrase. . . . Here, via a professor who has studied popularity and its effects, is a book that is frustrated with all the pretense. *Popular*, as its title suggests, wants us to talk about its subject—forthrightly and, perhaps more to the point, unabashedly. It wants us to question the power that popularity—status, in particular—exerts on our lives. It offers insights that are bolstered by research; it also, more broadly, gives the concept of popularity a specific language, and an insistent voice."

—Megan Garber, *The Atlantic*

"If painful memories of what cafeteria table we ate lunch at can potentially stick with us well into adulthood, what does that say about our culture's relationship to this thing called 'popularity'? That's the question all over the syllabus of Mitch Prinstein's first book, *Popular*, a study of how we, all the way down to our DNA, want to be viewed positively by our peers but how we go about it—through being liked, needed, amusing, or feared—affects our own health and happiness and that of the society we model from it."

—Kevin Smokler, *Salon*

"In this fascinating scientific study, Prinstein argues that popularity in the early years is more predictive of adult success and happiness than natural intelligence or family background. The hitch is that there are two kinds of popularity. Those who pursue popularity based on status rather than likability, argues Prinstein, end up unhappy. Those who are actually likeable—who work well with others, and are kind and generous—enjoy the most success. Prinstein argues that as society becomes increasingly fixated on fame, power, and wealth, it is important to understand the dynamics of how they are achieved—and how they aren't."

—*The National Book Review*

"Like 'homecoming' and 'curfew,' 'popular' is one of those words we tend to associate with high school; and understandably so, since that's the era of our lives when social status can be a daily crushing concern. But even in the thick of those angsty teenage years, you probably sensed that there was much more to the whole popularity thing than just prom court and class geeks. Like all social dynamics, it's complicated. Just how complicated is terrain tackled in a new book on the subject. *Popular* digs into the data and research around what designates popularity, and why it's so definitional—not just in our early lives, but through adulthood."

—Elizabeth Kiefer, *Refinery29*

"You might associate being popular at the office with fake smiling, sucking up to bosses, and playing Machiavellian office politics. Those tactics may actually boost one kind of popularity—your status—but will likely hurt the other kind: your likability. . . . There is years of research that proves that people who are popular when it comes to social preference are more successful, but you can easily think of examples from your own life and popular culture. 'I mean, it's amazing how much we give the benefit of the doubt to likable people, and how much we are willing to do for them and how much we just naturally think good things about them,' Prinstein said."

—*Business Insider*

"Prinstein aims to understand popularity; to reconsider our society's obsession with status; and to show how our desire for social approval can influence our choices. . . . Prinstein concludes by talking about the role of parents in trying to help their children become popular. . . . This highly readable study, which successfully blends science and anecdotes, is strongly recommended for public libraries."

—*Library Journal* (starred review)

"An intriguing treatise on how popularity works . . . Prinstein observes that the course of one's popularity through life is firmly established way back in first grade. However, he notes repeatedly, there are two kinds of popularity: one is an indicator of status and thus highly variable, while the other is likability. . . . An eye-opening look at the ways of the world."

—*Kirkus Reviews*

"It turns out that there's more to popularity than status. This book didn't just capture my attention; it also helped me understand why I wasn't cool as a kid, why I'm still not today, and why I shouldn't care."

—Adam Grant, *New York Times* bestselling author of *Originals* and *Give and Take*

"Fascinating, well-researched, and accessible, *Popular* will make you rethink every social interaction you've had since high school, and help you find greater success and happiness. Read this book, and you'll never think about popularity the same way again."

—Susan Cain, *New York Times* bestselling author of *Quiet*

"Is popularity overrated? Maybe not—especially if it's the right kind of popularity that we seek. In Mitch Prinstein's fascinating book, you'll learn all about the benefits and pitfalls of being popular and how to make popularity work for you in business and in life."

—Daniel H. Pink, *New York Times* bestselling author of *To Sell Is Human* and *Drive*

"*Popular* will show you how to build strong emotional appeal that enables you to stand out from the crowd and wildly succeed. More than ever, this book's advice is important to parents, future leaders, and go-getters everywhere."

—Tim Sanders, *New York Times* bestselling author of *The Likeability Factor* and *Love Is the Killer App: How to Win Business and Influence Friends*

"*Popular* deserves to be! A delightful and insightful analysis of the longing that makes us human."

—Daniel Gilbert, *New York Times* bestselling author of *Stumbling on Happiness*

"Were you popular as a kid? You no doubt have an answer to that, but Mitch Prinstein wants you to have two: Status is one thing, and likability quite another. The origins of both types of popularity are the topic of this singularly fascinating, extraordinarily well-written book. I read it cover to cover and learned as much about the science as I did about myself."

—Angela Duckworth, *New York Times* bestselling author of *Grit: The Power of Passion and Perseverance*

"We have all imprinted emotionally on the vicissitudes of our teenage years. Mitch Prinstein, in this compelling, page-turner, tells us why and also how we can shed the skins of our adolescence. Even better he tells us how our children can achieve meaningful popularity. A science-based Dale Carnegie."

—Martin E. P. Seligman, *New York Times* bestselling author of *Authentic Happiness* and *Learned Optimism*

"Who does not want to be more popular? When is that quest not in our best interest? Read Mitch Prinstein's fascinating new book *Popular* to discover new views on this vitally important topic. *Popular* offers a brilliant take on a largely misunderstood subject, shedding light on the type of popularity we crave versus the type that will improve our lives. Based on provocative psychological research, *Popular* will change how you think about your adolescence, your current relationships today, and ultimately help you become more truly happy in the future."

—Phil Zimbardo, *New York Times* bestselling author of *The Lucifer Effect*

"People seek happiness in all aspects of their lives and the quest to be popular is among the most common pursuits. We seek status and gratification from the crowd we run with, the stuff we buy, the street where we live, and the size of our bank account. Mitch Prinstein's *Popular* is a perceptive and inspiring examination of how these aims pale in comparison to the power of genuine, lasting social relationships."

—Sonja Lyubomirsky, professor, University of California, Riverside, and author of *The How of Happiness*

"It is hard to imagine a more important book for the popularity-obsessed times in which we are living. Few scientists understand popularity better than Mitch Prinstein, and no one has ever done a better job of explaining its nature, origins, and significance."

—Laurence Steinberg, author of *Age of Opportunity* and *You and Your Adolescent*

To SAMARA and MAX,
and to TINA,
the loves of my life.

CONTENTS

AUTHOR'S NOTE

I began working on this book in earnest about two years prior to its completion. But in a very real sense, my research began many years earlier. Perhaps as early as kindergarten. I was always drawn to the study of peer relationships and to psychological science more broadly. I recall my attempt to create an IQ test, using tater tots, on the lunch line in grade school; I posited stage models of adjustment to midterms while in eighth grade; and as a teenager, I developed my own taxonomy for different levels of popularity. These examples offer two revelations relevant to this book. First, I was always, without question, a psychology nerd. And second, long before I imagined I would ever write *Popular*, I had been collecting vignettes from people who never knew that their experiences would become apt examples in the pages that follow. To protect their privacy, and as is customary in the field of clinical psychology, I have thus de-identified all stories herein by replacing names and trivial, nonessential details. To further ensure confidentiality for some particularly sensitive examples, the stories of Steve and Peggy represent composites based on several similar experiences.

A few stories have not been de-identified. My star student at Yale is indeed named Daniel Clemens. Studies and quotes from public figures and celebrities similarly have remained unmasked. Last, details included in stories about my own life also remain unchanged, to the best of my recollection.

INTRODUCTION

It was a cloudy day in the fall of 1977, and the sounds of screaming children on a grassy field in Old Bethpage, New York, could be heard from blocks away. Boys and girls at the elementary school were contracting a mysterious and highly contagious illness at an alarming rate. With every passing minute, another child became infected and then immediately was shunned by their peers—cast aside by those they had called their friends just moments earlier.

Tiny pairs of plaid-covered legs were running as fast as they could to safety. The school grounds were freckled with youth scattering in every direction. Some hid behind trees, in the bushes, or under a set of monkey bars as they caught their breath for a few moments, and then took off again. Most of the teachers were nowhere to be found. The few that were outside simply watched as the children succumbed to the outbreak one by one.

I grew up in that town, and I was on that playground on the day of the epidemic. I remember yelling and rushing away as kids all around me were stricken. Then, finally, came a sign of relief: Doug and Jill, two of my classmates, announced that they had discovered a vaccine, one so effective that it could instantly eradicate the infection in any afflicted child. The cure was swift and powerful, but relapse rates were high. Soon another boy, David, announced that he also had access to a cure, but few took him up on his offer. We only sought help from Doug and Jill. By the end of recess, the Great Cooties Epidemic of Old Bethpage had ended—at least until the following day, when it began all over again.

I remember that day vividly, and many like it. I remember how much fun it was to run and scream without a care in the world. But I recall even back then my curiosity about kids like Doug and Jill. What made them so much more fun than everyone else? Why were they always the center of our attention?

I also remember feeling sorry for David, and how difficult it was for him to attract much interest from others. Why was he so often ignored?

The difference, of course, was that Doug and Jill were popular and would remain popular for the rest of their lives. David was not, and on that day, his standing in the social hierarchy became very clear to him.

There are relatively few Dougs or Jills in the world. Those people who seem to effortlessly become popular wherever they go—there's maybe just one or two in every classroom, company, or social group. There are likewise a small number of Davids. Everyone knows exactly who they are. Even at an early point in childhood, and most certainly by first grade, the popularity hierarchy is already established.

Most of us landed somewhere in the middle, and on some playground somewhere in our past, our relationship with popularity was born. Either we knew we were admired and began to worry about maintaining our special influence over others, or we recognized that others were more popular than us and began to yearn for more attention and positive regard from our peers.

Our positions in the social hierarchy seemed so important back then, and for good reason: popularity is the most valuable and easily accessible currency available to youth. It is salient to us at every age. I can still remember unpopular kids in elementary school crying when they weren't allowed to cut in the lunch line, while the populars had unfettered access. As we got older, our popularity dictated which peers were potential friends and which were strictly off-limits. Our cliques' seating preferences in the cafeteria were even organized along the status hierarchy. By high school, we barely spoke to—much less dated—anyone who was less popular than us. We would spend hours listening to adults chiding us to focus on schoolwork or eat our vegetables, but none of that mattered as much as whether the cool kids at school would greet us the following day.

Now, as adults, our parents' advice makes a lot more sense. Our grades really *have* affected our educations, our careers, and our financial resources, just as our eating habits have had implications for our health and vitality decades later. But is the same true of popularity? Did any of it *really* matter?

The answer is yes: it did matter then, and it matters now. It may surprise you to learn just how much we *should* still care about popularity.

Our popularity affects us throughout our lives, often in ways we don't realize. At some level, you may already perceive that to be true. Isn't it interesting that when we remember who was most or least popular back in high school, it brings up some of the same emotions today as it did back then? The mere mention of the word "popular" has the power to transport us back to our teenage years. We graduate high school, make new friends, find stable romantic relationships, and get settled in our careers, but somewhere deep inside, we know that some part of who we are today—our self-esteem, our insecurities, our career successes or failures, and perhaps even our happiness—is still linked to how popular we were back then. There's something about our popularity in youth that seems to remain a part of who we are, as if it's become deeply embedded in our souls forever.

Maybe the enduring power of popularity can be traced to the fact that those same dynamics are still a part of our daily lives. It may look a little different today as compared to our youth, but we still encounter most and least popular people in every office, every community group, every day on social media, and in every neighborhood. The factors that make adults popular are not much different from what seemed to matter back in school.

We may also still care about popularity because whether we want to admit it or not, most of us never overcame our desire to become more popular, and those old yearnings still have lasting effects today—not just on our own lives, but on attributes our society most values. In fact, this may be truer now than at any previous point in our history. Networked society offers the possibility of an interminable adolescence where, as never before, we can shine a light on those who are popular, create ways to emulate and interact with these individuals, and even raise our own level of popularity through new creative platforms that allow any average person a chance to become the most popular, even if only briefly. Our private lives are affected by these yearnings as well. Our unspoken desire to be popular changes the decisions we make, the kinds of relationships we form, and even how we raise our children, usually in ways we are not even aware of. If we're not careful, these yearnings can ultimately make us very unhappy.

Popularity is a topic that I and other social scientists have been interested in for decades, and the results from thousands of research studies have revealed a great deal about its origins and its significance in any number of social interactions. What we've learned is that popularity is something of a paradox: it is fundamental to human nature to desire to be more popular, but that doesn't mean that being popular is always good for us.

At around the same time that I was scurrying across the playground in Old Bethpage, something very interesting was taking place in the field of psychology. Until then the discipline had been dominated by Freudian-inspired notions of the id, the superego, and even unconscious libidinal urges. Most roads toward explaining our feelings and behavior eventually led to the mother and the ways that her child-rearing shaped personalities.

But in the 1950s through the 1970s, with a large number of veterans from World War II, Korea, and Vietnam needing psychological treatment, the US government began to fund mental health initiatives as never before. The National Institute of Mental Health was created, the Veterans Affairs system was built, departments of psychology were established at universities all across the country, and a far more thorough edition of the *Diagnostic and Statistical Manual of Mental Disorders* (*DSM*) was developed, based on scientific research.

Modern-day psychology was born, and with it came a surge in rigorous psychological science.

Much of the research sponsored at the time was oriented toward studies conducted to predict why some soldiers served honorably while others were dishonorably discharged, costing the government millions and endangering military missions. Psychologists examined subjects' combat experience, but also their IQs, school achievement, socioeconomic status, parent-child relationships, psychological symptoms, and histories of aggression. What they discovered was completely unexpected: one of the strongest predictors of soldiers' functioning in the military was how popular they were in primary school. In fact, childhood popularity predicted soldiers' behavior even after accounting for every other factor that investigators considered.

Within a decade or two, a number of other studies in nonmilitary populations yielded similar results about the power of popularity. More than childhood intellect, family background, prior psychological symptoms, and maternal relationships, popularity predicts how happy we grow up to be. Do we enjoy or dread leaving for work each morning? Are we in relationships that are fulfilling or conflicted? Do we regard parenting as a burden or a pleasure? Are we making important contributions in our lives? Do we feel as if we're valued members of society? The answers to these questions can all be traced back to the playgrounds of our youth.

A worldwide study conducted in my own research lab revealed that adults who have memories of being popular in childhood are the most likely to report that their marriages are happier, their work relationships are stronger, and they believe they are flourishing as members of society. People who recall unpopular childhood experiences report just the opposite.

Popular children grow up to have greater academic success and stronger interpersonal relationships, and to make more money in their jobs years later, while those who were not popular are at much greater risk for substance abuse, obesity, anxiety, depression, problems at work, criminal behavior, injury, illness, and even suicide. We now also understand that popularity changes the wiring of our brains in ways that affect our social perceptions, our emotions, and how our bodies respond to stress. As discussed in this book, our experiences with popularity can even alter our DNA.

Popular will examine how popularity actually affects us today—even when we don't realize it. We'll consider why popularity mattered among our ancestors tens of thousands of years ago and how it functions in the twenty-first century. Along the way we'll travel from the hallways of Google to our own homes and even deep down into the structures of our brains and our individual cells. By the time you finish, you may be surprised to learn just how strong a force popularity remains in our lives.

But it is not always the *most* popular people who are happier. That's because there is, in fact, more than one type of popularity. Anyone who's ever been to high school will recall that some of the most popular teens—the jocks, the cheerleaders, the "it" boy and girl—actually were hated by many. If that seems like a contradiction, it reflects the fact that most of the people high in one type of popularity are actually low in the other. The first type of popularity is a reflection of *status*—whether someone is well known, widely emulated, and able to bend others to his or her will. In adolescence, we called these kids "cool," but research suggests that they may be at high risk for a number of problems later in life. The other type of popularity is *likability*. It captures those we feel close to and trust, and the people who make us happy when we spend time with them. Of course, status and likability aren't only relevant in high school—they are central to the adult social hierarchy as well. But failing to recognize the distinction between these very different types of popularity, many spend their lives searching for the wrong one.

I wrote *Popular* with the goal of helping readers understand this timely and universal subject—one that touches all of us, and touches us deeply—and to offer insights that can help them in their daily lives in at least five ways. First, I hope to reach everyone who ever had a moment in school when they felt anxious, disappointed, or insecure about their level of popularity. I want this book to offer a framework to understand and reconsider those experiences, and to explain that the type of popularity that they so desperately felt they lacked may not have been all that it seemed.

Second, I hope *Popular* will promote a reconsideration of our culture's current relationship with popularity. Society has become fixated on status and all of its trappings—fame, power, wealth, and celebrity—even though research suggests that this is exactly what we should be avoiding if we want to foster a culture of kindness and contentment. This is concerning for all of us, but perhaps especially for today's youth who are being raised in a society that values status in new and potentially dangerous ways.

Third, I hope this book will help readers consider more carefully some of the choices they make in their own lives every day. How often do we make decisions that we feel will help us gain power and influence without realizing that we are inadvertently undermining our own true chances for happiness? How much energy do we waste investing in image management because of our misperceptions about how best to achieve social approval? How much is our lingering desire to be popular affecting our behavior without our even realizing it?

Fourth, I hope *Popular* offers parents the information they need to understand whether they want their children to become popular at all, and which kind of popularity is most likely to help them in the future. In a world where bullying and ostracism have become serious public health concerns, it is critical for caregivers and teachers to understand which youth will become bullies, who is most likely to be a victim, and what research findings tell us about how to best raise children today.

Last, I hope that *Popular* will help all readers who have been unknowingly reliving their high school years, repeating a pattern of interpersonal experiences that began with their concerns about popularity years ago. Too often, those who were unpopular continue to feel rejected throughout their lives, at home, at work, and even with loved ones. Those who were popular also are at risk for repeating the same patterns that may have worked for them then, but are not making them happy anymore. The more we understand about popularity and how it affects us throughout our lives, the more likely we are to break the cycle of interpersonal experiences that began back in school. And the better chance we have for meaningful, satisfying, and rewarding interpersonal relationships today.

PART I

The Types of Popularity That Affect Us Today

CHAPTER 1

The Adult Playground

Where Popularity Still Matters

> Popularity gets you nowhere after high school; matter of fact, it's the last thing on your mind.
>
> —*Anonymous*

On a Tuesday evening in October, about two hours outside of Chicago, a woman wearing a short skirt attempted to sit gracefully on a chair made for a small child. That woman was Paula, a friend of mine from college. When I first met her, Paula had brown, tousled hair and recently had lost some significant weight. Today, she is an ER nurse. She is married, has two sons, and has become a bit of a fashionista—always buying new shoes and trendy handbags. Nevertheless, she usually still thinks of herself as "that pudgy girl with the sloppy hair," and on that Tuesday evening, she texted me just before the start of the school board meeting at her son's middle school. "It's all coming back to me while I sit here. The teasing, the anxiety, the homework. I feel like someone may shoot a spitball at any moment. :)"

Paula was at the meeting to lobby for funds that would revitalize a gifted program she desperately wanted for her children. After six months of trying without any progress, she was losing patience. She'd written a coherent proposal, developed a budget, gathered data from comparable programs in nearby districts, and even asked a few teachers to testify on behalf of her idea.

"If we have a better gifted program, fewer parents will send their children to the local private school," she argued. "The retention of gifted children in the school system will lead to better test scores and a return to the levels of state funding we had three years ago. The program will essentially pay for itself." But the previous month, the board had allocated funds for a faculty lounge in the same school instead.

I checked in with Paula a few days later to see how her meeting had gone. She told me that just before it started, a woman named Susan showed up.

"She walks in, probably just to show off another new Birkin bag, and looks around the room like we're supposed to throw roses at her feet or something," Paula said.

Susan's daughter was in the same class as Paula's son. It was Susan's first appearance at a school board meeting. Several of the other parents in the room saw her and waved enthusiastically. One woman immediately ran over to give her a hug and cried, "Oh my goodness, it has been so long. We have to catch up!"

"Ugh, I got so annoyed when I saw how everyone kisses up to Susan," Paula told me. "But I gave her a hug, too."

The meeting started, and the board president began by soliciting ideas for how to help the school develop a higher profile within the district. A few minutes into the discussion, Susan stood up and addressed the room.

"I agree that we need to think about how to make our school stand out. I was visiting my sister last week in Michigan, and a few kids from the gifted program at her kid's middle school had just won a science tournament. The next thing you know, the school was in the paper, and the drug company that sponsored the tournament gave the school a big donation. Why don't we do that here? Do we even have a gifted program?"

Within thirty minutes, the board voted to approve additional funding for the program. Paula was both elated and furious—it was great news for her son, but in a few minutes, Susan had achieved what Paula hadn't been able to do in six months. Susan hadn't offered any new arguments or presented any research on school funding trends. But somehow, her ideas got traction.

"Everyone is always just so excited to do whatever Susan wants," Paula complained. "Sometimes I can't stand it."

Joe is a professor at a well-known university. He's been on staff for ten years, but was not supposed to be next in line for a promotion. His more senior colleague, Franklin, has been in the same position three years longer and has a more impressive record of scientific publications. In just the past year, Franklin obtained a prestigious grant to support his work, and a top journal featured one of his papers as its lead article, suggesting that his research is making a very important impact in the field.

Joe has also been publishing, but in journals of much lesser quality, and he has never been awarded a grant.

Nevertheless, everyone loves Joe. He always has something amusing to offer at faculty meetings. He regularly makes the rounds up and down the halls of his department, having energetic doorway conversations, and he's always open-minded to whatever opinions are expressed when department politics emerge. People reflexively smile when they see him.

That is not the case with Franklin, though. In fact, he is so contentious that his very name has become an adjective in the department, as in: "Let's add this to the consent agenda, so no one gets all *Franklin* about it."

At one faculty meeting, the agenda included a discussion about which of two courses should be added to the requirements for a second undergraduate major offered by the department. A committee that had spent the past three months developing the proposal outlined the pros and cons for each of the course selections, and then asked for comments and questions. As Franklin's hand launched up, the rest of the faculty shifted in their chairs and avoided eye contact with him.

"I don't know why we want a second major at all," he began. "I've been saying for years that this is a huge waste of time that puts a burden on our staff, and also on us. I spent three hours last week meeting with students about this, and I don't even know why we have it. One major is enough for our department!"

Groans could be heard all around the room. Many of the faculty lowered their heads, ostensibly to check something on their phones. After a moment of uncomfortable silence, the committee chair opened the discussion to other comments. A few people praised the committee for its work and expressed a clear rationale for which course should complete the major requirements. A consensus quickly became evident, with enthusiastic nodding around the room.

But Franklin was not convinced. "Look, I think this is a huge mistake," he said, interrupting the next speaker. "You are all going to wish you had stopped this second major when you had the chance," at which he defiantly picked up his iPad and tuned out for the rest of the meeting.

Two weeks later, a senior professorship opened just above the level occupied by both Franklin and Joe. It was Joe who received the promotion.

Jennifer is a successful statistician who works at a federally funded research center that is testing new cancer drugs. By age thirty-five, she already had become the director of her unit at the institute and the president of a national professional society for statisticians, and she had even been invited to the White House as a member of an expert panel. She also is deeply in love with her wife of fifteen years, an oncologist.

But Jennifer is not happy. In fact, on many days she's pretty down on herself. Even though she knows she is doing well professionally, she just can't shake the feeling that she is somehow inferior to her colleagues. The same despondency affects her relationships. Her wife often tells her how much she loves her, but Jennifer feels as if she is incessantly being judged and criticized. Even with friends or coworkers, she senses that everyone has made plans but excluded her. *Everyone is just so arrogant*, she would think. *They're no better than me.*

So, when Jennifer was recruited to lead a team on a new high-profile grant in North Carolina's Research Triangle, she was more than happy to move. She chose a little neighborhood in Chapel Hill called Southern Village. Ever the statistician, she loved how this community had been developed based on modern urban planning research. The constellation of apartments, town houses, and single-family homes, which collectively encircled an old-fashioned town square, was designed to foster community engagement and social interaction. The urban planning principles seemed to work—the town square indeed became a hub of almost utopian friendly exchange, like a scene from *The Truman Show.* On the first Wednesday of each month, the neighborhood sponsored a dog parade. On Friday evenings, the community assembled on the green in the center of the square to watch movies and share a picnic dinner. *This is just the place to feel at home*, Jennifer thought.

But after six years there, not much had changed for her. Jennifer still listened to her coworkers make happy-hour plans, but she was not invited. When she went to the green on movie nights, she resented that everyone who came by talked more to her wife than to her. And she was particularly annoyed every morning by the sight of the neighbors who would stand at the foot of her driveway chatting with one another. "I don't know what I ever did to them," she once told me, "but they never ask me to go running, or to yoga, or anything—even if I am standing right next to them!"

Alan is forty-six years old and has a weakness for pie. He has a very nice office in downtown Sunnyville but he hadn't been at his desk all week. Instead, he sat in the last booth at the local diner to catch the view from the huge bay window right next to his table. On a clear day, this was an ideal spot to see the whole shopping district downtown, and on this particular afternoon, he had covered not only his table but the one next to it with file folders, Post-its, and empty cups of coffee strategically placed on top of papers.

No one at Sunnyville Diner seemed to mind. One of the waitresses, Lateesha, waved at him when she began her shift.

"The day hasn't really begun until I see you!" Alan called out. Lateesha smiled while playfully holding a dish towel over her face.

When Donna, the hostess who had recently separated from her husband, came to his table, he held her hand in both of his and asked, "How are you holding up?"

Even the chef gave him a nod and a smile as he walked to the front of the diner. "Best pie yet!" Alan told him with his mouth full.

At about 5 p.m., Alan was greeted by Mike, a colleague from his former real estate development firm.

"Hey, looks like you've moved in," Mike joked. "Working on a pitch?"

"Yup, north side of town. Ten acres, mixed-use development, plus a new hotel," Alan replied, pointing to the coffee cup at the edge of the table. As Mike questioned him about the project, Alan used a laser pointer to trace the perimeter of the property, the stream that would cut through it, and the new set of apartments, marked by a sugar dispenser in the middle of the table.

Mike hadn't blinked in at least a minute as he listened to Alan's plan and finally shook his head. "You have no fear, man. The north side? Really? Here in Sunnyville? You know they turned us down when we pitched there last year. 'This generation will never see development in that part of town,' they told us. Good luck, you're going to need it!"

Alan's presentation to the town council lasted over three hours. And for most of it, things did not look good. Just fifteen minutes into his presentation, two council members interrupted him to say that they were simply not going to be able to support the project.

"This isn't a sound investment for Sunnyville," one of them asserted. "The implications for the traffic and road repair alone are far too substantial to seriously consider any type of mixed-use development in that part of town."

But Alan persisted, armed with graphs, town records from the archives, and the testimony of experts from nearby properties he had developed who were ready to comment on his successful track record. But mostly, Alan had a patient, nondefensive, and unwaveringly enthusiastic demeanor as he calmly described every detail of the planned development. When his estimate of the project's finances was disputed, he smiled, took a step back, and walked his inquisitor through his figures. When the town council members challenged his ideas for possible commercial uses of the property, Alan was firm, but open-minded. When they questioned his proposed timeline, he made a joke and agreed with their assessment.

By 9 p.m., the council members were ready to allow questions from the town's residents in attendance. One spoke critically of the proposal and also shouted an insult directly at Alan. He took it in stride, even self-effacingly. When other citizens praised him, he was modest, and when they embarrassed themselves with incomprehensible questions, he rescued their dignity. Finally, after thirty minutes of discussion, it was time for a vote.

The proposal passed unanimously. The onlookers applauded as Alan closed the biggest deal of his career. Many were excited about the changes coming to their town. But as some shook his hand to congratulate him, it almost seemed as if they were rooting more for Alan than the proposal itself.

After everyone left, Alan remained in his chair for a few moments, in stunned disbelief. Mike had witnessed the entire meeting and now walked over to offer his own congratulations.

"I am so glad I pulled those old town records," Alan said. "I think that may be what got them."

Mike shook his head and patted his friend on the back. "It wasn't the records," he said. "It wasn't the experts, and it wasn't even the breaks you offered them. We did all of that last year, and they never agreed to a single proposal. It was *you*, man. They didn't vote for the project, they voted for *you*."

Everyone knows a story like these. Some of our coworkers and neighbors are consistently successful, and not for the reasons we might expect, while others don't get their way no matter how hard they try. We also all have peers who feel excluded in every context, while others have mysterious confidence and consistent social success. We may think we left the mores of high school behind us, but popularity is still very much a part of the adult playground. It is that one factor that no one really talks about, yet it makes a big difference in our lives. Popularity dynamics affect our careers, our success in meeting our goals, our personal and professional relationships, and ultimately our happiness.

The ongoing importance of popularity in adulthood was a surprise even to me, until I learned a lesson from my own students.

In August 2001, something strange was taking place on the campus of Yale University. I had recently been hired as a professor in the department of psychology, and I was about to give my first lecture for a course I had developed about popularity among children and adolescents. Yale didn't have a preregistration system, so anyone who showed up the first day of class was welcome to enroll. The course had been assigned a small classroom on the central campus—about thirty-five students were expected to attend.

But as I approached the building, I noticed a crowd had gathered at the south side of the lecture hall. I assumed a fire drill was being conducted, so I hung around for a while and started to chat with the students. But I soon realized that no alarm had been sounded—they were waiting for my class. All of them!

I made my way through the throng outside the building, standing wall to wall down the hallway, and stretching up the entire staircase until I finally reached the tiny classroom. The whole way I was still questioning: was everyone really there to learn about popularity? By the next session, the registrar reassigned the course to the Yale Law School auditorium, the largest available space on campus, and by the end of the first week, one out of every ten undergraduates had enrolled—over 550 students. During the course of the semester, I was contacted by university administrators, scientific advisors for national youth organizations, and ABC News. The word was out: "popularity" was popular. But why?

At first, most people reacted to the huge enrollment in the class in similar ways. More than one of my colleagues said to me something along the lines of, "Of course it's crowded—this is Yale. These are the students who were terrorized by high school bullies, and they are all in your class to learn better social skills."

But it turned out that this explanation wasn't true at all. The class had a huge range of students. Certainly, some had been rejected as kids, but others were extremely popular. Some were the children of American senators and national advisors; others were top collegiate athletes. One student was a movie star, a few were musical prodigies who had already traveled the world, and others were summer aides at the White House. The group included future doctors and lawyers, scientists and politicians, economists and Fortune 500 CEOs. One became a bestselling author and another a Rhodes Scholar.

"What are you all doing here?" I asked the students as the semester progressed.

They told me that although they had long since departed the playground and the school cafeteria, they never left the world where popularity matters. During their summer internships, they saw it continue to play out in boardrooms, operating rooms, and classrooms. The basketball players witnessed it on the court, and the legal aides told me how it made a difference on juries. Even congressional interns perceived how popularity affected our government's legislative decisions. But mostly, they saw it in themselves—knowing that whatever degree of popularity they enjoyed or endured as kids would probably come back to haunt them again. In a very real manner, our experiences with popularity are always occupying our minds. We never really left high school at all.

Years later, I was curious to learn whether popularity still mattered in the adult lives of my students in that first popularity course I taught back in New Haven. I knew just who to call.

Even with hundreds of students in the class, Daniel Clemens

stood out as the one everyone knew, respected, and liked. Just mentioning his name seemed to bring a smile to the face of any professor or student on campus. A nationally ranked All-American tennis player and star student in high school, he had arrived on campus as brilliant as everyone else at Yale. But there was something that made him distinctive even in this impressive group. He was unusually kind, extremely respectful, always positive and energetic, and yet among his peers he was also regarded as incomparably cool. He was the most popular student in my popularity class. By the end of his senior year, he was awarded a Rhodes Scholarship.

Today Daniel is in his thirties, and he's turned out exactly as you might have expected—caring, energetic, modest, and likable. In the past decade or so, Daniel has founded and sold several multimillion-dollar businesses. If you have ever used Google Docs, Daniel is one of the people you can thank, as his was one of the companies that helped create the live-collaboration capability of the application. After years working on strategic initiatives at Google, he's now a sought-after investor and board contributor to many of the most successful CEOs and entrepreneurs around the globe. He's also a frequent keynote speaker at business schools and an advisor to entrepreneurs throughout the country, and he counts former US presidents, members of Congress, prime ministers, and CEOs of some of the most well-known global brands like Google and Apple as his close personal friends.

Daniel believes that popularity is very much a part of the adult playground, affecting the innovation and productivity of corporations all over the world. He perceives something very adolescent in the workplace that reminds him of my class almost every day, he tells me. It's a dynamic that plays out in every meeting and influences how every decision is made.

"Here's what happens," Daniel explains. "After a meeting, everyone gets together in twos and threes around the watercooler, and then you hear what people *really* thought. And it's all the stuff that didn't get talked about at the meeting at all. I'm always amazed at the big difference, and I wonder, why the delta?"

Daniel's theory is that efficient decision-making in business has become hampered by popularity, or rather the fear of losing it. "People don't want to lose status or have people dislike them," he says. "There's a lot of norming in a company, people going with the herd, following others. People are afraid to say what they think. I find it really interesting how much we overestimate how secure those around us are, and how much this still plays out for people in their thirties, forties, and fifties. They still need that validation from their peers. They really want people to like them, and when they think others don't, it stings them for days, or months."

Daniel also believes that popularity has a lot to do with our happiness. "We did a study at Google," he recalled. The results boiled down to two findings. More than raises, or promotions, or perks, there were two things that predicted who was happy and who was not. One had to do with the frequency of constructive feedback employees got from their managers. But the second was simply how much people felt they had someone—anyone—who liked them. "It's the small things, the human things, that make organizations flourish and make people happy," Daniel says.

"It's funny," he explains. "We teach writing and arithmetic. We expect folks to do very well in science and reading from a very early age. But the ability to establish great relationships with others seems to be every bit as important to success if not more, yet it's not taught in a formal way. We usually learn about relationships by trial and error—how to get along with peers and how to be popular. For those who can do it, great. But for others, it is a lifetime of struggling, never understanding why their peers have issues with them."

Popularity is a part of life that we experience every day, in every type of social situation. And the way that we experience popularity in one context tends to be related to the way we connect to others in all parts of our lives.

But there's a catch: most people don't realize that there are two different types of popularity—one that helps us, and one that can potentially harm us, leaving us stranded in adolescence. And ever since high school, we have never come to terms with which kind we want.

CHAPTER 2

Boorish Bully or Likable Leader

There's More Than One Type of Popularity

It was the early 1840s, and the doctors of General Hospital in Vienna were worried. For reasons no one could understand, hundreds of women who delivered babies at the hospital were developing an extremely high fever and dying. The fever occurred most often among new mothers on an obstetrics unit staffed by physicians. Those who gave birth on a second unit, run by midwives, had much better rates of survival.

The doctors carefully analyzed both units, taking note of the differences in doctors' and midwives' delivery practices, the units' atmospheres, and even the women's physical positions during labor. They systematically tested one hypothesis after another to account for the deaths, but they could not identify a determinate factor. Mothers on the doctors' unit continued to develop what was referred to as a "puerperal fever" and die. Soon pregnant women in Vienna pleaded to be admitted to the midwives' unit. Some even chose to give birth on the city streets. Remarkably, even those who delivered outside the hospital were more likely to survive than those under medical care.

Then a young physician named Ignaz Semmelweis began working at General Hospital. Semmelweis was a trainee from a wealthy family, and his colleagues quickly selected him as chief resident. Over time he earned respect from his associates and supervisors for his medical knowledge, his upper-class background, and his medical proficiency. His reputation spread throughout the entire city, and people wanted to meet him just to hear his opinions.

Semmelweis soon developed a theory to explain the mysterious deaths. He observed that the doctors who worked on the obstetrics unit also performed autopsies. Many of these were conducted on individuals who had died of puerperal fever, after which the attending physicians would proceed immediately to the obstetrics unit. Semmelweis hypothesized that puerperal fever in the new mothers was caused by "cadaver particles" that somehow spread the disease from the dead bodies.

He suggested that his colleagues routinely wash their hands with an antiseptic solution following each autopsy to reduce contagion to women on the obstetrics unit. He also urged doctors to disinfect all medical instruments that had been used in autopsies. In essence, Semmelweis developed a theory of infection by germs that guides medical practice to this day.

His suggestions worked. The mortality rate among the mothers on the physicians' unit fell to around 1 percent, the same rate as the midwives'. Dr. Semmelweis was hailed as a hero, but despite all his fame and status, medical historians report that people did not especially like him. Howard Markel, a distinguished professor and director of the Center for the History of Medicine at the University of Michigan, reports that Semmelweis frequently "hurled outrageously rude insults to some of the hospital's most powerful doctors who deigned to question his ideas." He "publicly berated people who disagreed with him," according to another account, and loudly branded those who challenged his ideas "murderers."

His supporters pleaded with him over many years to publish his findings, so others could review and promote his practices. Yet he refused, stating that his discoveries were "self-evident," and that there was no need to defend them to those who were "ignorant." When he did eventually agree to publication, after a decade of resistance, the piece was filled with hostile rants that personally attacked his critics, their intelligence, and their character. He stated that his peers did "not even understand the limited truth," dismissing them as "wretched observers" of medical conditions, and judged that Germans' disagreement with his principles rendered "the obstetrical training in Berlin worthless."

Dr. Semmelweis had high status and influence. He was well respected, revered, and powerful. He was popular. But he was also a bully, and thus loathed by many of his peers.

One hundred fifty years later, three girls walked into the library of a small suburban high school in southern Connecticut. All had blond hair and all were dressed impeccably, if not a little provocatively for fifteen-year-olds on a school day—tiny T-shirts, short skirts, and matching sneakers with bulky pink socks. Their arrival was noticed by just about everyone.

The tallest girl, Alexandra, entered the library first, while her two friends followed dutifully a few paces behind. Alexandra moved with the confidence of a star, without a trace of adolescent awkwardness. The aisle between the study carrels was her runway, and she walked it erect with long strides and a gaze fixed toward nothing specific ahead. When one of her friends asked her a question, she responded without turning to face her. Occasionally she offered a passing glance or wave to a classmate, who stared up at her with wonder.

Alexandra had come to the library to participate in a research study on popularity conducted by my lab. My assistants stood in the doorway of a private room, waiting for a dozen or so participants, a few of whom were already working diligently at a large conference table. Before my assistants could ask for her name, she entered the room and announced, "I'm Alexandra Cort." The other students looked up immediately.

Alexandra's friends, meanwhile, seated themselves on chairs outside the private room, staring aimlessly at the stacks around them. When my assistants informed them that they were free to leave, one replied, "No, we'll stay here. We're here with Alexandra Cort."

"Yeah," the other boasted. "We're her best friends."

"She will be here all period," an assistant pointed out. "Don't you want to get some lunch?"

"No, we want to wait for her. We'll skip lunch."

"Actually," the assistant explained, "it's important for our study that the participants are not distracted. Would you mind waiting for your friend in the cafeteria?"

Rolling their eyes, the girls slid their chairs some twenty feet away from the room, sat down again, and began to whisper to each other.

Our data eventually revealed that Alexandra was the most popular girl in the tenth grade. In fact, she was the first person selected by almost every single participant when we asked them to name the most popular kids in their school.

But she also was one of the most despised. About 65 percent of her classmates—by far more than anyone else in her grade—picked Alexandra as the student who was most likely to gossip about others, use her friendships as a way of being mean, give others the "silent treatment," and say hurtful things behind others' backs. About half of her classmates identified her as one of the students they liked least.

Even her friends obediently waiting for her to complete her participation in our study were overheard whispering about her. "Alex is so conceited," one remarked. "I know," replied the other. "Like, I don't even want to go with her to the mall this weekend."

Anyone who is popular is bound to be disliked.

—*Yogi Berra*

How can someone be popular when they are not even liked? The very idea seems like a contradiction.

Yet when we think about "popularity," we tend to immediately think of people who have an outsized reputation—people like Ignaz Semmelweis and Alexandra Cort. Anyone who has been to high school remembers exactly who the popular types were: the cheerleaders, the athletes, the wealthy kids, or those whose parents held high-profile positions in the community. Even as we disliked them, we grudgingly emulated them. In my high school, no one would be caught dead without an Ocean Pacific T-shirt and everyone talked about the latest Duran Duran video, because those were exactly the things the popular students told us were cool. But in most cases, these kids weren't even our friends.

If we consider someone we don't like as being popular, then what does "popularity" really mean?

This is a surprisingly difficult question to answer. Bill Bukowski, a Canadian psychologist who has studied popularity among youth for decades, traces the etymology of the word "popular" to the Middle French (*populier*) and Latin (*popularis*), which originally referred to ideas or politicians that were "of the people." A "popular movement" was thus one that rose from among the masses, rather than from their leaders. By the sixteenth century, the word "popular" was adopted by the English to refer to prices or resources that were "accessible to commoners," such as the "popular press." But in the past four hundred years, the term "popular" began to blend the concept of plurality with the idea of something valued and preferred. By the seventeenth century, "popular" referred to anything widely adopted but also "well regarded." Today, of course, this usage is reflected in the ubiquitous online lists that have co-opted the phrase "most popular" to rank anything and everything—baby names, vacation destinations, dog breeds, diets, YouTube videos, stocks, ice-cream flavors, and so on. There are even lists for the most popular Nobel Prize Laureates, sexual fetishes, Catholic saints, cat names—it's endless. I assume that the criteria for what makes sexual fetishes and Catholic saints most "popular" differ considerably. So what does "popularity" really mean?

This contemporary notion of "popularity" as anything or anyone that is favorably viewed by many others is more complex than it appears, because there are different ways that we may feel approvingly toward something. Even in the 1600s, popularity could refer to that which was "well liked," "admired," or "desired," which all express different sentiments. Consequently, there are various kinds of popularity that are now studied in the social sciences.

When we remember what "popular" meant in high school, we are invoking the type of popularity that social scientists believe more accurately reflects *status*. Status is not a measure of how well liked a person is, but rather of his or her dominance, visibility, power, and influence. Interestingly, status does not become salient to us until we reach adolescence, but it tends to establish itself as a meaningful kind of popularity for the rest of our lives.

A second type of popularity reflects *likability*. Based on findings from social science, it is this type of popularity that we should genuinely care about. Even very young children understand likability. Research shows that as early as the age of four, children can report exactly who their most popular peers are and can do so reliably. But these popular toddlers are not necessarily powerful, dominant, or highly visible. They are, rather, the kids that everyone likes the most. Likability continues to be relevant to us throughout our lives and has been shown to be the most powerful kind of popularity there is.

In 1982, John Coie, a psychologist at Duke University, conducted a now-seminal series of experimental studies that began by giving children a list of all of their classmates' names and asking them two simple questions:

"Who do you like the most?"

"Who do you like the least?"

Psychologists refer to this procedure as a "sociometric assessment." For each of these questions, participants can nominate as many people on the list as they wish.

Coie and his then-assistants, Ken Dodge and Heide Coppotelli, asked over five hundred children to answer those two questions. The results were interesting for a number of reasons. First, Coie found that children who were very well liked might also be just as strongly disliked. In fact, likability and dislikability are independent measures of regard. We can be both liked and disliked at the same time. We can also be neither.

Second, the scientists found that children differed greatly in the number of times they were named at all, regardless of which question was being asked. Some children seemed to be especially visible in their classrooms—they were cited often when their peers were asked to name the kids they liked *or* disliked. Other children were just the opposite: it was as if their classmates barely knew they were there.

This study was not the first time researchers had asked children these questions. But Coie and his team were the first to use the answers to create five categories, or "sociometric groups," that are the foundation for how we now think about the different faces of popularity. Their results have been replicated in hundreds of research studies among children and adults all over the world.

Coie's groupings can be pictured in a two-by-two matrix. "Likability" is plotted on the vertical axis, while "dislikability" is plotted horizontally. The more times a child is picked as "liked the most," the higher his or her name would appear. The more times a child is nominated as "most disliked," the farther to the right his or her name would go.

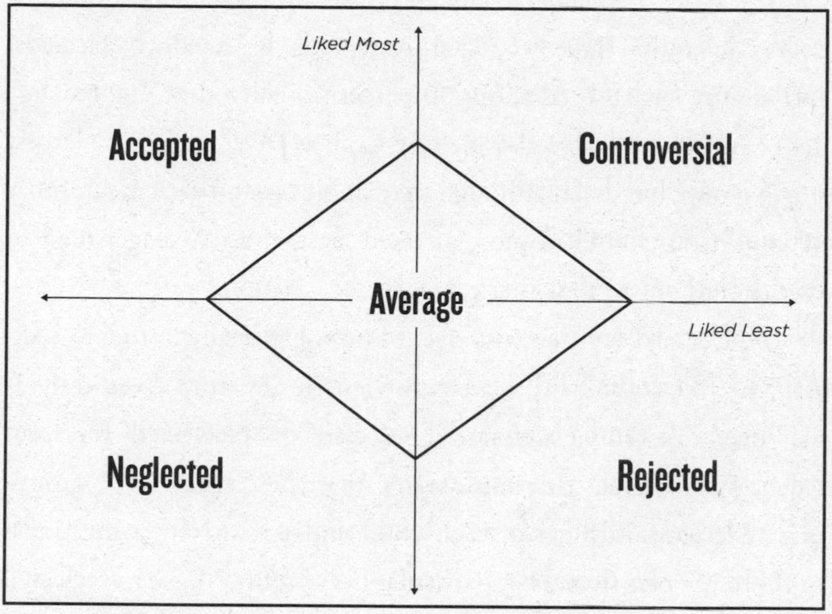

Figure 1. Sociometric Groups

Coie and his colleagues found that some children received an unusually high or low number of nominations, and this qualified them for one of four sociometric groups in the corners of the matrix. Children in the top left quadrant were highly liked and rarely disliked. Coie described this group as "Popular," but they also can be designated as "Accepted," because the type of popularity they enjoy is based purely on who is most likable. The opposite quadrant, at the bottom right, included those who were "Rejected"—liked by few and disliked by many. Children who rarely were nominated as liked *or* disliked, the invisible children, gathered in the lower left box and were referred to as "Neglected." By contrast, the group in the upper right box—those who were widely liked and disliked in roughly equal measure—were among the most visible members of the group, and make up the "Controversials," the peers we either love or hate. Controversials are relatively rare and make up the smallest of the sociometric groups. Taken together, Accepteds, Rejecteds, Neglecteds, and Controversials total about 60 percent of all youth. The remainder of his subjects were classified by Coie as "Averages"—the largest single group. Note that although they do not get an extreme number of nominations as liked most or liked least, most Averages tend to veer toward one of the other categories.

These labels may feel reductive, I know. Especially in today's society, when we try so hard to adapt any environment to meet individuals' needs, describing anyone as "Rejected" or "Neglected" can seem harsh. Such characterizations assume that these sociometric groupings reflect an attribute of each child and not merely a mismatch between the person and her particular peer group. Might a Neglected child be better liked if he was placed among different peers? Might someone who is Rejected become popular if given a fresh start?

This is exactly what Coie wondered, so he designed a follow-up study to test whether children's groupings would stay the same if they were placed in a new context. He started by inviting ten-year-old children to his research lab to participate in playgroups. These groups were not randomly composed: each included four children from four different schools, none of whom had met before. One child in each group was Accepted in his originating school, one was Rejected, one Neglected, and one Average. (Coie excluded Controversials, since they are uncommon.)

For one hour each week, the children met to play together in much the same way they might in class or at recess. They gathered in a room that had been stocked with games, Legos, toy cars, inflatable boxing gloves, markers, paper, and so on. First, each group engaged in a structured activity supervised by an adult. Next, they had unsupervised time for free play. Then, once playtime was over, it was time for the researchers to unobtrusively measure each child's popularity. They did so in a particularly clever way.

Rather than make the point of their experiment too obvious, they asked one of their trained research assistants to drive each participant home at the end of every weekly session. During the ride the researchers first engaged in normal conversation about the child's interests and hobbies, but before they reached their destination, they asked him whom he liked the most in his playgroup, followed by whom the child liked next best, and so on, until all their playmates had been named, including the child they liked least.

At the end of Week 1, Coie and one of his graduate students at the time, Janis Kupersmidt, examined the compiled results of these interviews and discovered that there was absolutely no relationship between how well liked children were at their own schools and how well liked they were within the group of unfamiliar playmates. The new configurations truly offered a fresh start. A week later, the researchers conducted the interviews again and still found no correspondence between the children's likability in the playgroup and at their respective schools.

But by the third playgroup session, a remarkable similarity emerged between the popularity of each child in his group and at his original school. It only took three hours of play for Accepted children to become accepted again. Rejecteds were once again the most disliked, and Neglecteds again proved themselves unlikely to be picked as most *or* least liked. The study continued for another three weeks, during which the patterns grew even stronger.

Subsequent research has revealed that the factors that cause us to be accepted by peers are fairly universal and enduring—they have the potential to make us liked or disliked again and again, even as we change settings, for the rest of our lives. When Coie and Kupersmidt reviewed the videotapes from the first two weeks of their experiment, they noticed that in their new playgroups, the Accepted and Rejected children had already begun talking far more than their Average and Neglected counterparts. When Accepted children spoke, they were setting the norms for the group, gently reminding others of the rules, suggesting new games, and coming up with innovative ideas for how to make toys more interesting. But when Rejected children talked, they were more likely than the others to insult, threaten, tease, and boss around their peers. Rejected children also were the least likely to listen to directions when participating in the adult-structured activity. It was no surprise that children attained the identical level of popularity so soon after meeting brand-new peers. They behaved in the same ways that had determined their likability in their original schools.

Shortly after I began teaching my first college class on popularity, I had an opportunity to witness this phenomenon for myself. It was about midway through the semester when I got a call from an ABC News producer who wanted to film a replication of Coie and Kupersmidt's classic experiment. My students and I received permission from parents at a local day-care center to film a group of three-year-olds who had known the peers in their respective classrooms for only a few months. Interviewing each child just as Coie and his colleagues did quickly revealed who among them was Accepted, Rejected, Neglected, and Average. We invited one child from each sociometric group, kids from different classrooms who had never played together, to gather in the school gymnasium. We then began to observe their interactions for what was expected to be a few weeks of play sessions.

But in this case, it took only about thirty minutes before the children's previous popularity was revealed. In less than an hour, the child whose classroom peers had nominated her as Accepted had begun leading the others in a game with an oversized ball, and the child who had been picked as Rejected was excluded. I did not continue to study this group, but researchers who have worked with children over many years have found that over half of those who are categorized as Accepted, Rejected, Neglected, Controversial, or Average in elementary school continue to fall into the same group over five years later in high school, even those who have switched schools and become part of a brand-new group of peers.

Does the type of popularity we experience in our youth remain constant for the rest of our lives? Some say that we can hit the popularity reset button when we go to college, where we are suddenly surrounded by a far more homogeneous group of peers, at least in terms of academic achievement and ability to follow adults' directions. In many European nations, this occurs in secondary school, where teens are already grouped by educational tracks.

But for most of adulthood, we find ourselves again in groups that are involuntarily assembled—peers who have been placed together for reasons other than common friendship, educational level, or familial relation. Then it is like grade school all over again. It doesn't take long until groups of Accepteds, Rejecteds, Neglecteds, Controversials, and Averages begin to emerge. Often, the group we land in as adults is the same one we were in as youths, and this can have remarkable implications for us.

It was not long before the holidays when employees of a large international tech company learned of an upcoming corporate "reorganization"—in other words, a major round of layoffs. In all, about 30 percent of the workforce would be let go by the end of the year. Three weeks after the announcement, forty-five hundred employees drove to work on the day that most would learn their fate.

One of these employees was a guy named Billy. I know him quite well. Billy had started working at the company about five years earlier, shortly after he finished graduate school at Harvard. Billy has two kids, a son who looks exactly like him and a daughter who is a clone of his wife. They had just agreed to buy a new house, and before they knew anything about the reorganization in Billy's company, they had scheduled their closing on the day after layoffs would be announced.

Billy's unit within the company is located in a building that has adopted an open floor plan, a well-lit bull pen of conference tables, stand-up desks, and free-floating file cabinets, with occasional cubicle dividers that reach only chest high. Everyone can hear their colleagues' conversations, and there is no mystery about who is meeting with whom. It might as well be the school cafeteria all over again.

Billy usually chooses a desk close to the perimeter, alongside a wall of full-length windows that overlooks the parking lot. No matter where he sits, however, Billy experiences a lot of traffic at his workstation. People come by to say hello in the morning, congregate after difficult meetings to debrief and commiserate with him, and gather at lunchtime to decide where to eat. Even a casual visit to the office would reveal that he is one of the most well-liked people on his floor.

On the morning of the layoffs, Billy sat nervously at his desk waiting for a representative from human resources. He tried hard to focus on his work, but it was almost impossible to ignore the chatter of his coworkers as they paced and gossiped down the hall. Once his colleagues saw that he had arrived, Billy's desk was surrounded by peers who wanted to hear his predictions, and for the next hour, no one got any work done.

Sitting across from Billy's desk was Carl, a tall, lanky man in his mid-forties who had been working at the company for twelve years. Carl did not take part in the chatter. In fact, he rarely talked at all. Billy describes Carl as one of the "heads-down" people in the office. He is quite good at his job—his work is always on time and carefully completed—but he just isn't very showy about it. He stays at his desk, he rarely eats lunch with others, and while he always pays attention in meetings, he rarely participates.

Carl's workstation is well ordered and uncluttered. His desk has a few neatly labeled file folders tucked in the corner and a mug filled with about a dozen identical pens. On most days, he offers a brief nod and courteous smile to everyone as he walks through the break room to get his coffee, then sits at his desk and works undistracted until lunch. But on the day the layoffs were announced, Carl seemed agitated. He kept his cell phone close at hand, sending periodic texts to his wife as he overheard rumors. Occasionally he got up from his desk and disappeared for fifteen minutes at a time, but no one noticed.

On the far side of the room, sitting by himself, was Dan. Dan is in his late fifties. He is pleasant enough, generally gregarious and enthusiastic, but something about him seems a bit off. In dozens of little ways—none remarkable on their own, but collectively quite noticeable—Dan doesn't seem to be tuned in to others. While his peers share minor details of their personal lives as they chat in the break room, Dan discloses just a little too much information about his marital woes, making others uncomfortable. When friendly banter leads to a volley of quips around the conference room table, Dan hogs the ball, getting carried away with his own story. He even looks like an outsider, wearing wrinkled khakis and white sneakers in an otherwise preppy-dressing office. It's not a difference he seems to notice.

Dan had no idea whether or not he would be laid off, he told me, but he certainly was curious what others thought about his fate. He roamed the floor peering over the shoulders of colleagues who huddled together to make predictions. In most cases, they continued their conversations without widening their circle to include him, and he continued to walk from group to group.

The one person in the office who didn't seem nervous at all was Frank, the slick, well-groomed assistant whom Billy calls one of the "manage-ups" of the firm. Frank is in his mid-twenties, far junior to most of his colleagues but well known by all. He is the epitome of charm and polish—smooth and funny but never really offering much of substance. He is quite helpful to any superior who needs his help ("Sure thing . . . happy to do it . . . no sweat"), but when a fellow assistant asks for a favor, Frank is downright rude ("Your problem, not mine"). As he walks to his desk, Frank offers an eager nod to almost everyone he passes. Some greet him back enthusiastically, while others nod curtly. While his colleagues fret over the upcoming layoff announcements, Frank sits back calmly and plays a game on his phone.

In this company, Billy is Accepted, just as he has been for most of his life. He describes himself as an introvert—he would prefer to play golf alone than to network at a company party. But likability is not necessarily related to either introversion or extroversion. Like many Accepted people, Billy is likable because he has the ability to read the room—any room. His ideas aren't always better than others', but he knows exactly when in a meeting to offer them, and he often gets the credit. Just slightly faster than his colleagues, he recognizes when there is an emerging consensus or conflict. He's good at tuning in to the emotional underpinnings of his coworkers' statements. But perhaps most important, Billy is adept at using his social skills to help others feel connected to him.

He does so in a number of ways. First, Billy is great at asking astute questions. Studies show that people who ask many questions of each other when they first meet—a highly effective way of scanning for an emotional connection—are more likely to have high-quality relationships even months later. When you first meet Billy, his questions clearly communicate that he wants to know more about you, and he finds most everything you say to be interesting, important, and relatable. Billy's social behavior signals that he cares about the herd. People want to talk to him because they believe that Billy wants to talk to them. That makes him likable.

Second, Billy has a terrific sense of humor. This trait also is a function of reading the room well, because a good joke requires understanding the current mood or sentiment, and exaggerating or twisting it for comic effect. More fundamentally, humor offers biological benefits. Laughter is associated with the release of dopamine and endorphins that promote euphoria and improved immune response—and people like others who help them feel good.

Third, just like the Accepted children in Coie's studies, Billy is described by others as someone who is trusted, has many friends, seems fair, happy, polite, patient, and knows how to share. And as research on Accepted children would predict, Billy generally has had a very successful life. Studies show that when Accepted children become adults, they have higher self-esteem, make more money, and have better-quality relationships with friends and romantic partners. They even grow up to be physically healthier than their less accepted peers. The power of likability persists above and beyond the effects of all kinds of factors that we usually think are most important, like intelligence, socioeconomic status, and healthy behavior.

Carl is Neglected. In childhood, the Neglecteds watch their peers play from afar, remaining behind a fence poking a worm with a stick, rather than joining the others. Or worse, they attempt to take part in a game of hide-and-seek, but no one tries to find them. Some Neglecteds are anxious—desperately eager to be a part of a group but rarely confident enough to initiate interactions with others. Studies show that as adults, Neglected people are a bit slower to begin dating or establish secure, committed relationships, and they usually choose professions that do not rely heavily on interactions with others. They are unlikely to become public speakers, salespeople, or recruiters.

Still, many Neglecteds do very well in adult life. Some manage to quell their anxieties, while others simply prefer to spend a great deal of time alone. There is also evidence that being Neglected may be more associated with one's particular environment than it is for other groups. In Coie's studies of children's sociometric groups over a five-year period, the Neglected category was the least stable. While most

Rejecteds and Accepteds remained so over time, Neglecteds were just as likely to ultimately land in almost any of the sociometric groups six years later, though they almost never became Controversials.

Dan is Rejected. The Rejecteds have been the category most studied by clinical psychologists, because peer rejection turns out to be a very important predictor of mental health difficulties throughout our lives. Research has found that Rejecteds can be divided into two subgroups. One includes those who are highly aggressive. Rejected-Aggressives become angry, rude, or defensive when upset. On the playground, the Rejected-Aggressive child is the boy who hits someone who took his toy without asking, or the girl who excludes just one classmate from her party. In a business meeting, it is the person who is so desperate to be heard that he or she cuts off and undermines others. In the community, it is the individual who gossips about neighbors when he or she feels wronged.

A key characteristic of the Rejected-Aggressives is that they often don't realize that their behavior is inappropriate. Many do not even know they are rejected, and in fact, Rejected-Aggressives often believe that they are the group's favorite. Many aggressive people are not rejected. But about half of those rejected are also aggressive, and these Rejected-Aggressives have far worse outcomes than those who are only aggressive or only rejected.

Dan is actually a Rejected-Nonaggressive, a group that violates the social norms in any number of nonhostile ways. Some Rejected-Nonaggressives are disliked merely because they look unusual or come from a different background than most of their peers. Others are rejected because they engage in odd behaviors. Still others have not matured as quickly or in the same way as others. In Dan's case, his problem was being too smart in a world where being smart can be very uncool.

Dan's intelligence wasn't always an obstacle. In elementary school, he was his teachers' favorite, often called on to tutor classmates who had difficulty with math. By third grade, he won a district-wide math tournament and remembers receiving a standing ovation from his peers at an elementary school assembly. He was the first to be singled out by the principal whenever she visited Dan's classroom, and his peers, recognizing his special status among their teachers, were always eager to play with him on the playground.

Of course, this all changed for Dan by middle school. Suddenly the same low-achieving classmates whom he used to tutor started to call him names, and Dan became a nerd, a pariah. It seemed as if every academic award he received only further branded him a geek in the eyes of his peers, and by tenth grade, he became so mercilessly teased by his classmates that it became easier for him to live in his own little world—deliberately oblivious to whatever his peers thought was cool.

Dan's story is typical of what I have found in my own research. Following over two hundred children until they reached adolescence, Annette La Greca and I found that at age nine, high-achieving children are typically the best liked of all. Teachers love them, they are terrific at solving social problems, and their peers are excited to play with them. These children enjoy high self-esteem and the lowest levels of depression, anxiety, and loneliness compared to their peers. But six years later, these same kids reported precipitous declines in their emotional well-being. As a group, they were the most depressed, socially anxious, lonely, and insecure of all adolescents.

What changed? Not their intelligence—they were still the smartest kids in class, achieving the highest grades. But by their early teens, their peers' attitudes toward high achievement transformed, and the smart kids suffered the social and psychological consequences. Getting good grades and trying hard in school is exactly what adults want kids to do. In other words, these kinds of behaviors reflect adults' values. In childhood, kids think adults are "cool," so acting in accordance with adult values is cool, too. In adolescence, however, we are programmed to look toward our peers more than our parents. And there could be nothing more "uncool" than doing what your parents want. So among teens, getting good grades or trying really hard to achieve suddenly attracts ridicule and scorn.

Of course, many highly intelligent people like Dan find a place to feel comfortable in adulthood, when there is a bit less stigma to being smart. Others lose the US presidency to George W. Bush, who may have been the less qualified candidate in 2000 but seemed more likable to the American people than Al Gore. Still others feel alienated for the rest of their lives and find a way to simply ignore their peers, because it is too painful to feel so different.

In adolescence, this latter strategy worked well for Dan. By deliberately disregarding what others thought was cool, he could evade the sense of inferiority he felt among his classmates. He decided that he didn't care what his peers valued, because they didn't value him. By adulthood, however, this strategy started to backfire. On performance reviews, Dan was rated as competent, loyal, and timely, but also judged to be "not a team player" and "difficult to work with," and to have poor "agility."

How about other Rejected children, who may have been disliked for any number of reasons other than being too smart? Research findings tell us that being rejected is one of the most consistent risk factors for a whole range of later psychological symptoms—depression, anxiety, substance use, even criminal behavior. Of course, not every Rejected individual experiences mental illness. But many such children do continue to feel shut out even as adults. Somewhere—at work, in their communities—there is a group that they try to avoid or feel uncomfortable being around. They may opt out of dinner parties or social events, for instance, if there's a risk of being made to feel inferior again. Like Dan, they may find a spouse and have a few close friends, but they perpetually fear being marginalized. Alternatively, many find a vocation or a workplace populated by others who themselves were Rejected or Neglected. Some become so skilled at engineering their contacts with others that they report no longer feeling very rejected at all. But old feelings of insecurity continue to haunt them when they are thrust outside their comfort zone.

Rejecteds also may feel innately unworthy, anxious, or angry. These feelings can manifest themselves subtly, through a continual need for reassurance from loved ones, a sensitivity to signals that they're being teased or excluded, or fear when meeting people who remind them of their childhood tormentors. It's common for Rejecteds to develop a push-pull relationship with the world around them, often judging others as a way to feel superior, yet all the while dependent on positive feedback to gird their own fragile self-esteem.

Frank, the social-climbing assistant who manages up so persistently, is a Controversial. In childhood, the Controversials are often the class clowns—everyone's favorite peer when part of a large group, if not necessarily someone whom people are eager to invite into their circle of close friends. These individuals can be very adroit socially but are also quite aggressive. Many describe them as Machiavellian—strategically using their social skills when it serves them, but also willing to knock others down to get what they want.

We don't know a great deal about how Controversials fare over time. They are relatively difficult to find and as such are often excluded in research studies. But available evidence suggests that although they achieve short-term gain, they do not do well in the long term. One study revealed that out of almost three hundred girls who were categorized as Accepted, Neglected, Rejected, Controversial, or Average in the fourth grade of a low-income community, it was the Controversials who were most likely to become teen moms. In fact, compared to all teenage mothers, the Controversials were youngest when they gave birth.

Research also has shown that Controversial children grow up to be especially likely to have high *status* in adolescence—that's the other type of popularity we will explore in this book.

It was nearly noon when a representative from human resources finally stepped off the elevator and onto the floor where Billy, Carl, Dan, Frank, and almost a hundred other employees sat in gloomy anticipation. As if in a scene out of *American Idol*, the representative read off three lists of names, directing employees to separate rooms to learn their fate. Billy and Frank were sent to the same room. Carl was in another, and Dan was in the third.

After about twenty minutes of waiting, the workers in Billy and Frank's room began to whisper, and soon rumors were circulating. Finally, the human resources director entered, shut the door behind her, and informed them that they were all safe. They were expected to return to work immediately.

She next entered Carl's room and notified this group that while their positions were being eliminated in the corporate reorganization, they each would be offered one-year contracts with a subsidiary. It was not a great outcome, but it was better than unemployment.

"I knew I was in trouble," Carl recalled. When the executives debated who would stay and who would go, he said, he understood that "I wasn't anybody's boy." Others hypothesized that Carl was among those who were asked to move because he was connected to so few others, which meant that his departure had the lowest likelihood of upsetting the office network.

Dan's room held the fewest workers. All were told that their duties had been reassigned, and they were expected to vacate their desks by the end of the week. Although Dan was smart and did his job well, there was no question that he would be laid off on that grim day. He just never seemed to fit in among his peers.

Of course, the decisions made regarding Billy, Carl, Dan, and Frank were based on a complex array of factors. Work performance, seniority, organizational needs, and future projections were taken into consideration. But were they all that mattered? Substantial evidence suggests that it is our likability that can predict our fate in so many domains of life. Likable people continue to have advantages, and dislikable people will almost always suffer.

Likability is an important type of popularity, but it is not what we typically think of when we judge who is most popular. What we usually imagine has much more to do with status. For some people, it is possible to be popular in both respects—to have power, influence, prestige, dominance, and also to be a person that everyone likes. But this is rare. Research studies measure status by using a different type of sociometric assessment, asking subjects to identify peers who are "Most Popular" and "Least Popular," rather than whom they like the most and least. Findings reveal that only about 35 percent of those who are high in status are also highly likable. Many of the rest are Controversial.

Ignaz Semmelweis's high status afforded him the opportunity to investigate a major medical crisis and ultimately propose a theory that had the potential to advance knowledge and save lives. When his peers adopted his new methods—washing their hands and disinfecting surgical instruments between procedures—hundreds of mothers were saved.

During his lifetime, however, Semmelweis never received the credit he deserved for his major medical breakthrough. Howard Markel, the University of Michigan historian, writes that Semmelweis's shrill, harsh behavior ultimately led doctors in Vienna to stop washing their hands following autopsies. Soon mothers began to die again, at an even higher rate than earlier. In 1850, Semmelweis quietly resigned from General Hospital. It was not until over a decade later that Louis Pasteur conducted a series of experiments revealing the existence of specific disease-causing bacteria, which changed medical practice forever. In the meantime, thousands of women and babies died in Vienna, and Dr. Semmelweis himself passed away at the age of forty-seven—purportedly from an infection.

Alexandra Cort's story similarly suggests a troubling outcome for those high in status. As part of our research, we continued to follow her and her peers for a few years after our first meeting. On measures of status, Alexandra was by far the most popular student in her grade all the way up to graduation, even as she continued to be rated by many as someone they liked the least.

But that was her downfall. It was because of her high status that she was invited to every party, where she drank, smoked pot, used ecstasy, and even experimented with cocaine. Her grades dropped, and while her friends from the library were admitted to four-year universities, Alexandra was left behind. Her friendships eventually became strained, and her boyfriend broke up with her as he prepared to leave for college.

When we last collected data for our study, the most popular girl in school was lonely.

CHAPTER 3

The Problems with Popularity

What's Wrong with What We Want?

In the center of Rome, nestled comfortably among historic landmarks like St. Vincenzo's Church and the United Colors of Benetton, sits the Trevi Fountain. It is a glorious site, with over one hundred thousand cubic feet of water pouring through its aqueducts hourly. Every day it is surrounded by people who marvel at its beauty and listen to its endless roar. They take pictures, they sit nearby to have coffee, and the vast majority throw in a coin to make a wish. About three thousand euros' worth of coins are tossed into the fountain every day, representing thousands of wishes from all over the world.

What does everyone typically wish for?

I wish to win the lottery.
I wish I were ten pounds thinner.
I wish to become famous.
I wish for a promotion.
I wish to fall in love.
I wish my family happiness and health.
I wish for no more war or suffering.

What would you wish for? Research studies have posed this question to adults from all over the world. Some studies have reframed the idea by asking people to report their "fundamental motives"—in other words, the deepest desires that drive their behavior. Others have investigated life longings, or what Germans call *Sehnsucht*. Still other researchers have analyzed subjects' most important "aspirational goals."

Results from all these studies reveal that while our wishes depend a bit on our age, our gender, our personality, and even where we are when we are asked, we all basically want the same things. Psychologists can group all of our wishes into just two main categories.

One of these categories includes our "intrinsic" desires—wishes that make us feel good without needing any external recognition or feedback. Psychologists posit that these intrinsic goals are inherently fulfilling because they make us feel as if we are honoring our own internal values. They promote psychological growth and self-actualization—in other words, they make us the best people we can possibly be. Intrinsic goals include our desire to feel connected to others, to find love, and to be healthy and happy. Altruistic wishes (e.g., desiring happiness for our loved ones or an end to world hunger) are a reflection of our intrinsic desires, because when we seek to help others, it feels good, even if no one else is aware of our benevolent intentions.

In one study, a group of psychologists asked 405 young adults, "If you could have three wishes, what would you wish for?" The results revealed fewer intrinsic wishes than might be expected. About 13 percent wished for happiness, and 12 percent wished for social intimacy, including "positive relationships with family and friends." Only about 8 percent chose an altruistic wish. Others (6 percent) made a wish pertaining to physical health or the health of a loved one; this type of wish becomes more common as we grow older.

The other category of wishes has a great deal to do with popularity. This is not the kind of popularity based on likability, but rather one grounded in status and all of its trappings. Researchers refer to these types of wishes as "extrinsic," because they are defined by a desire to be regarded favorably by others. Extrinsic desires are satisfied only when other people notice us and give us positive feedback, so fulfilling them is out of our own control.

Common extrinsic wishes are craving fame and attention (e.g., "to be admired by many people," "to have my name be known by everyone"), as well as power and dominance ("to be able to influence people"). Extrinsic wishes also include those qualities that we associate with high status, like beauty ("to have people comment how good I look") and excessive wealth ("to have many expensive things"). No matter how the questions are posed or who the participants are, research reveals that at least one of the subjects' top three wishes usually is extrinsic, with fame or attention being particularly common. Power (especially for men) and beauty (for women) are also typically in the top five. Ultimately we all want to be admired and influential—and maybe even a little envied.

Is this so wrong? Is it shallow? Immature? Maybe a little vain? Is there a part of us that still wants to live out our high school glory days, or fulfill a wish that was never granted in adolescence? Do we really still want this type of popularity?

I must confess, although I am not terribly active on Facebook, I do have an account that enables me to keep up-to-date with friends and colleagues who might otherwise fall out of touch. I occasionally post a picture of my family, and after a few days, and several pestering emails from Facebook, I log back in to see what I have missed. At the top of the screen is a little icon showing me that there has been activity on my account. When I click, it announces that dozens of people have "liked" or commented on the photo I posted. I didn't upload the picture just to accrue some impressive number of "likes," but I can't help but feel a little uplifted knowing that so many people saw and approved of something I offered. Of course, this recognition has nothing to do with people actually liking me, despite Facebook's clever use of the word. It is, rather, a simple way for them to indicate that they saw my picture, and it made them smile. It seems that the fundamental purpose of "liking," retweeting, or offering any other form of endorsement on social media is to join the herd that says, "I see you. I notice you. I approve of you." It is a way of granting people high status—showing them that they are visible and admired by many. And the tactic works. When I see the number of "likes," it makes me feel . . . well, popular. It seems juvenile to admit it, but it offers a little bit of a rush, a small pat on the back, a feeling of being reinforced.

We typically look down on people who openly crave high status. Seeking this type of popularity is the kind of pursuit we associate with preteens and boy bands. We even use derogatory names for adults who seem to brazenly pursue status, like "status-seekers," "wannabes," or "fame-mongers."

But is it wrong to desire high status? It's certainly more socially advantageous to have this type of popularity than not. Imagine attending a party where everyone is excited to talk with you, amused by what you say, and impressed by how great you look. Consider how gratifying it would feel if, at every work meeting, your ideas were heralded as the most inspired and influential. Think how special you would feel if people were excited just to meet you and talked favorably about you afterward. Who wouldn't want to be venerated by all their peers? This recognition appeals to all of us, just as all of us do secretly feel a little boost when we get "likes" on our Facebook page, or when we receive lots of invitations to parties and get-togethers. Why? It's not appealing because we are still vying for a spot on the "Most Popular" senior celebrities page in our high school yearbook—it actually has a much deeper basis. Our pursuit of status can be traced back to the most primitive of origins.

Deep within our brains, in a part of the limbic system that sits below the cerebral cortex, is a region that has been part of our anatomy for thousands of years and is found not only in humans but also in other mammals. It's part of a network of coactivating substructures, but the area that may have most relevance is called the ventral striatum. The ventral striatum is a hub in our brain's reward center and as such plays a major role in making us feel good. It responds to all kinds of rewards, from the promise of money to the high that comes from using drugs. But beginning in adolescence, the ventral striatum becomes especially activated when we experience rewards that are social in nature such as attention and approval from others. One of its chief functions is to make us care about status.

The ventral striatum is among the first parts of the brain to change at puberty. This is highly adaptive. About the time that our output of testosterone and progesterone begins to surge—even before our voices change and our sexual interests develop—our bodies prepare us to become autonomous. A first step in doing so is to help us separate from our parents and become more interested in our peers.

This interest is stimulated by a cocktail of neurochemicals. Feelings, sensations, urges, and behaviors are all triggered by the activity of central nervous system neurons. These each have receptors keyed to specific hormones, neurotransmitters, or other substances that signal the neuron to fire or not. When we are about ten to thirteen years old, pubertal hormones stimulate neurons in the ventral striatum to grow additional receptors for two brain substances in particular.

One of these is a hormone called oxytocin, which increases our desire to connect and bond with our peers. Receptors for oxytocin proliferate in many mammals at the onset of adolescence. Even mice prefer time with other teen mice over adults when they begin to mature—a fact that can bring comfort to millions of parents who wonder why they have suddenly become such an embarrassment to their tween children. The second substance is dopamine, the same neurotransmitter that produces the pleasure response triggered by many recreational drugs. Together these neurochemicals make tweens suddenly feel an urge to obtain "social rewards"—feedback that makes them feel noticed, approved, admired, and powerful among peers.

But that's not all. Our brains are not only designed to make us feel good when we have high status—they are also programmed to make us pursue it. The reason for this is that the ventral striatum rarely acts alone. It's part of a group of regions that neuroscientists like my colleague Kristen Lindquist call the "motivational relevance network." Kent Berridge, a neuroscientist from the University of Michigan, is an expert in the motivational relevance network and has studied the brain's likes and wants—in other words, what feels good and why we so doggedly pursue more of it. His work has revealed that the ventral striatum sends neural outputs to locations throughout the brain, such as the ventral pallidum. The ventral pallidum translates our likes into a strong motivation to act—to get more of what we want. In other words, it affects our behavior and can also affect our emotions. In fact, the ventral pallidum has been linked with a variety of addictions and the emotional attachment we may develop to things we know are not so good for us.

Some of the connections that govern our likes and wants also occur in the cortex, the region of the brain that sits atop the subcortical regions we share with many other species. The cortex is where we think—a process that includes consciously recognizing what we like and deliberating whether or not to pursue it. Among adults, thinking helps restrain us from becoming too obsessed with any of our desires, such as popularity. By our mid-twenties, the rest of our brain has caught up to the early-developing ventral striatum, and the cortex helps us act sensibly, enabling us to resist the urge to fulfill every want.

But many neural connections also occur below the cortex, like the ones between the ventral striatum and ventral pallidum. Berridge explains that these subcortical connections can lead us to pursue certain behaviors without realizing we are doing so, and later, we may even reflect upon them as being irrational—like becoming giddy when we see a celebrity, or blurting out our desires when it is inappropriate to do so. In fact, subcortical connections are so strong that we begin to "want" not just those things that directly give us social rewards, but anything that has been paired with social reward, Pavlovian style. We soon begin to want things that simply remind us of high status, such as beauty or excessive wealth, whether or not they will actually benefit us. Berridge refers to these links as "motivational magnets."

If you talk to any adolescent, it is easy to see how their wants are related to a craving for social rewards and high status. By the time we are thirteen, it seems as if there is nothing more important to us than this type of popularity. We talk about who has it. We strategize how to get it. We are devastated when we lose it. We even do things we know are wrong, immoral, illegal, or dangerous merely to obtain status, or to fiercely defend it. Adolescents are virtually addicted to popularity—at least the type based on status.

This is exactly what we learn when my graduate students and I meet with teenagers to study their behavior with peers. In fact, this predilection seems to be becoming even more pronounced now that teens can enter a social rewards lottery with every mouse click on social media. When we talk with teens about what's most important to them, it seems all we hear is a craving for, and strategy to attain, social rewards.

"I want the most Twitter followers in my school," one subject tells us.

"If I post a pic on Instagram, and it doesn't get, like, thirty 'likes' in the first few minutes, then I take it down," another says.

"You have to 'like' whatever your friend posts right away or you are not being a good friend," explains a third.

"Why?" we ask them. "Tell us why your social media profiles are so important."

"It's like being famous" is a typical response. "It's cool. Everyone knows you, and you are, like, the most important person in school."

Or, "If you're popular, if everyone is talking about you, you can go out with whoever you want. You can be friends with anyone. It just, like, feels good."

Is this obsession with social media also true of adults? We all know those who use it as fervently as today's teens—posting incessantly, soliciting attention in the form of "likes" and retweets, and so on. In fact, the ventral striatum remains just as active in adulthood. Granted, as we age we are better able to control these impulses. But for the rest of our lives, we will still experience the drive to gain social rewards and to have high status. The more we learn about the brain, the more we discover how much this desire for status can change us, without our even realizing it.

What did you do today to raise your status? Did you pick out attractive clothes to wear so others would notice you? Did you put on an expensive watch that makes you feel powerful or prestigious? Maybe you sent an email to colleagues that you hoped would leverage your influence at work. Or perhaps you just posted on Facebook or Twitter. These are all pretty obvious things we might do to make us feel as if we have higher status, and we're usually pretty aware of what we are doing when we do make choices like these to gain social rewards.

But is that all? What else reflects our status yearnings? It turns out that our ventral striatum is linked to a much wider range of our behaviors and emotions than we once thought.

For instance, research shows that when we read about high-status people, talk about them, or even just look at them, those actions are sufficient to activate the social reward centers in our brains. In fact, we tend to gaze at high-status peers (of the same or opposite gender) much longer than we look at others around us. In other words, without our even realizing it, our brains habitually orient us toward status all day long.

We also experience social rewards when we believe that someone we admire likes us in return. Anyone who has ever fantasized about meeting a celebrity and then becoming best friends can relate to this concept. This is not a far cry from the high school yearning to have the most popular kid notice us, and it all can be traced back to the same adolescent surge in our desire for social rewards.

Chris Davey and his colleagues in Australia and Spain tested this idea in a study of adults. They asked participants to review a series of photos of people they had never met before and then to indicate how much they admired each individual. They were led to believe that the subjects in those photos did the same to them. Next, they were placed in an fMRI (functional MRI) scanner and shown the photos again, but this time given information about whether each of the individuals in the photos admired them in return. The reward centers of the brain became active whenever participants believed that others esteemed them. That finding makes sense, as being admired provides us with social rewards. But the most interesting result of the study was that those same brain regions were most strongly activated when participants believed they were admired by their own favorite peers. Gaining approval from those we look up to seems to be particularly valuable to the reward centers.

Research also shows that when we are tempted by social rewards, we are particularly likely to act impulsively. This may explain why so many of us have done regrettable things when we are in the presence of high-status peers.

This was most recently demonstrated by Leah Somerville at Harvard and B. J. Casey at Cornell, who adapted a computer game to determine whether we lose some of our inhibitions when faced with social rewards. The game was simple: participants were asked to press the space bar on a keyboard when they saw one stimulus on-screen, but not when they saw another. When this game is used with letters as the stimuli (e.g., press the space bar when the letter *R* is displayed, but not when the letter *J* appears), it can help make a diagnosis of ADHD. But in their study, Somerville and Casey replaced the letters with pictures of smiling or neutral faces, and the participants were placed in an fMRI to have their brains scanned. The researchers found that the sight of smiling pictures offered social rewards—after all, a smile is an instinctual cue of approval, like the approval we get when we have high status. Most relevant, however, was that in the presence of these social rewards, participants performed much more poorly at the task, suggesting that they weren't able to control their impulses as well. This was especially true of subjects who were adolescents or older. No one is immune to this effect—ask my wife and she'll tell you about the time we ran into one of my favorite actresses, and I began fawning like a twelve-year-old fan. There is something about status that naturally reduces our inhibitions.

The promise of social rewards can even change our own most basic attitudes and preferences without us even realizing it. Stanford student Erik Nook and psychologist Jamil Zaki investigated what happens in our brain when we conform to others. In their study, Nook and Zaki initially asked adults to report on their liking of different foods (chips, candy, fruits, vegetables), which were displayed in a series of photos. After they rated each item, participants were then shown a statistic that ostensibly reported the average rating of the previous two hundred study participants for the same food. The statistic was bogus, of course, but it enabled the investigators to examine the brain's response to the opinions of others. As expected, corroboration produced activity in the ventral striatum. We experience social rewards simply by learning that others agree with us.

The investigators then took their experiment one step further. After the participants were presented the bogus feedback, they were asked to rate each food again. Nook and Zaki wanted to see if any of the subjects would change their assessments after hearing how their responses lined up with those of others, even for something as inconsequential as food preferences. Their findings suggested that this is exactly what happened: most everyone conformed to others at least to some degree, but most interestingly, the people most likely to conform were those who had the largest responses in their ventral striatum in the first part of the experiment. The results demonstrated that not only are we biologically primed to enjoy feeling that others agree with us but those of us who have the most dramatic social reward response are especially likely to conform to the views of others. This all takes place outside of our conscious awareness.

Our desire for social rewards doesn't only affect our behavior. It also has significant effects on our emotions, even our most fundamental feelings about who we are. Adolescence, the stage in our lives when our biological cravings for status are suddenly heightened, is also the period when we first develop our sense of identity.

Ask young children how they feel or what kind of person they are and they will offer answers that are based on whatever happened to them in the last few minutes or hours. But in adolescence, we become more capable of thinking about ourselves in a way that cuts across time and recent experiences. We develop a stable sense of self, and the juxtaposition of our identity development with the rapid increase in ventral striatum activity leads to a process psychologists call "reflected appraisal." In other words, we begin to base our self-esteem not on how we feel, but on how we gauge that others approve of us. If everyone in homeroom thinks that we're cool, it means that we *are* cool. If we are teased or ignored by our peers, we don't interpret it to mean that they are being mean or rude; rather, we take it as evidence of our own unworthiness. In adolescence, our self-concept is not merely informed by how our peers treat us but is fully dictated by such experiences.

Reflected appraisal continues into adulthood, too, but for some more than others. Many people's sense of identity seems to be overly influenced by the last bit of positive or negative feedback they received. Hearing that someone likes them makes them feel like a good person, while exclusion turns them into total failures. Some are so invested in having high status (whether fame, beauty, power, or wealth) that it seems as if their entire identity is dependent on it. Neuroscience research supports these observations. We now know that neural outputs from the ventral striatum lead to our brain's "emotional salience" network, including the amygdala and parts of our hippocampus. These regions influence our emotional arousal, our most meaningful memories, and our experience that something has affected us in a personal and profound manner. Consequently, when we crave social rewards, we don't feel casually about it but view it as the basis of our self-worth. We may even begin to believe that status is synonymous with contentment. If we are not famous, powerful, beautiful, wealthy, or influential, then we must be worthless. This is not a great recipe for happiness.

Do you still long for status? Do you desire motivational magnets—things that you associate with high standing, like beauty or great wealth? How often is your behavior driven by a yearning for extrinsic reward, and to what degree do you allow your inner experience of happiness and self-worth to be influenced by your popularity among peers?

> It's much safer to say popularity sucks, because that allows you to forgive yourself if you suck.
>
> —*Cameron Crowe*

The truth is, we all want to have a certain degree of status. It is a natural product of our neurochemistry and our developmental history. Enjoying social rewards—feeling the high of exalted status—and seeking even more of it is perfectly normal. It's when we begin pursuing high status excessively that we can get into trouble.

In contemporary society, there are at least four ways that our pursuit of popularity through increasing status has gone awry.

POPULARITY PROBLEM #1:
How Far Will We Go for Status?

In 1939, a five-year-old girl named Valerie Jane disappeared. For an entire day, her family, neighbors, and the police searched tirelessly for her, but to no avail. The little girl had recently become curious about animals and particularly concerned with one puzzling question: how could something as large as an egg come out of a hen—an animal with no obvious opening to accommodate it? To answer her question, Valerie Jane quietly crawled into a henhouse, covered herself with straw, and lay motionless for the entire afternoon until she watched one of the fowl lay an egg. Only then did she emerge and return safely home.

Valerie Jane grew up to be Dr. Jane Goodall, who at the age of twenty-six quietly entered the Gombe Forest of Tanzania to observe chimpanzees—our closest evolutionary cousins, which share at least 90 percent of our DNA. Over the years, Goodall's discoveries challenged accepted notions in ethology, revealing that many behaviors originally thought to be unique to humans are also common in other species.

Goodall discovered that chimpanzees want to be popular, too. They don't brag about how many Twitter followers they have, but they do use status to determine which individual gets first access to resources. Among many animals, the most popular members of a group are young and able to maintain loyalty from others. High-status males typically are strong; females are socially shrewd. Popular chimps get first pick of food and mating partners. Status therefore offers chimpanzees a survival advantage: the more they are attuned to status and driven toward the social rewards it offers, the better chance they have at meeting their basic needs.

Goodall has described a day in the life of a sanctuary built by her foundation to help chimps and other primates return safely to their natural habitat. On a beautiful spring day in the Republic of the Congo, one of these chimps, a female whom Goodall calls Silaho, met some of the new sanctuary residents. Silaho had been transferred there a few months earlier, and in the time since, she had established a community among ten others. She was indisputably the "alpha" of the group. But then three new chimpanzees arrived. Naturally, Silaho did what any host might do when greeting guests: she violently attacked them into submission. Later, she did so again. Ultimately, Goodall explains, Silaho and three others in her group teamed together and tormented the visitors until they fled to the opposite side of the island. These three new chimpanzees remained ostracized from the rest of the community for months, while Silaho's status remained intact. Goodall, along with many other ethologists studying species in every corner of our planet, suggests that aggressive behavior is one very effective way that animals establish dominance and status among their peers. It is their natural instinct to do so.

Seven thousand miles east of Congo, anthropology professor Don Merten was observing a group of cheerleaders in an American high school. In this school, the cheerleaders ruled. Others looked up to them, they had first access to the most popular boys, and they set the trends that many other girls followed.

When an unpopular girl decided to join the cheerleading squad, Merten reports, the other girls reflexively behaved aggressively toward her. They teased her. They ostracized her. They made sure that her reputation was besmirched across the entire grade.

The cheerleaders knew their treatment of her was mean, and even recognized that it would earn them reputations as stuck-up snobs. It didn't matter. Merten's research suggests that the function of aggression is to protect the exclusivity that defines status itself. It is a necessary evil to maintain dominance. The cheerleaders explained to Merten that allowing a lower-status girl to join their group would come with a cost—a decline in the squad's status. His work subsequently demonstrated that each time a high-status teen acted aggressively in school, whether toward someone in his group or even someone similarly high in status, it was to preserve the social hierarchy. A punch in the face or the start of a nasty rumor was an act of dominance, letting victims and onlookers alike know the boundaries that defined status in that school. Threats to the social order are sanctioned by publically forcing submissiveness.

Psychologists refer to this type of hostile behavior as "proactive aggression," and research suggests that it is highly reinforcing. Unlike other uses of aggression that are hot-blooded, impulsive, and uncontrolled reactions to anger or frustration—also known as "reactive aggression"—proactive aggression is cold-blooded, calculating, and targeted precisely toward those who threaten the perpetrators' dominance. Proactive aggression is goal oriented, and the goal is to obtain or defend status.

Bullying is the best-known expression of proactive aggression. One bully in the PBS documentary *In the Mix* explains its function well when he says, "I've made fun of people when I am with my friends. I am not going to lie. The reason why I did that is to laugh—to make my group laugh. To put me on a higher pedestal. Even though I don't do it on a constant basis, it does kind of boost you up a little bit."

We conducted research involving two hundred tenth graders at an American high school and saw this behavior directly. Every participant in the study received rosters of all grade-mates to help them identify those peers high in status and, separately, those high in aggression. We asked them who hit, pushed, threatened, or physically intimidated their peers; who excluded, ostracized, or conspired to abandon others; and who spread rumors or threatened to end friendships as a form of retaliation. We also asked the adolescents whom they liked most and least among their classmates.

It was not hard for teens to pick out the mean boys and girls. Participants knew exactly who fit each description, and their reports were remarkably consistent. For each peer whom they described as aggressive, we asked our subjects to explain why they thought these individuals acted aggressively—out of frustration (reactive aggression) or to get something they wanted (proactive aggression). A little over a year later, we collected the same information again from the same group of adolescents.

The results from our research, and similar studies in the literature, demonstrated what Jane Goodall learned from watching chimpanzees: acting aggressively was one of the surest ways for teens to increase their status. But this was not true for every form of aggression. Those who were described as reactively aggressive had low status and were also less likable. But proactive uses of aggression had just the opposite effect: although the bullies were disliked, their use of proactive aggression was associated with increases in their status.

Do adults also use aggression to boost their status? Certainly. This type of behavior can take place at the individual level, like badmouthing a neighbor to make ourselves seem a little more worthy of attention, or in public, such as when Donald Trump's poll numbers rose following every insult he lobbed at a reporter or opponent. Sometimes it is even global, as when a nation attacks a weaker foe to assert its dominant position. In each of these cases, the use of aggression is shortsighted, because while it may result in a temporary boost in status and offer a little jolt of social reward, it is not ultimately fulfilling the wishes that really matter.

POPULARITY PROBLEM #2: Have We Granted Some of Our Peers Too Much Status?

On June 24, 2005, something took place on US television that captured the attention of news outlets all over the world.

It was a typical episode of the *Today* show, the cheerful morning news program, until host Matt Lauer introduced his next guest. Other than a prior incident involving Oprah, a buoyant couch, and an energetic discussion about his then-fiancée, Tom Cruise was known mostly for being a talented actor with a remarkable string of box-office blockbusters to his credit. But in this interview, Cruise was asked to share his opinions about mental health treatment options. For the latter half of his fifteen-minute interview, Cruise discussed his beliefs and those of the Church of Scientology about postpartum depression, the use of Ritalin to treat symptoms of ADHD, the history of psychiatry, and a fellow celebrity's choice to seek mental health services when experiencing distress.

Of course, several other items were in the news that same day that might have garnered some attention. Norma McCorvey, the woman dubbed "Roe" in the landmark *Roe v. Wade* abortion rights case, was testifying before Congress; the Senate was close to approving comprehensive energy legislation; and partisan bickering regarding the United States' response to 9/11 had reached a fever pitch. But the event that got the most coverage in the media was this interview with Tom Cruise. The story ran for several news cycles all over the world. Articles about it appeared in the *New York Times* and the *Washington Post* up to a week later.

Did we all really care what Tom Cruise had to say about such serious issues simply because he has high status?

Several years later, television star Jenny McCarthy began appearing on talk shows to discuss her new book, in which she claimed that a vast medical conspiracy was covering up a link between vaccines and her son's autism. To be fair, a parent's coping strategies and search for meaning in the face of a child's devastating diagnosis is perfectly understandable. McCarthy never claimed to be a scientist and freely admitted that the evidence supporting her beliefs came only from her "mommy instincts." Just as we cannot blame Tom Cruise for offering his strongly held opinions about postpartum depression, we cannot fault Jenny McCarthy for trying to help parents as earnestly as she knew how.

But the fact that she was a celebrity did have an impact on the power of her opinions. In his book *The Panic Virus*, Seth Mnookin reports that Jenny McCarthy's theories on autism "singlehandedly push[ed] vaccine skeptics into the mainstream." She appeared on television for weeks—not on entertainment programs but on news shows. She sat on panels alongside physicians from the American Academy of Pediatrics, and journalists discussed her ideas as seriously as they did reports on scientific studies and a statement disputing the vaccine theory issued by the Centers for Disease Control and Prevention.

The public not only listened but even changed its opinions. The more McCarthy talked about her distrust of the medical community, the more parents began adopting the same skepticism, eventually making decisions against their own pediatricians' advice. Mnookin reported that following McCarthy's televised appearances, the number of parents declining vaccines for their children skyrocketed.

It's one thing to enjoy watching celebrities when they entertain us. It's another entirely when our fascination with these high-status figures begins to affect our own behavior, even irrationally.

But even this phenomenon can be explained by the changes that occur in our brains during adolescence. In modern society, celebrities are our highest-status peers—they have all the visibility and prestige we associate with status, based on qualities like attractiveness and excessive wealth. Of course we want to watch them. We care about their lives, their physical appearance, and their courtships and breakups just as intently as we paid attention to the popular teens in high school. Our obsession with status is biologically programmed, and if it seems juvenile to be concerned with such topics, or to consume celebrity-themed media, it is because they remind us of the time in our lives when our unrestrained cravings for social rewards first blossomed.

We are also biologically susceptible to conform to celebrities, simply because of their high status. Marketing executives have long relied on this predilection. The use of celebrities' images or voices to encourage the sale of goods and services, for fund-raising efforts, and even for endorsements of political candidates has been a standard strategy for decades.

But the leverage of high status to capture our attention and change our behavior can go too far. It might occur when celebrities' private lives are exposed in greater detail than we would ever want known about ourselves. Even then we continue to watch, effectively signaling the media that such stories will drive viewership. The death of Princess Diana while being pursued by paparazzi is the most notorious example of this. Exploiting high-status figures can also become excessive when celebrities are asked to weigh in on matters outside their expertise, such as during political campaigns or even in congressional hearings. The time may have come for us to stop and question what our exaltation of high status says about us as individuals and as a society.

POPULARITY PROBLEM #3:
Is Our Desire for Status Excessive?

In 2001, political scientist Robert Putnam published *Bowling Alone*, a book based on his landmark essay that examined social changes in American life over the last four decades of the twentieth century. His research suggested that we are in a period of rapid change, one that seems to involve a shift toward placing an even higher value on status. Putnam found that the public's conception of a "good life" evolved from a desire to contribute to society to a need for wealth and status. In 1975, 38 percent of respondents indicated that a good life would include "a lot of money"; by 1996, that number had risen to 63 percent. During the same period, the proportion of people who wanted a vacation home, more color TVs, and "really nice clothes" doubled or tripled. Meanwhile, aspirations for a good marriage, children, and feeling connected to others have slightly declined.

Similar results were obtained by Cornell University historian Joan Brumberg. Her research analyzed personal diaries from the past hundred years, examining private thoughts to reveal how desires have changed over the past century. Brumberg reports that young women in the 1890s resolved to take more interest in others and refrain from focusing only on themselves. Their goals were to contribute to society, build character, and develop mutually fulfilling relationships. Yet in diaries from the 1980s and 1990s, young women record their intentions to do whatever is necessary to lose weight, find a new hairdo, or buy new clothes, makeup, and accessories—presumably, to attract more attention and approval from others.

Fame is in. Power, influence, and prestige are hot. Character, kindness, and community? Not so much.

What has made us so much more status-hungry? The answer involves a wide range of factors.

In 1943, Abraham Maslow proposed a hierarchy of needs, each of which would be fulfilled only after those lower on the list had been satisfied. First, we strive for basic survival requirements, like food, shelter, safety. Next, Maslow argues, we seek love and affection. We then pursue what Maslow called "esteem," which is effectively equivalent to status—defined as a desire to have others admire and accept us. Does our increased yearning for status today reflect the conditions of an advanced society, where hunger and isolation are increasingly rare? To some extent that may be true. Certainly in some regions of the world, we have become more prosperous and interconnected (at least superficially) than we ever have been. If Maslow is correct, then striving to attain status could be good news, for according to his theory, once we have satisfied the need for "esteem," we can then advance to the final stage of this needs hierarchy—self-actualization.

Another explanation for our rising need for status is that it simply reflects our increasingly individualistic culture. In *Bowling Alone*, Putnam extensively discusses Americans' declining sense of community, which has been replaced by a norm of autonomy and self-reliance. At the turn of the twentieth century, Western society was based far more on cooperation and partnership than it is today. In the field of labor, especially in the industrial era, few tasks could be accomplished without a large assembly of partners working together. In the neighborhoods of the early 1900s, an egalitarian community ensured the safety and comfort of all. While a higher status may have conferred benefits in those contexts, allegiance to and cooperation with a group was nevertheless a necessary part of life.

Contrast this with our work and home lives today. There are far fewer jobs that require a community of workers to cooperate simultaneously to reach a goal. In fact, some of our jobs don't even require us to be in the same building or time zone. In our domestic lives, many of us don't know our neighbors. Most of our needs can now be met via a smartphone and an internet connection. In a culture where our sense of community is waning, and mutual reliance is less necessary, has our proclivity to share been supplanted by a desire to have more than others? Does individualism give rise to a craving for high status?

If this is true, we would expect the pursuit of status to be greater in individualistic societies than in collectivistic cultures, which emphasize group harmony more than personal rank. The communitarian worldview is more common in the Far East, and stands in stark contrast to the "me culture" that now characterizes most Western nations.

It's a difference I couldn't help but notice on a trip I took from

New York to Japan years ago. As I rode the subway to New York's Kennedy airport, I was surrounded by people who wore their individual differences like a badge of honor. Their clothes, their hairstyles, and their behavior all seemed to shout "Look at me!" The subway from Tokyo's Narita airport was notably different, however. It was striking to see how similarly everyone dressed and behaved, particularly the adults. In a society that values communal accomplishments over individual ones, attempting to stand out may be not only unnecessary but downright disruptive. A few days later in Nara, the home of the Great Buddha temple, I stopped by a gift shop selling religious souvenirs. Each was customized with a personalized wish, and common choices translated to sentiments like "helping my family" and "contributing to society." I couldn't help but wonder what wishes would be top sellers in the United States.

We tested the cross-cultural relevance of status in my own lab by simultaneously examining the two forms of popularity, likability and status, in the United States and China. With graduate students Chris Sheppard and Sophie Choukas-Bradley, I analyzed data gathered from fifteen-year-olds in both countries. The data were collected by our colleague John Abela in two Chinese communities, one in urban Changsha and the other in rural Liuyang, while I gathered it Stateside using identical procedures. Over eight hundred adolescents in both countries were asked to identify the school peers they liked most and least, as well as the ones they thought had highest and lowest status. To our surprise, the concept of status did not translate well. In fact, there is no Mandarin word for "popularity" that has the same meaning among adolescents in Western nations, so we had to use phrases to describe likability and status that were recommended by native Chinese speakers and experts in the Mandarin language.

When we examined what these two samples of adolescents living over seventy-five hundred miles apart told us, our findings suggested that popularity may be at least partially rooted in culture. In the United States, status and likability were very distinct attributes—there was only modest overlap between those teenagers high in one quality and those high in the other. But in China, adolescents who had high status were often also those who were judged to be the most likable. In fact, in the United States, our results revealed that high status was associated with those who were highly aggressive. But in China, we found exactly the opposite—highly aggressive teens were low in status. In a culture that values community, status may not be all that important.

A third possible explanation for our increasing status obsession may be related to the mass media, but not exactly in the way you might think. Among scholars in communication studies, the media is referred to as a "super-peer," given its commanding role in not just reflecting but establishing our values. It is the peer we read, watch, and heed. The media is not just the vehicle that gives us access to our high-status peers but is a high-status peer itself. Getting attention from this super-peer is a major sign of status and a guarantor of huge social rewards.

According to this theory, our increased desire for status reached a turning point in the 1980s, when the media became a peer that never slept. A society accustomed to interacting with a single daily newspaper and a few dozen radio and television programs suddenly found itself presented with thousands of options to receive content twenty-four hours a day. As the media's power increased exponentially, it started to use every angle it could to make sure that its audience remained motivated to keep tuning in.

On June 1, 1980, CNN, the first twenty-four-hour news channel, debuted in the United States. Sociologists Joshua Gamson and Denis McQuail observed that this presented a challenge to producers needing to fill airtime, to ensure that viewers would stay engaged as long as possible. McQuail wrote that journalists were required to produce stories that were "supposed to be creative, novel, original, or unexpected [news], yet produced with extreme regularity and often against much more demanding schedules than apply to other industries." To do so they relied much more heavily on a reporting strategy that had worked in the past—stories reporting the news disguised as stories about people. Theories suggest that this shift in framing had a tremendous effect on our desire for status.

Profiling personal stories is a simple and effective way to add an emotional element to any unfolding event. If we are presented with a story about climate change's effect on the polar ice caps, we might switch the channel. But if a teaser promises the tale of a family trying desperately to survive flooding in its hometown as a result of global warming, we are more likely to tune in. With the demand for twenty-four hour content, the focus on "real people" went into overdrive, and soon, we, the public, became characters in the news more than ever before. For a few minutes anyone could be at the center of the media's focus, the most "visible" person of the hour. What once seemed like a great distance between us and those who were revered as high-status individuals now suddenly seemed like not such an obstacle.

As the gap between us and our higher-ranking peers narrowed, we became even more obsessed with status. The public's voyeuristic curiosity about the lifestyles of the rich and famous, the proliferation of tabloid "entertainment/news" programming, and the development of reality TV and social media may all be traced to the sudden accessibility of high status for virtually anyone. When we saw our peers achieve social rewards we once thought inconceivable, it became almost impossible to wish for anything else.

Today it seems as though members of the public have morphed from narrative devices used to tell the news to the news itself. We have witnessed the rise of celebrities whose fame seems to be based only on their status, so that what they do, say, and think is now newsworthy in itself. The concept even extends beyond the popularity of people and includes the value we now ascribe to the status of products and businesses in ways that have changed modern marketing and industry. Perhaps it's time for us to reflect on whether we care a little too much about status, as it is frightening to think where we are headed.

POPULARITY PROBLEM #4:
We Think Status Will Make Us Happy

Today we live in a Warholian world, where we all bid for our brief moment of highly visible status. In the United States alone, over $11 billion a year is spent on plastic surgery. Books about how to earn excessive wealth and prestige regularly appear on bestseller lists. Even in our private lives, in moments when we should be working or connecting with loved ones, we post and tweet, with the not-so-subtle hope that we will garner status. The mid-2010s saw the emergence of consulting firms whose sole purpose is to help individuals increase the number of their social media followers. Will all this time, energy, and expense dedicated to raising our status actually pay off? Will high status actually make us happier?

The answer is no . . . or more accurately, mostly no. I hedge here because the outcome depends on how we approach the question. If we consider the consequences of low status—the fate of those who are widely disregarded, perhaps due to significant deficits in wealth, power, or beauty—then naturally we conclude that it is associated with risk for many types of difficulties in life. It's not merely that low status serves as a marker for these other determinants of despair. It has been associated with outcomes like depression even when accounting for the effects of socioeconomic stress or cultural disadvantage as predictors in their own right.

But most of us do not seek status as a practical way to make ends meet or to help alleviate personal shortcomings, just as most do not wish to reach only the middle of the bell curve. Rather, we long for high status, which, somewhere deep inside, we continue to believe will make us happy.

But what if that conviction is wrong?

Recent research has documented exactly what it's like to have high status, and it's not a pretty picture. In one study, psychologists were able to interview over a dozen of the "most popular" peers in our society whose names would be instantly recognizable—a group that included movie stars, CEOs, TV actors, a state governor, music legends, NBA and NHL athletes, journalists, and even a former child celebrity. No matter what their background, those with the highest status in our society all tell a very similar story, one that plays out in a series of stages.

Stage 1: Elation. *The attainment of high status is accompanied by a whirlwind of attention and adoration.*

"The first thing that happens is that everything and everybody around you changes . . . And you can feel it filter down to whatever your inner circle of friends is," explained one subject. The attention also comes with perks: "The access is unbelievable." "Suddenly, you're worth something. You're important." "When you reach a stage financially when you don't need freebies, that's when freebies are thrown to you."

The experience is variously described as a "guilty pleasure," a "high," and a "rush."

Stage 2: Overwhelmed. *Most people find their sudden rise in popularity becomes almost too much to deal with.*

As another subject warned, "Fame 101 is needed to teach people what's coming: the swell of people, the requests, the letters, the emails, the greetings on the street, the people in cars, the honking of the horns, the screaming of your name. A whole world comes to you that you have no idea is there. It just comes from nowhere. And it starts to build and build like a small tornado, and it's coming at you, and coming at you, and by the time it gets to you, it's huge and can sweep you off your feet and take you away." Not surprisingly, this quickly leads to . . .

Stage 3: Resentment. *The attention becomes irritating.*

"You are an animal in a cage," the movie star said. "If you're sitting at a sporting event in a seat and you're on the aisle . . . all of a sudden you have someone on your left arm kneeling in the aisle [wanting to talk to you]. I want to push them down the stairs."

Stage 4: Addiction. *The ambivalence regarding popularity becomes almost too much to bear.*

If you've ever watched *E! True Hollywood Story*, you'll recognize this stage as the moral of each episode.

"I've been addicted to almost every substance known to man at one point or another, and the most addicting of them all is fame," said one celebrity. As is true of any addiction, a number of people become dependent on their next hit, hating themselves for wanting it but desperate to have it anyway. Some high-status individuals never get beyond this phase, and their lives become an endless chase for an ever-greater high. If it eludes them, they become the junkies who will do almost anything simply to get even one last taste of the notoriety that they so desperately crave. The cycle can become debilitating, because unlike other addictions, it inherently requires the participation of others to satisfy the craving for status.

Stage 5: Splitting. *The high-status individual realizes that his popularity is not based on his or her actual character at all.*

"You find out there are millions of people who like you for what you do. They couldn't care less who you are," acknowledges one well-known figure, while another says, "It's not really me . . . it's this working part of me, or the celebrity part of me . . . So, I am a toy in a shop window."

Some report that they are forced to form split personas to retain any real sense of a genuine self-concept—a version of themselves that is for the public, and a version they can maintain with family and friends, while their true self remains somewhere trapped in between. Over time it becomes harder and harder for them to even remember which is real. One subject reports he has "two different dialogues—the one that I'm thinking and the one I'm saying . . . [I can't be] as authentic as I'd like to be . . . to show my true self."

Stage 6: Loneliness and Depression. *At this stage, there is no one who really knows the high-status individual at all.*

As one respondent explains, "I've lost friends . . . just by all this adoration that comes whenever you're in public, [my friends] feel less. They feel inferior . . . You're special and they aren't. You're extraordinary and they're ordinary . . . and the next thing you know, they'd really rather not have anything to do with you. And you understand them. You have to."

Philip Burguières, CEO, president, and director of at least a dozen large, international energy conglomerates over the years, spoke about this isolation often. "I estimate that 50 percent of CEOs, at some point in their lives, experience depression. I receive calls about it daily, and at least twice a week I meet CEOs who are struggling or have struggled with depression," he said. Rock star Dan Reynolds of the band Imagine Dragons has described his rise in status in similar terms: "[I've been] depressed as hell . . . It's lonely when your life changes like this . . . I've lost all my friends . . . the relationships feel false." Olympic swimmer Ian Thorpe recalls how "The cancer of attention [contributed to my depression]. People sometimes don't think you have a right to feel like this because you've been famous or successful."

Stage 7: Wishing for Something Else. *Celebrities have everything that many other people wish for, but lack the one thing they desire most.*

"[Popularity] is an intrinsically untrustworthy dance partner—it could leave you at any time . . . so it's a very mysterious thing," explains one. "Anyone who comes through that dance partner to you is also mysterious. Why? Why do they want me? Why are they interested in me? . . . You start double-guessing yourself. I find I put up a kind of a wall around me, and I just deal with people up to that wall but not inside of it."

One cried while explaining, "I worry about my son, because I don't want him to think of me, because I'm famous, as being any more special than he is. And I wonder sometimes if he's going to confuse fame with worthiness or value as a person, that if he doesn't grow up to be someone who has celebrity or fame, he is somehow not recognized or not worthy of people's respect or admiration. I think a lot of people confuse it. In our whole culture, people confuse it."

In response, these high-status individuals decide to invest in something that feels authentic. For some, it's humanitarian work or charity; for others, it's stumping for a cause. But for many with high status, it's genuine human connection that they long for more than anything else. Relationships with people who care about them for who they are, accept them, and want to spend time with them. It's awfully ironic: while the rest of the world is wishing for status, those who have it are wishing for likability—the type of popularity that is so much easier to achieve.

How about those kids with whom we grew up who were "most popular"? They didn't all end up becoming sports heroes or celebrities, or in high political positions. How did they turn out? Recent scientific data has addressed this question as well. Joe Allen and his colleagues at the University of Virginia sought to track down the "cool" kids from one of their high school samples to see whether having elevated status led to long-term benefits or problems. Allen's study had begun with a group of youth who were just about to enter high school. They were thirteen years old—pubescent, naive, and in the throes of the usual adolescent awkwardness. Some had high status, but most did not. Using a variety of measures, Allen determined which were most popular and also which seemed to care most about having high status.

As anyone who has attended high school might expect, these high-status adolescents were among the first in their grade to get involved romantically with others; the first to show signs of minor deviancy, like shoplifting or sneaking into a movie without paying; and the most likely to have physically attractive friends. These are the qualities that many adolescents consider to be "cool," and sure enough, it was these kids who were named as "most popular" by their schoolmates. Allen and his colleagues labeled this group the "pseudo-mature" teens.

Ten years later, Allen and his team tracked down all the participants in the initial study to see how the pseudo-mature teens had matured compared to their peers. By now the subjects were in their twenties and dispersed far from their hometown of Charlottesville. Allen's lab flew around the country to meet with each participant, interview his or her friends and romantic partners, collect public records concerning them, and even gain permission to follow each participant's social media profiles as another source of data. The result was one of the most comprehensive studies ever to examine relationship development from early adolescence to young adulthood.

What they discovered was that the pseudo-mature participants who seemed to have it all at thirteen were no longer doing as well. In fact, they seemed to be experiencing many more difficulties than their formerly low-status peers.

Allen found that by their twenties, the high-status kids were significantly more likely to abuse alcohol and marijuana, and to have higher likelihoods of serious substance-related problems, like DUIs and drug-related arrests. Even after considering their socioeconomic status and adolescent use of alcohol and marijuana as possible predictors, it was their focus on high status as teens that was significantly related to these adult outcomes.

Having high status at age thirteen also predicted poorer-quality friendships later in life. Allen asked each participant in his young adult study to bring a close friend to the research lab. These friends were able to tell the researchers a great deal about the subjects' lives. Results indicated that those with high status at age thirteen had a more difficult time making friends in adulthood, and those friends they did have said they didn't much enjoy that friendship.

High-status teens also were less likely to be involved in satisfying romantic relationships as adults. When those relationships broke up, they were more likely to believe that it was because their partners did not find them to be "popular enough" or "part of the right crowd." Caring about status at age thirteen seemed to be related to a lifetime of seeking more popularity.

Similar results have been found in longitudinal studies of adults. In their studies on extrinsic goals—the kinds of wishes that focus on being well regarded by others—psychologists Richard Ryan and Tim Kasser found a curious link with life satisfaction and well-being. They studied people's wishes in countries throughout the world, including North America, Russia, Croatia, Germany, and South Korea. Their findings were remarkably consistent no matter where the research was conducted: those who wish for intrinsic rewards, like those that come from close and caring relationships, personal growth, and helping others, report far greater happiness, vitality, self-esteem, and even physical health. But wishing for extrinsic goals—fame, power, excessive wealth, and beauty—is associated with discontent, anxiety, and depression. When Ryan and Kasser likewise followed their research participants over time, it was those who wished most strongly for status who were the most likely to be faring worse later in their lives.

So, what is the point of seeking status in the twenty-first century? We don't need it for the same reasons we did when our brains first developed. In most contemporary societies, humans can access vital resources like food simply by visiting the local market. And with the advent of computerized dating sites and fruity alcoholic cocktails, finding a willing mating partner also is easier in the modern arena, even for those who are not the "alpha" member of their group.

But our ancient brain wiring has us yearning for status nevertheless, and over time we have created new and sophisticated ways to help satisfy those cravings every day. Society has fostered the illusion that by spending enough time, money, and energy, anyone can attain high status.

But that's not the kind of popularity that will make us happy. Perhaps it's time for us to realize that status is no longer worth wishing for.

PART II

The Surprising Ways That Some Types of Popularity Can Change Our Lives

CHAPTER 4

Herds and Headaches

How Our Bodies Are Programmed to Care About Popularity

An old house sits at the top of a wooded hill, a cape of fog swirling around it in the darkness. The only light comes from a single window shrouded with overgrown vines and a broken shutter. Inside lies a man in a tangle of sheets on a bed with a headboard as tall and heavy as a tombstone. He is frail, wheezing, yet desperately clutching something made of glass. His dry, crusted lips part; the sound of air slowly escapes his body.

"Ro . . ." he moans. "Rose . . ."

His eyes open suddenly, staring straight ahead with

pain, fear, then anger. He finally finds the strength to utter:

"Rosenbaum!"

From his hand drops a frame holding a picture of his childhood bully, Damien Rosenbaum. It falls to the floor, the glass shattering to pieces as the last sound of air emerges from the limp body above . . .

OK, none of this actually happened. But it could have. Recent evidence suggests that being unpopular can be hazardous to our health. In fact, it might even kill us.

That's because our bodies are literally programmed to make us care about popularity. More on that later . . .

First, a quick quiz:

Do you own an iPhone/iPad?
Do you drive a Honda?
Have you recently bought something from Amazon?
Do you use a Gillette razor?
Have you purchased anything made by Disney recently?
Did you drink a Coca-Cola product this week?
Do you have a Gmail address?

If you answered yes to at least one of these questions, then you're pretty much like most of the rest of the world. It is part of human nature to follow trends. The above list was adopted from a report on the largest global brands, and while some of their success reflects the fact that they offer excellent products and services, it also has to do with popularity. We like to follow the herd, and we tend to rely on one another substantially when we make our own choices. There is something about popularity that is inherently appealing.

Princeton sociologist Matthew Salganik and his colleague at Yahoo!, Duncan Watts, conducted a series of experiments to test just how strongly drawn we are to popularity. In one study, over twelve thousand participants from North America, South America, and Europe were asked to visit an internet site to rate some new music and download it for free. The site wasn't real but was developed by the experimenters to make it look similar to iTunes. Through this study, Salganik and Watts were able to examine how our taste in music relies on that of others.

Participants were initially presented with a list of forty-eight unfamiliar rock songs. They were instructed to listen to each, rate it from one to five stars, and then, if they wished, download the song for free. In this first phase of the study, the experimenters simply collected data on the popularity of each song. For instance, "She Said" by the group Parker Theory was by far the most popular—15 percent of all participants who heard it chose to download it. "Florence" by the group Post Break Tragedy was the least popular, with only 1 percent of listeners downloading it. Much like on iTunes, the researchers used these data to create a list of the songs organized by their popularity. "She Said" was listed first, with the most downloads, and "Florence" was last.

Then, the experimenters began their study on conformity by testing what might happen if they manipulated the ranking of each song. For their next group of participants, they simply inverted the data on each song's download rate: "Florence" was now ranked as the most downloaded choice, while "She Said" was the least. With this manipulated ranking posted, the experimenters opened the music portal again and watched to see how each song's apparent popularity affected the participants' musical choices over time. As you may expect, popularity mattered—the download rate of "Florence" increased tenfold, while that of "She Said" plunged to only 2 percent. And as more people downloaded "Florence," it was made to seem even more popular, leading in turn to even more downloads, while "She Said" remained at the bottom of the pack.

Results like these help explain why popularity itself has become such a valued business commodity. Marketers know that we tend to follow the herd, so they rely on who or what is popular to influence our behaviors.

Have you read an article online recently? You may have noticed that the headline is no longer the only thing placed at the top of the page meant to attract our attention. There's often also a row of icons above each article, one for each social media outlet, with a running tally showing how often the piece has been emailed, "liked" on Facebook, tweeted, and so on. Lists of "trending topics" have become common, too—not just on social media, but on news outlets as well. This information is intended to pique our interest, as if the popularity of the story among others should make it more enticing to us. The tactic is not much different from a TV commercial that touts the "number one movie in America" or the "leading brand of headache medicine." In each case, we are called to follow the herd.

We are in turn prompted to tell others what we liked, or bought, or preferred, so that the herd can follow us as well. As we finish reading an article that impresses us, we are prodded to "like" it or email it to our friends. Likewise, when we buy products, we are asked to post the news to our Facebook feed. I can't imagine that my friends would be interested in knowing that I just bought shaving cream, but I can understand why the manufacturer wants me to tell them I have. We associate popularity with quality.

Why is this strategy so effective when, logically, it doesn't make much sense? Why should I care about what everyone else is reading? I want to read what interests me, not what appeals to ten thousand complete strangers. I want to watch movies that match my own tastes, and I assume that my own body's physiology is the most important factor to consider when choosing a medicine.

One explanation is based on the idea that we feel essentially similar to others, thus, we assume that whatever the herd likes, we'd like, too. Or perhaps our natural proclivities toward popularity come from our sense of community and our desire to feel connected. If everyone is talking about a news item, or a movie, we don't want to be left out of the conversation.

It's interesting that despite all reason, we remain naturally tuned in to popularity. Yet this instinct doesn't always help us. Sometimes our tendency to follow the herd can have serious consequences.

Economists suggest that the lure of popularity has been responsible for some of the most peculiar and damaging trends in history. In 1841, Scottish journalist Charles MacKay wrote about the human impulse to follow the herd in his famous book *Memoirs of Extraordinary Popular Delusions and the Madness of Crowds*, in which he examined the tendency for an asset to gain in value well beyond its intrinsic worth simply because it is perceived as popular—a phenomenon we now refer to as a "market bubble." In one chapter, he recounts the great fervor that ignited in the early seventeenth century over a particular tulip species that had been imported to Holland. This blossom offered no apparent superior value in its beauty, scent, or longevity when compared to indigenous species, but its popularity grew nonetheless. As this passion for the tulip spread from the aristocrats to the middle class, and eventually to those with scant means, the flower's value soared, ultimately garnering huge sums for even a blossom weighing less than a gram. Reportedly, this type of tulip became so valuable that visitors to Holland were imprisoned if they unwittingly damaged a bulb. Such "overvaluation" of a commodity based on its popularity rather than on its actual worth is the basis for an unsustainable market, and is the same phenomenon that accounted for the stock market's dot-com bubble of the 1990s.

As more Dutch were afflicted by what MacKay called "Tulipomania" and the popularity of the flowers increased, prices continued to rise. The Dutch assumed that citizens from throughout Europe would share their enthusiasm, bringing increased value to their investments. Tulip dealers accordingly mortgaged their homes and spent their fortunes to purchase more bulbs, while businessmen began neglecting other profitable industries. Of course, the tulips never turned out to be worth anything near what people had paid for them, and when the flower's price dropped dramatically, the collapse of the market bubble ultimately threatened the entire Dutch economy. MacKay concluded, "Men . . . think in herds; it will be seen that they go mad in herds, while they only recover their senses slowly, and one by one."

In my own research, I have found that the instinct to embrace the popular can lead to behaviors with even worse consequences. My work has been designed to understand how herd-following patterns begin when we are young, and specifically just how far youth will go to be like one another. What will adolescents do when they are told that their popular peers endorse behaviors that are dangerous or illegal, and how will they react when they are asked to be mean toward one another, even though they know it is morally wrong to do so?

In one study, my former colleague and now Stanford psychologist Geoff Cohen and I examined a range of risky behaviors. We asked kids about drinking alcohol, having sex without a condom, smoking marijuana, and using harder drugs, like heroin and cocaine. We also questioned them about bullying, dangerous eating behaviors like bingeing and purging, and using hormones and drugs to change their body shape.

In the United States, about one of every four adolescents has used alcohol before the age of fourteen, 25 percent have had five drinks in a row before high school graduation, one in five smoked pot before age fourteen, and 40 percent of teens report that they did not use a condom the last time they had sex. More than one out of ten say they have fasted just to try to look thinner. These are all remarkably risky behaviors that strongly predict which teens will become pregnant before graduating high school, grow up to have substance abuse problems, develop serious eating disorders, and even get cervical cancer.

Of course, when we asked adolescents in our study whether they would be likely to engage in these behaviors, the vast majority told us that drugs are bad and that everyone should use a condom, be nice to others, and keep a healthy attitude about physical appearance.

We then invited each of these same subjects to participate in a simulated online chat room along with three of their most popular fellow students. In fact, it was not a real chat room at all, but a computer program we developed using intricate graphics and timing to convince adolescents that they were talking live with the cool kids from their own school. The others in the chat room were phantoms, or "electronic confederates," that we identified as highly popular by listing the first name and last initial of actual grade-mates in our participants' school. Our deception worked. At the end of the experiment, when we revealed our procedures, our subjects told us they really believed they were online, and even reported excitedly that they believed they knew exactly which of their peers was taking part in their chat.

In this counterfeit chat room, we again asked adolescents the same questions about risky behaviors, but this time, we had the fictitious peers take part first and report that they would be very likely to engage in each bad habit. Our participants were then asked again to respond to the same questions, first while they believed their peers were watching their responses, and then after they had ostensibly logged out of the chat room, so we could make sure they weren't just showing off for the cool kids.

What we found was that simply knowing that their popular peers would be likely to drink alcohol, smoke pot, or have unprotected sex was sufficient to change adolescents' answers—and dramatically so. Suddenly our participants were far more apt to say they would engage in all these behaviors than they had been when they began our study. Even when they had logged off and were told that none of their peers were watching, our subjects continued to state that they would pursue those risky actions.

We then took the study one step further. Rather than simply asking adolescents what they would do hypothetically, we gave our participants the chance to actually do something they shouldn't do in real life. After responding to a few simple questions about hobbies and interests within the chat room, during which we manipulated the responses of one confederate to seem a bit deviant from the others, we offered our participants the option to vote one of their "peers" off the experiment. They were instructed that for someone to be kicked out, he would have to be voted off by all of the others in the chat room unanimously. They were also told that the evicted participant would lose out on the chance to meet the others, and would not receive the reward we offered for completing the task.

In each case, the subjects were asked to cast the deciding vote: the fate of their peer was in their hands, and they had the choice to be kind or to be mean. What they didn't know was that, in this case, the individual they were voting off wasn't a real person. They were also unaware that the other votes were fabricated.

Once the subjects saw that their popular peers had voted against one of their own, eight out of ten of our participants voted to evict as well.

Why are we so likely to follow the herd?

> On a sunny day in the year 60,000 BC in what is now southern Europe, a lone female enters a crowded cave where others are sitting down to eat their latest kill. But when she attempts to take her place at the rock where her hominin friends usually eat, she is shunned. It is the time of the full moon, and the others at her rock have a rule that on these days, females must wear fur clothes. This particular woman is wearing a wrap made of animal skin.
>
> "You can't sit with us!" the women seem to grunt. Finally, with no place else to eat, she leaves the cave,

> walks a few dozen yards, and sits alone. Moments later, she is attacked by a wooly mammoth and is never heard from again.

OK, this didn't happen, either. But research suggests that there may be something about unpopularity then that has a lot to do with the humans we have become today.

Back in 60,000 BC, we were not the only humanlike species on the planet. Anthropologists believe that in addition to the beings who had migrated out of Africa and closely resembled our own species today, there were Neanderthals in the north, Denisovans in Asia, and even a small humanlike species called *Homo floresiensis* in Indonesia. Yet only we humans ultimately survived. We endured not because we were the strongest—in fact, the Neanderthals were a bit larger, with bigger teeth, and probably could have won any battle against relatively weak humans. It wasn't because we had bigger brains, either.

There is one quality that is unique among humans and has been credited to be a fundamental factor in our evolutionary advantage. While some species became larger, or stronger, or able to withstand more severe temperatures, it was we humans who learned how to work together. Anthropology research reveals that, unlike other hominins, humans had the genes to form and comprehend complex vocal sounds. Language ability formed the basis for more sophisticated social interactions. Soon we became a species that could organize into groups and network with our peers in ways that were far superior to those of the others.

Living as a herd offered many survival advantages. By working as a community and sharing tools, we could hunt more effectively. By sharing the spoils of the hunt, we could eat food while it remained fresh and safe to consume. Joining together in groups enabled us to warn and protect one another when predators threatened. We soon evolved to become acutely sensitive to social cues, and through the process of natural selection, our species eventually favored only those who were attuned to the herd. Those individuals who remained solitary became extinct.

It's been thousands of years since we needed one another to survive our daily lives. Rarely does someone today venture out to Starbucks alone only to be attacked by a woolly mammoth. But the vestigial effects of our evolution as social creatures are still visible in many subtle ways. Have you ever wondered why yawns are contagious and the menstrual cycles of women living together synchronize? Some hypothesize that even these phenomena reflect our genetic programming as a social species. The herd worked most effectively when everyone was able to move as a single unit and stop together for resting, mating, or childbirth. Today, we still have instincts that make us become tired simultaneously or fertile at the same times.

So what happens if we don't follow the herd and choose to remain alone, isolated, unpopular?

Over the past several decades, scientists have demonstrated that being unpopular can actually be harmful. It's not hard to imagine how solitude can lead to emotional difficulties. Those who are ostracized, alienated, bullied, or victimized are more likely to experience loneliness, low self-esteem, anxiety, and depression. But there is now also evidence that being unpopular may even have dire consequences for our physical health—to the point that it can kill us.

Julianne Holt-Lunstad, a psychologist at Brigham Young University, recently conducted a meta-analysis—a study of studies—combining the data from 148 prior investigations. Each asked the same basic question: does being unpopular increase the risk of death? Collectively, these studies included 308,000 participants between the ages of six and eighty from all over the world. Each included two basic procedures. First, the investigators measured the size of participants' social networks, the number of their friends, whether they lived alone, and the extent to which they participated in social activities. Then, they followed each participant for months, years, and even decades to track their mortality rate.

The results revealed that being unpopular—isolated, disconnected, lonely—actually predicts mortality rates. But perhaps even more surprising is just how powerful these effects can be. People in the study who had larger networks of friends had a 50 percent increased chance of survival by the end of the study. It didn't matter whether the participants were male or female, whether they had health problems to begin with, or where in the world they lived. Being disconnected from the herd substantially increased the risk of death.

But not every kind of connection was equally important. And this finding was key, because it gives us a clue as to which type of popularity really matters.

Simply living with someone, or having a spouse, was related to increased life expectancy, but not very significantly. It was those people who actively participated in their social lives and had *good-quality* relationships who seemed to benefit the most. In other words, it was those individuals who had relationships that the *most likable* people tend to have that seemed to have the advantage. Their chance of survival was 91 percent higher than those who were essentially alone. In other words, almost twice the number of popular people were alive at the end point of the study as those who were unpopular. This is a highly significant finding. Comparing these figures to research on established health risks suggests that being unpopular more strongly increases our chance of death than does obesity, physical inactivity, or binge drinking. In fact, the only factor comparable to unpopularity as a health hazard is smoking!

How could our social lives, or lack thereof, kill us? Could effects like these be accounted for by intentional self-harm? Perhaps those most socially isolated, ostracized, or friendless are especially likely to commit suicide?

This is certainly true. In the United States, suicide is the second leading cause of death in adolescence and young adulthood; it remains one of the top ten causes of death until the age of sixty-five. One of the most common risk factors for suicide attempts is feeling lonely, like a burden to others, or like one doesn't belong. Among adolescents in particular, ostracism from a peer group is an especially strong predictor of suicidal behavior. We are painfully reminded of this every time we hear of another teen who commits suicide after being tormented in school or online.

But remarkably, intentional self-harm does not account for the link between unpopularity and mortality. In Holt-Lunstad's meta-analysis, studies that measured death by suicide were excluded.

In fact, recent evidence suggests that those who are socially disconnected are at risk for a wide range of physical health problems that can cause death. In 2016, Kathleen Mullan Harris, a sociologist at the University of North Carolina at Chapel Hill, examined how social connections might predict coronary artery disease, hypertension, cancer, and stroke. Her research accessed data from four large, nationally representative samples that collectively included about fifteen thousand Americans between the ages of twelve and eighty-five. As with Holt-Lunstad's meta-analysis, Harris's group examined first social integration and then a range of physical health indices between five and twelve years later.

What Harris found was that having friends or a romantic partner, socializing with neighbors, and volunteering substantially decreased the risk of physical illness. Those who were socially isolated when the study began were most likely to develop high blood pressure. They were also most likely to have high levels of C-reactive protein in their blood—a harbinger of inflammation-related health problems, like rheumatoid arthritis, inflammatory bowel disease, and heart attacks. None of these findings seemed to have any relation to participants' gender, race, educational attainment, income, history of smoking, alcohol use, physical activity, stress, or depression. Of course, it is impossible to ascertain whether it was unpopularity that *caused* these health problems per se, but the results are among the most powerful to suggest that even after accounting for so many other possible explanations, social isolation seemed to be the most powerful prognosticator of illness years later.

We now know at least a few reasons why being popular, even as adults, is more important than we ever imagined. One simply has to do with the psychological effects of unpopularity. Being disliked means that we lack social support, so in times of stress, we have no one to turn to, to help us out of trouble. In one study of women with breast cancer, simply participating in a support group with other patients was a significant predictor of life expectancy, even after accounting for other possible factors that could have explained these effects.

The effects of popularity can even be seen in our body's physiology. Recent evidence suggests that our connection to fellow humans has a strong effect on cortisol—a hormone that is produced as part of the autonomic nervous system in response to stress. Cortisol can be beneficial—in the face of a looming attack, it maintains the fight-or-flight response. When this hormone is released, our hearts pump more blood to our muscles, our airways expand so our brains can get more oxygen, and our body fat releases blood sugar so we can maintain our energy while we bolt or battle.

But cortisol has a Goldilocks-like quality: too much or too little can wreak havoc on a wide range of bodily functions. High levels of cortisol weaken our immune systems, leading to obesity, heart disease, gastrointestinal disorders, and even infertility. They can also damage the cortisol response system itself until it is no longer responsive to stress, much like overused shock absorbers compromise the performance of a car. Too little cortisol puts us at risk for chronic fatigue, asthma, rheumatoid arthritis, eczema, and so on.

Can popularity affect cortisol levels, and thus place unpopular people at greater risk for dire health consequences?

My graduate student Casey Calhoun and I set out to determine whether that was the case. We invited about two hundred adolescent girls into our lab and measured a wide range of their prior social experiences. Then, we exposed them to a minor stressor and measured the cortisol in their saliva to assess whether the social experiences of these girls would influence how their bodies responded to stress. We did so by asking each girl to face a camera with a feedback screen and deliver an impromptu speech. A young male onlooker sat directly in front of them, ostensibly judging their performance. Giving a speech is a very safe task commonly used by social scientists to induce stress and provoke cortisol output.

As we expected, many of our participants had mild elevations in cortisol while giving their speech but quickly recovered to normal levels within fifteen to twenty minutes, a normal span of time. But some subjects as young as twelve already had abnormal responses. Their bodies produced too little cortisol, indicating an under-reactive stress response system. This was a sign that their brains were not prepared to handle stress, which put them at risk for developing later health problems.

Why did these girls have inadequate cortisol responses? One of the strongest predictors of this reaction was the extent to which they had been teased, excluded by others, and called names by peers in the past. It didn't matter how old they were, or how many other stressful things they had experienced in their lives. The results also were not accounted for by their race, ethnicity, or symptoms of depression. The more unpopular they were, the more their cortisol response systems were severely compromised.

If unpopularity prevents our bodies from responding adequately to stress, then do social connection and support help us react more adaptively? We examined this question in a second study also involving adolescent girls and a speech task. But in this experiment, we asked girls to bring their best friends along.

After the subjects delivered their talks before the video camera, the girls, naturally, discussed them. Many of their friends were very supportive of their effort, listening carefully, helping the girls feel better about themselves after the speech, and being generally empathic. But the friends of some other girls were less responsive, and in fact, a few were so focused on themselves that they barely engaged in mutual conversation at all.

In this experiment, we focused on those girls who had an overreactive cortisol response to stress—also an indicator of future health difficulties. For this group, cortisol levels spiked after the speech and remained high for far longer than they did for other girls in our study. But we found that the more girls' friends were supportive after the talks, the more quickly cortisol levels reverted to normal. Overall, our results demonstrated that social experiences have remarkable power over our stress response system.

More recently, psychologists and neuroscientists have learned that the link between our membership in the herd and our health may go even deeper. It is not only when we feel stressed that being socially connected matters. Being unpopular may be sufficient to harm us on its own.

> Mary Sue's life changed forever late one afternoon. It was a nice day, and in fact, all days were nice for Mary Sue. She walked to school, sat with her friends at lunch, and then came home to milk and cookies that her mother had left out for her. Everything about Mary Sue's life seemed perfectly pleasant. But there was something out of the ordinary. Mary Sue and everyone in her entire town existed in shades of black and white: their hair, their eyes, their clothes, their skin—everything.
>
> When evening came, Mary Sue did her homework at a desk in the corner of her room, a cardigan draped over her shoulders and a pair of horn-rimmed glasses hanging

> from a chain around her neck. It started to get chilly, and she crossed the room to close the window. Down on the street she saw a boy she liked standing and looking up at her. He reached down, lifted a rock, and then sneered as he threw it at Mary Sue's window. The rock landed in the middle of her bedroom floor, surrounded by shattered glass.
>
> As he drove off with a group of laughing friends, Mary Sue stood in shock. How could something so horrible happen? Why would she be the target of a deed so . . . well, so unpleasant? Then she felt something she had never felt before: her heart ached; tears ran down her face. Suddenly, Mary Sue's hair turned blond, her eyes became blue, and her lips pink. That act of unkindness had not only broken Mary Sue's heart but seemed to change every cell in her body. Neither Mary Sue nor her town would ever be the same . . .

OK, this scenario also is adapted from a movie. But is an experience such as Mary Sue's strictly fiction? How does rejection actually get under our skin and transform us?

Have you ever noticed that when people talk about feeling lonely, rejected, or unpopular, they tend to use words typically associated with physical illness? Terms like "heartbreak" or "homesick," emotional "scars," and "hurt" feelings are common to many languages. Are these just expressions, or is there something about unpopularity that can actually do us physical harm?

UCLA neuroscientist Naomi Eisenberger wondered the same thing and took a special interest in the question of whether unpopularity may affect us in more fundamental ways than we are aware of. She conducted a series of studies designed to examine the regions of our brain that become activated when we experience social rejection. She did so by having her participants take part in a computer game designed to simulate a negative interaction with peers.

Imagine playing catch over the computer with two other players who, you are told, are in nearby rooms. On-screen are two stick figures, one on each side, representing the other players, and a hand in the center representing you. To take part in the game you hold a joystick, and when someone throws a ball to you, you catch it, and then choose to whom you would like to throw it next by moving the joystick left or right.

This game is called Cyberball, and it was developed by researchers to understand social experiences. In Eisenberger's study, subjects were scanned in an fMRI machine while playing. But unbeknownst to them, there were no other actual participants in the game—the stick figures were controlled by a computer simulation program. For about ten minutes, the program ensured that the ball was thrown to each player an equal number of times.

But then, without explanation, the program made it appear as though the other two players had decided to exclude the study participant from the game. Imagine watching as the ball is tossed back and forth, over and over, but never to you. Eisenberger let the game go on in this manner for another ten minutes.

During this latter period the researchers noticed something interesting happening: according to fMRI results, the parts of the brain that were activated during this part of the experiment were the same as those that are involved when we experience physical pain. Two regions in particular surprised Eisenberger—the dorsal anterior cingulate cortex (dACC) and the anterior insula (AI). Of course, the participants playing Cyberball did not experience any actual pain. The part of our brains responsible for the sensation of burning, stinging, or aching is elsewhere. But it is the dACC and the AI that work with our sensory input to interpret those sensations and tell us if we're feeling something extremely unpleasant. In fact, these regions are part of the most powerful alarm systems in the brain, motivating us to escape the source of our pain at all costs. In short, Eisenberger found that at least some regions of our brain experience unpopularity in the same way that they respond to physical distress—a phenomenon that she refers to as "social pain."

Subsequent research found that these same regions are activated during a whole host of social rejection experiences. As soon as we fear that we might get rejected from the group, our brain sends the most powerful signal at its disposal to warn us and motivate us back into the fold. Worrying about a breakup, seeing pictures of someone being teased, remembering a lost friend or loved one, or even just thinking about being negatively judged by others in the future all seem to implicate the same brain regions.

The neural overlap between social pain and physical pain has been identified in several other studies as well. For instance, research has found that those who have a low tolerance for physical pain also seem to be more sensitive to interpersonal rejection, and vice versa. In one experiment, Eisenberger even found that taking a Tylenol can actually reduce the sensation of social pain. Our brains try to ease the pain of headaches and heartbreaks in the exact same way.

Unpopularity also is felt in millions of other places in our bodies simultaneously and just as quickly: within our cells. Every day we lose millions of cells as they die off, and new ones are born, built to specifications dictated by our DNA. But there's an interesting thing about DNA: it contains far more information than is needed for any given cell. Some of its genes are turned on, while others are left off, depending on where in our bodies the cell is located. It's kind of like when you buy a computer that has a lot of software preloaded—some has already been activated to help make the computer run, but other software just sits on the desktop, dormant, waiting for you to double-click it.

So, if a cell is located in a kidney, the parts of DNA with the blueprint for a kidney cell are activated, while the gene that determines, say, the color of eyes remains inactive. This is useful—we don't want an eye growing out of our kidney—so that part of the DNA strand literally coils up and moves to the edge of the nucleus, far from the center where DNA gets double-clicked.

Recently, neuroscientists discovered that unpopularity affects that mechanism. At the first sign that we may be banished from the group, our DNA unravels and reorients. In fact, social rejection experiences activate a surprisingly large number of genes, while also deactivating many others.

UCLA psychologists George Slavich and Steve Cole, experts in the field of human social genomics, have described DNA as being "exquisitely sensitive to social rejection." They studied what happens immediately after we've been dumped by a romantic partner, excluded from a social event, rejected by a stranger, or even simply told that we may be socially evaluated by others we care about. Within forty minutes, they found, a wide array of changes in our DNA can be detected in the blood. Only a few dozen out of at least twenty thousand genes turn on or off in these moments, but even that small number seem to play a very significant role.

According to Slavich and Cole, these activated genes have a radical effect on the immune system. Some are linked to the body's inflammation response, which comes in handy when we need to heal wounds or fight off bacterial infections. Slavich and Cole suggest that this response to rejection may be nature's mechanism to help those who were unpopular. Millennia ago individuals who had no peers to protect them faced a high risk of an untimely death due to injury or attack. Those whose bodies preemptively activated a "pro-inflammatory" response that would be ready to heal them from any impending wounds were the most likely to survive. Ultimately, evolution favored bodies that were quickest to respond, and thus most sensitive to rejection.

Other genes implicated in this process are related to viral protection; social rejection seems to deactivate these DNA. Slavich and Cole suggest that those who had no peers to protect them no longer had a great need to be protected from viruses—who would infect them?—so their bodies conserved energy by reducing their vigilance to infection.

But today our lives are different. There's no longer a great need for our immune systems to respond to the dangers associated with loneliness. Being unfriended on Facebook doesn't require a systemic inflammation response. Our bodies, however, continue to respond as they did sixty thousand years ago. Today humans suffer from a wide range of diseases related to chronic inflammation, like cancer, asthma, Alzheimer's, Crohn's, hepatitis, lupus—the list goes on and on. We're also very likely to catch a cold.

Our DNA doesn't reorient itself only when we actually experience severe social rejection. Such changes occur even at the most subtle suggestion that we may be shunned. There's even research to suggest that our pro-inflammatory genes are activated when we merely imagine being rejected, or when we play a video game that simulates our being left out.

Why, then, don't we all fall ill after every heartbreak and betrayal? It's likely that we *do* experience an inflammatory response on such occasions, but only in a few cells out of the thirty-seven trillion in our bodies. It's those who are chronically rejected who may suffer harm from these hypersensitive cells. Slavich suggests that unpopularity, even if it occurs over a period of just a few months, may be sufficient to trigger an entire "molecular remodeling" of the body as cells are gradually replaced by those containing DNA that's hypersensitive to social rejection.

Is this a cause for concern?

Holt-Lunstad, the BYU psychologist who conducted the meta-analysis on popularity and mortality argues that despite all of our attempts to feel more connected than ever, including the creation of online social platforms to facilitate more interpersonal ties, we have never felt more lonely. Today, we are more likely to live alone, marry later in life, and move farther from our loved ones than ever before. In just the past twenty years, the number of people reporting that they feel they have no close confidant has tripled.

Our species is programmed to care about popularity. But we may be searching for connections in all the wrong places. What does this mean for our future?

Thomas was walking through a city surrounded by others, but still he felt alone. He could see those around him and even talk to them, but none of it seemed real. Soon, he realized that he was not really connected to other people at all. He was actually strapped to a computer, linked to others at their computers, all networked within a matrix of simulated interactions. Everything was mediated by technology, although everyone secretly longed for genuine social interaction. They built ever more complex programs to help them network across the globe, rapidly share information, and simulate real human discourse. But it didn't work. It just made the people feel farther apart. Thomas and a small group of others discovered the truth—that their lives had been taken over by the machines—and dedicated themselves to bringing the world back together again, so no one would be alone, and no one would be unpopular.

This sounds like a movie, too, right? But it is a true story.

CHAPTER 5

The Popularity Boomerang

How We Create the World We Live In

It was early in the morning. The crowd was jittery. Sitting in a large auditorium at Emory University were hundreds of young students on their first day of law school. For most, this was the start to the career of their dreams. Soon a professor would arrive onstage and begin explaining what the next three years of life would entail. In the meantime, the students shifted in their chairs, offered overly animated introductions to those sitting nearby, and imagined their futures as legal titans.

Seated at the back of the large hall were Jeff and Steve, who hadn't yet met. Steve was tall and sandy-haired, and wore gold wire-rimmed glasses. He had a new leather laptop case with an Emory logo. Jeff wore jeans, a plain brown T-shirt, and a Yankees baseball cap that couldn't quite contain the thatches of curly red hair escaping out its sides and front. He was about to introduce himself when Steve leaned over to pull a few papers from his briefcase and accidentally dropped them onto Jeff's shoes.

"Damn it," Steve mumbled as he reached under Jeff's seat to retrieve them.

"I got it. No problem!" Jeff said as he handed over the pages. "Hey, I'm Jeff." He pointed to Steve's briefcase with the Emory logo and asked, "Did you go here for undergrad?"

"No. Brown," said Steve, who then turned away to review his papers.

Steve and Jeff didn't subsequently spend much time together in law school. They would go on to have very different careers and markedly different lives.

Steve had graduated near the top of his class at Brown and had substantial experience as an intern at a law firm in Providence. Through his mother's professional connections, he had met the governor of Rhode Island on several occasions, drafted briefs for a few high-profile cases, and had a letter of recommendation from a federal judge who predicted his "meteoric rise through the ranks of the legal profession." Steve was nervous on his first day of class, but confident in his future and focused on his desire to become a judge before he turned forty.

Success did not seem as certain for Jeff. He had decided to apply to law school only a few months before he graduated from the University at Albany, SUNY. He was more interested in soccer than his classes while at school, and despite his high intelligence, he did not have the grades to make him an obvious lock for top law schools. Yet throughout college he had received many invitations to join his professors' research labs or intern at their legal practices, offers he usually declined. It was one of those professors who had ultimately convinced Jeff that he should apply to law school. "Your energy would work well in a firm," the professor told him. "At the large firms, being an attorney is about relationships as much as it is about the law. You'll be happy there." But as Jeff sat in the auditorium on that first day, he asked himself, *What am I doing here? Do I even want to* be *a lawyer?*

Steve remained focused throughout his entire law school career. He studied, he clerked, and he built his résumé. For his part, Jeff always seemed to be off socializing with classmates—grabbing coffee, going out on dates, chatting in the hallways. One afternoon in their first year, Steve looked out the library window and saw Jeff laughing with a group of classmates. He returned to his studies, proud of how disciplined he had been to reach this point in his career.

Today, almost two decades later, Jeff is doing far better than even he ever expected. A senior partner at a well-regarded firm in Atlanta, he is the first to arrive at the office every morning, not because he has to be but because he can't wait to see his colleagues and do the work he loves. He's an outstanding attorney.

Things did not work out as well for Steve. Despite a terrific start in law school, over time he gradually lost his confidence and ultimately his interest in the field. He started as an associate at a mid-level firm back in Rhode Island where he'd previously worked as an intern. But he was in over his head, and after a couple of years of middling performance, he and a colleague decided to start their own practice. After a year without much success, he left. He picked up a few cases here and there, but eventually he grew annoyed. He currently works from home doing part-time consulting for a local real estate agency and is quite unhappy about how his career turned out.

Steve's and Jeff's unexpected professional outcomes are just the kind of thing that drives college admissions committees crazy. Who will be the surest bet to succeed? On the first day of law school, Steve was clearly the more qualified, focused, and confident student, with a trajectory that predicted success. Jeff's path was far less clear, and few would have forecast that his achievements would exceed Steve's, yet he is by far the more competent attorney and the happier person in his job today.

This same issue faces anyone hiring new employees. Beyond what is on applicants' résumés, what is the factor that helps distinguish those who will flourish from those who will fail?

After accounting for all of the usual qualities that contribute to well-being and success—intelligence, socioeconomic status, school achievement, physical health, mental health, and so on—there is one factor that has remarkable power to predict life trajectories. It predicts which children thrive. It predicts which employees succeed. It even predicts who enjoys more rewarding romantic relationships and better physical health. It was the one factor that Jeff had but Steve did not.

That factor is likability—not status, but likability. But perhaps more interesting is *how* likability affects us.

"I think it's favoritism!" one parent chastised me before I began a talk at a local high school about my research on the power of likability. "Some people just get all the breaks—life is handed to them on a silver platter."

"People are biased," a friend who works in a large accounting firm insisted. "Everyone loves going to happy hour with Terri at my office, so when they are asked who is good at their job, they all say her. Meanwhile, the rest of us work our butts off, and no one notices."

"It's a con job" is another argument I've heard. "If a guy is really smooth, friends with everyone, making them all laugh, then he is probably up to something. It's a fake."

As it happens, they're all wrong.

Likable people are not just *perceived* to be better at their jobs, more satisfied, happier, and more fulfilled. They actually *are* all those things. The reason is that likable people live in a different world from the one inhabited by their unlikable peers. It is a world of their own making, and it produces a chain reaction of experiences that molds their lives in dramatic ways.

It's a world worth understanding, because following the example of likable people might just change our lives.

Psychologists have been investigating the power of likability for decades. A host of studies began when researchers first found that some children were consistently nominated by their peers as classmates who were "liked the most," far more often than they were picked as someone that classmates "liked the least." These are the Accepted children discussed in Chapter 2. But the power of likability is not only evident among children—Accepteds can be identified at any age. Peer relationship dynamics are remarkably similar across the life span, from four-year-olds in preschool to senior citizens in retirement communities. Accepteds also can be found in any context—the classroom, the office, the softball team, places of worship, the PTA. All include some people who seem effortlessly, immensely likable.

Findings regarding the long-term benefits enjoyed by Accepted people are abundant in the psychological literature. In 1987, developmental psychologists Jeff Parker and Steve Asher summarized dozens of research studies in their now-seminal review of the long-term effects of likability. Their results revealed that compared to the Rejecteds, Accepted children grew up far less likely to drop out of school, commit crimes, or experience mental illness as adults. In another study, Penn State psychologist Scott Gest and his colleagues asked 205 children in grades three through six to report on one another's likability. Then, ten years later, Gest asked all of the participants to report on how their lives were going. The children initially picked as most likable by their peers grew up to be most likely to be employed and to have gotten promotions. The likable kids also had better odds of being in long-term, satisfying friendships and romantic partnerships. Such findings seem to be universal—similar results were obtained in a seven-year study of youth in Shanghai, China.

But studies like these often provide more questions than answers. The one I hear most frequently is: Does any of this research *prove* that likability itself leads to positive outcomes? How do we know that the same factors that make people likable aren't the *real* reasons they are also happy and successful?

In fact, research does tell us that there is indeed a specific set of traits that almost guarantees that an individual will be very well liked. It's a fairly obvious list, and it is generally similar for adults and children.

The most likable people are those who cooperate with others, are helpful, share, and follow the rules.

Likable people are generally well adjusted.

They are smart (but not too smart!).

They are often in a good mood.

They can hold up their end of a conversation.

But they make sure to give others a turn to speak, too.

They are creative, especially at solving awkward social dilemmas.

And perhaps most important: they don't disrupt the group.

Are these the behaviors that are actually responsible for making people happy and successful? Or is there something about being likable—about being popular—that improves our lives directly?

From a scientific perspective, the ideal solution to these questions would be to conduct a randomized clinical trial—in other words, to manipulate a classroom so that one random group of kids became Accepted while others were Rejected. After some period of time, investigators would be able to see how members of each group turned out. You'd have to tell the students, "Remember, these are the kids you really like, so make sure you treat them well. These other kids you don't like so much. Make sure you are not as excited to be with them for the next few years!" Fortunately, researchers are bound by a code of ethics that prohibits them from experimenting with people's lives this way.

But back in 1968, a third-grade schoolteacher named Jane Elliot did attempt something comparable with her classroom in Iowa shortly after Martin Luther King Jr. was assassinated. Her famous "brown eyes, blue eyes" demonstration was designed to teach children about discrimination, and it lasted only a few days. On the first day, she randomly selected children with brown eyes to be "superior" to those whose eyes were blue. She instructed the brown-eyed group not to sit with blue-eyed children or play with them, and she pointed out their foibles. Meanwhile, she offered extra attention and praise to the students with brown eyes, and instructed them to play enthusiastically with one another. It should be noted that her demonstration was intended to illustrate the effects of prejudice, not likability, and Ms. Elliot herself purposefully contributed to the disparity between brown- and blued-eyed children to demonstrate the widespread assumptions of inferiority that are leveled at minority groups.

Nevertheless, it's interesting that after only one day of being more liked by their peers, the brown-eyed children began acting more confidently and doing better in schoolwork. The blue-eyed children, meanwhile, became timid, glum, and isolated. They were even less likely to correctly answer quiz items as frequently as they had just the day before. When Ms. Elliot reversed the conditions of her experiment the following day—the blue-eyed children were now deemed superior to those with brown eyes—she found the same results.

Could the effect of likability have similar effects over a lifetime? Is likability really related to our long-term happiness and success? Or is there some other variable that accounts for both?

Absent the use of a randomized clinical trial to study the consequences of likability, researchers have relied on longitudinal research—studies that observe people, sometimes over years or decades—to examine how experiences early in life may predict outcomes much later. Longitudinal research makes it possible to analyze all types of possible predictors of later happiness and success, and then determine which of these factors are relevant to predict life outcomes. It's also a useful approach to verify whether it is likability that predicts life outcomes or some other factor—a "third variable"—that may be responsible for both.

These third variables are important to consider. Have you read that scientists found a strong link between increases in ice-cream sales and the growth in murder rates? Although it would be tempting to assume that one causes the other—perhaps the sugar high from ice cream sends people running from Baskin-Robbins in a homicidal rage—the link can actually be explained by a completely separate "third" variable: hot weather.

Is the apparent link between likability and later success also due to a third variable? It doesn't seem so. Study after study has revealed that even after accounting for the effects of IQ, socioeconomic status, mental health, or any of the behaviors that make us likable, there is something about being Accepted that directly predicts how happy, fulfilled, and even successful we are years later.

One study examined more than ten thousand Swedish youth and then followed them over the next thirty to forty years. The children's likability was measured at the age of thirteen along with a host of possible factors that could explain both their likability and later outcomes. Researchers measured each subject's IQ, aggressive and disruptive behavior, history of physical and mental illness, parents' level of education and income, and even the child's future goals. After accounting for all of these possible influences on adult outcomes, it was likability that predicted happiness, employment, and income decades later. In fact, compared to those who were well liked as kids, those who were rejected were two to five times more likely to be unemployed or request welfare assistance. Likable children even grew up less prone than others to be diagnosed with diabetes, obesity, high cholesterol, or high blood pressure.

Studies also have looked at the value of likability by examining how it might predict *changes* in our lives. This approach offers another way to determine whether likability might have a causal effect. After all, Accepted children might grow up to seem happier than others because they were happy in the first place, while Rejected children might seem as though they became depressed adults because they were depressed to begin with. In fact, their sad demeanor may have been one of the factors that led to their being rejected.

In my own research, as well as that of many other psychologists, this possibility also has been tested. For instance, in one study of adolescents conducted in my own lab with then-postdoctoral fellow Julie Wargo Aikins, we collected information from over 150 tenth-grade students to measure likability and depressive symptoms. After all the students in the study picked who in their class was liked most and least, we asked each participant to identify any symptoms of depression they might have via a standard checklist used by clinicians. About eighteen months later, we gathered data from the same group again. Our results revealed that some adolescents already had signs of depression during our initial survey. By the time they were about to graduate high school, however, many more participants reported depressive symptoms, and it was the Rejected tenth graders who were significantly more likely to fall into that category. Conversely, being likable predicted improvements in mood over the same period, even among teens who were happy when we first saw them.

What is it about likability, then, that has such a powerful and enduring effect on us?

It's a sunny day on the campus of the University of North Carolina at Chapel Hill. As I stand by the "pit," a gathering spot right next to the student union, I see about two hundred students walking toward me, all wearing identical hot pink T-shirts. People stare at them and take pictures with their phones as the mob reaches me and then stops.

I am wearing the same pink T-shirt. The students are all enrolled in my course on popularity, and we are taking part in an annual experiment designed to help us understand the reciprocal exchange of "transactions" that continually occur between ourselves and our environment. Our experiment does not concern popularity per se, but it is a demonstration of what psychologists call the "transactional model"—the chain reaction involving how others act toward us, how we behave in response, and how those responses in turn elicit new behaviors among others all day, every day, for our entire life. The transactional model refers to a give-and-take between what we put out into the world and how everyone else responds to it. My experiment was intended to demonstrate how our lives can change with even one simple adjustment to this dynamic.

For the first day of the experiment, the control day, students are asked to wear their normal clothing while they keep a written record of their social interactions and their mood. Every hour or so, they jot down whether they initiated any conversations with others, whether they met anyone new, and how they felt at the time—happy, bored, sad, anxious, et cetera.

Then, on day two, we make a minor adjustment—all my students and I don the same T-shirts. Each year we create a design together to attract maximum attention. Sometimes the shirt has been neon green. In other years, it's bright orange or hot pink. On the front is a message that's a little cheeky, sometimes an in-joke for the class. One year it read, "Everyone at UNC Likes Me!" and another, "Most Popular." But the T-shirt is not really designed to make us likable. The primary objective is to guarantee an atypical social experience for a single day—to trigger novel transactions. When a few hundred people are walking across campus wearing the same eye-catching attire, we are all guaranteed unusual treatment. People stare, chuckle, or even roll their eyes, and many approach us to ask what the T-shirt means.

What we want to know is how this new treatment changes our own behavior, and maybe even influences how we feel. Again, students are asked to record their own behavior and mood, hour by hour. They then review their data and write a paper about their findings. I ask them to discuss not only the two-day experience, but to hypothesize what their lives would be like if they figuratively wore that distinctive shirt every day.

Students invariably write that they are shocked by how much their own behavior changed on T-shirt day. They are even more surprised to see how those changes created a cascade effect—their behaviors caused others to respond in unexpected ways, which prompted their own uncommon reactions, and so on, in an endless feedback loop. Shy students, for example, approached people they had hoped to talk to for weeks. During these conversations they felt more confident, happy, and optimistic. They were surprised to discover that their peers laughed at their jokes, seemed interested in what they had to say, and even invited them to hang out again.

Angry students, who didn't usually feel very connected with others on campus, couldn't believe how often they smiled on the day they wore the T-shirt. To their surprise, others smiled back, and suddenly they didn't feel as angry or lonely. Some reported that it was the first time in weeks that they had chosen to leave their dorms and go out to mingle with others on Franklin Street, Chapel Hill's famous strip.

Students who typically stared down at their phones as they walked across campus looked up on that day and offered friendly nods to others as they walked by. Their peers nodded back, and my students reported that they felt an increased sense of community, so much so that they were even more likely to raise their hands in other courses. Overall, the consensus of the members of the class each year is that when the world treated them differently, even just for a day, it changed their behavior and their feelings in surprising ways. One student wrote, "If I wore that T-shirt every day in my childhood, so to speak, I would be a different human being now."

This experiment offers an opportunity to learn how much our own behavior and mood can be affected by altering how we approach the world even for just one day. It also helps explain the power of likability, because being likable changes not only how people treat us, but ultimately how we grow and develop over the course of our own lives. Stated simply, likable people are treated very well. And not just for a single day, but every day.

Of course, this may be true for people of high status as well. Like those who are likable, those with the other type of popularity are the objects of a great deal of positive attention. But that's where the similarities end. Unlike those high in status, it is those high in likability who have more friends, fuller social calendars, and more genuinely positive interactions.

From the perspective of the transactional model, each of these friendships and social engagements offers another opportunity to practice and learn increasingly sophisticated interpersonal skills. Research demonstrates that likable children indeed develop advanced social skills faster than their peers. Among nine- to ten-year-olds, for instance, likable kids are the first to form emotionally intimate friendships while others are still engaged in juvenile play. When they are a few years older, likable youth are among the first to participate in monogamous romantic partnerships, while their peers are still experimenting with fleeting teen crushes. Of course, developing refined social skills makes these adolescents that much more likable, thus advancing the cycle even further.

The same transactional model explains why being disliked can result in a lifetime of thwarted opportunities and disadvantage. Research reveals that there are many behaviors that lead to being disliked. We can alienate others by acting aggressively, breaking social norms egregiously and unapologetically, acting selfishly, or "oversharing" our own problems in a manner that places self-interest over the needs of the group. But as much as these behaviors can affect a disagreeable person in the moment, it is their impact on other people—the transactions they initiate—that are responsible for the enduring problems experienced by dislikable people.

This can be a difficult concept to accept. It's easy to blame being rejected on circumstances beyond our control, like our victimization by others or the general unfairness of life. Certainly, that can be true. But the transactional model suggests that some of our happiness and success, or misery and failure, are the direct result of how we've conducted ourselves in our daily social interactions.

While likable people live in a world in which they are treated well, unlikable people are avoided, ridiculed, or victimized. In early childhood, Rejecteds are less likely to be invited to playdates and birthday parties, or even to take part in games. Each time this occurs, it represents a missed opportunity to learn new social skills. Of course, lacking social skills only makes them that much more unlikable, perpetuating a sad and damaging cycle. Not surprisingly, by middle school, Rejected children are less adept at following group rules, negotiating conflicts with friends, or knowing how to take turns in large conversations. By adolescence, they are among the last to begin dating and often have limited their friends only to others who were similarly rejected in childhood.

This cycle can start as early as kindergarten. A study by Jennifer Lansford of Duke University examined the transactional model within a group of 585 children who participated in her research between kindergarten and third grade. Over this four-year period, the investigators interviewed participants and their peers a total of twelve times, which offered a chance to study rapid transactions during a critical time in these children's development. Their research tested the notion that our behavior is not only a product of how others treat us, but also a major influence on our future social success.

Lansford and her colleagues asked peers to report the likability of each child in her study, and teachers were asked to rate each child's aggressive behavior at school. Her team also interviewed each child to learn about one of their social skills. Specifically, the researchers examined a type of bias that leads some people to see the world as aggressive and hostile in contexts in which most don't perceive it that way at all. (More on this bias in Chapter 6.)

The results demonstrated just how powerfully likability can affect long-term growth and development. As one might expect, Lansford found that the more children behaved aggressively, or saw the world through "aggression-colored" glasses, the more rejected they were by peers by the next study time point. But importantly, she also found the reverse was true: the more rejected the children were, the more aggressive they became over time. Of course, this in turn led them to become even more alienated from their peers, causing these Rejected children to see the world as even more hostile than they had before. For instance, when shown video scenes that most of their peers thought were benign, those who were rejected became increasingly likely to see acts of cruelty, while those who had been accepted had an increasing tendency to see the same videos more favorably. Naturally, this difference in social skill was related to even greater differences in likability in the following years, and so on.

The transactional model also explains how Jeff became a much more competent and content attorney than Steve. His character was evident even as the two men sat together in the crowded auditorium on the first day of law school. While Steve seemed oblivious to the people around him, Jeff was all introductions, smiles, and handshakes. Standing to reach the rows in front of and behind him, he had brief conversations with many students that day.

"You're from Chicago?" he asked one. "My uncle lives there!"

"I play soccer, too!" he said to another. "We have to find a league around here!"

Jeff has always been naturally helpful, happy, and kind. He is one of those individuals who can say almost anything to anyone, no matter how difficult or potentially painful, and do so with a genuine grin, some charm, and a self-effacing chuckle. Merely being with him makes a person feel as if they are among the most likable, interesting people in the room.

Because he was so well liked in law school, Jeff was invited to join many study groups, where he encountered a wide variety of perspectives. His likability also led professors to initiate discussions with him outside class, which is how Jeff learned more details about course material than had been presented in lectures. With this additional knowledge, he felt more confident to speak up, which elicited even more opportunities to study with other students, meet with faculty, and so on. Within a year, he was selected as the student representative to faculty meetings, and later became a representative to a national conference of attorneys. All these interactions had a major impact on how Jeff experienced law school. His initial likability as a student started the cycle that led to his success and happiness many years later.

Steve also was enrolled at Emory but didn't seem to be attending the same law school at all. The academic world he occupied did not involve study groups, meetings with faculty, or leadership positions. When he was asked by classmates for his input, he was evasive and cold, fearing that their success might come at the expense of his own. Students felt tense around Steve and before long just avoided him altogether. When he disagreed with something in class, his hand launched up like a missile, and his comments were more focused on demonstrating his own knowledge than recognizing valid points made by his peers. When assigned to a group project, Steve asserted his ideas without regard to how he might have disrupted an emerging consensus. Ultimately, with decreasing opportunities to study with others, his first-year grades were lower than he expected, and his confidence was shaken. This contributed to a cycle of decreasing engagement in school, further drops in performance, and so on. Steve's dislikable nature made law school a lonely place without many opportunities to learn, which ultimately affected the lawyer he became.

The Steves of the world might find this chapter depressing. It may seem to offer confirmation of their belief that the deck was stacked against them, starting with those first awkward social encounters as children. Now, after a lifetime of negative transactions and lost social opportunities, the challenge to behave more likably may seem insurmountable.

That's not quite right. The transactional model may tell the story of how Steve reached his unhappy outcome, but it also suggests a path toward change that can be easy to follow.

It may offer some comfort to know that being disliked in the past will affect us only insomuch as we allow it to dictate how we behave today. Even the smallest adjustments in our current behavior can change our future—a friendly overture to a passerby, a single act of kindness, or even something as simple as a smile. It may seem trite, but there's now compelling evidence to suggest that transactions occur at a level that is beyond our conscious awareness. Without us even realizing it, we are tuned into even the smallest of social cues and being influenced by others' likability all day long.

Imagine walking into a research lab to take part in a psychology experiment. You meet someone in the waiting room about your age who is there to participate in the same study. You try to strike up a conversation, but she barely makes eye contact. She grudgingly answers your questions, but her arms are folded across her chest, and she seems unemotional, sour, flat. After a while one of the researchers comes in and tells you it's your turn to begin. You are accompanied to the lab and are asked to discuss your own feelings and interests as the experimenter evaluates you.

Now imagine the same experiment, except this time the person you meet in the waiting room looks you in the eye, smiles, speaks easily, and answers all your questions in a friendly manner. The content of your conversation is not any different, but she now projects confidence and enthusiasm—she is, in short, likable. After a few minutes you are summoned to the lab, where you are evaluated by a researcher just as described above.

It turns out you've been tricked—the person you met in the waiting room isn't a fellow participant in the study but is an experimental "confederate," instructed how to act by one of the researchers. The ruse is designed to covertly test how a social interaction with a person, likable or unlikable, affected you. Depending on which version of the experiment you took part in the one with the confederate being likable or with her being dislikable—your own behavior, your mood, and even your interests will have been affected.

How could a mundane encounter with a total stranger have such a striking effect? It is the result of a phenomenon known as "social mimicry," which is the tendency to instantaneously copy others without meaning to or even being aware that we're doing so.

Social mimicry has subtle yet pervasive effects on us. Studies like the one above have demonstrated that if you were placed with the confederate who kept her arms folded, you would be significantly more likely to fold your arms yourself. If she frowned, you would likely do so as well. The same is true for the speed and tone of your speech. Neuroscientists have found that such inadvertent mimicry is likely due to significant overlap in the parts of our brains that are involved in perception and physical action. This explains why mimicry also occurs after simply asking people to *think about* how others behave. In one experiment, participants who were asked to imagine elderly people even walked more slowly afterward.

Perhaps most interesting, social mimicry can also unconsciously affect our emotions, which helps explain why we prefer to spend time with likable people and avoid those who are awkward, mean, or sad. We've all had the experience of meeting a negative mood magnet—someone who radiates despair and pessimism wherever he or she goes. Even after they depart, we find ourselves feeling down, too, maybe wondering why we're in a bad mood. Scientific studies have confirmed this phenomenon as well. After just a few moments interacting with sad, socially awkward confederates in experiments, participants commonly report feeling the same way themselves. Their shift in attitude is not simply a matter of having sympathy for the confederate, either. In one study an experimenter read a boring text in a sad manner, and that was sufficient to make participants feel sadder as well.

The effect occurs even when we are trying our best to be upbeat and friendly. At a speed-dating event in Belgium, experimenters asked participants to rate their own mood and their interest in being matched up after each of ten rapid (four-minute) dates. Findings revealed that after dates with an awkward, sad individual, participants themselves reported a decrease in their own happiness and energy, as well as far less interest in meeting for a second date.

Results like these suggest that for gloomy, unlikable people, the world itself is truly quite dreary. Every interaction they have is a bit sadder than it has to be, without them realizing how their own behavior affected others' moods and made it more likely they would be rejected again in turn.

Meanwhile, happy, likable people seem to be perpetually surrounded by positivity, cheerfulness, and acceptance. Their upbeat nature is so infectious that we feel they bring out the best in us, and we seek out opportunities to be in their presence—all the while unaware that their mysterious "positive energy" is simply the work of social mimicry. Even their laughter is contagious, which accounts for why TV shows have laugh tracks. Hearing others laugh makes us more likely to do so.

Can we use social mimicry to trigger a new pattern of transactions, perhaps even promoting a new chain reaction in our lives? It's hard to say, as there hasn't been much research examining the longer-term effects of mimicry. So I decided to try an unofficial experiment of my own.

As I sat at my computer drafting this chapter, my internet service was interrupted, and I ultimately realized I would have to call my service provider for help. As anyone who has reached a technical support line can guess, I spent the next several hours first navigating the touch-tone purgatory of automated menus and then ultimately arriving at my own personal hell—an endless series of customer service agents prepared to walk me through all of the obvious steps I already had attempted to fix the problem. Needless to say, by the time the first hour had elapsed, I was not behaving in an especially likable manner.

I wondered what would happen if I attempted to change the

terms of the transaction. Over the next hour, as I spoke with at least another half-dozen technical support agents, I decided to systematically vary my behavior. With some agents, I acted like a Rejected: I was aggressive, impatient, and even oppositional. I'm quite certain those agents did not like me very much. With others, however, I responded like an Accepted: I was upbeat, helpful, and even took an interest in those with whom I spoke. They, in turn, took an interest in me.

Of course as one might predict, the more likably I behaved, the kinder the agent was in return. When I was more socially aversive, however, the agent was equally curt. My behavior didn't only affect how each agent acted toward me but also the quality of his support. In each instance when I acted in a dislikable manner, agents listened less intently and were more error-prone. When the agents liked me, I received more helpful suggestions.

But there were also some results I did not expect. Being likable didn't only affect the behavior of the agents I spoke with; ultimately, the transactions had a surprising impact on me as well. As I inquired and learned about the foreign on-call center, I became genuinely interested in my agents' lives, felt more optimistic about a potential solution, and my patience with the process increased. This naturally promoted greater investment in seeking a solution from the agents, and the whole experience was suddenly far more tolerable.

When acting in a dislikable manner, however, I could feel my blood pressure rise and I even became annoyed with unrelated tasks I attempted while on the phone. I likely missed the chance to learn how to troubleshoot the problem myself, and I suspect it would have taken much longer for my service to be restored.

Being likable didn't just change how others felt about me, it changed my happiness and success as well. Once I noticed this, it was amazing to witness how easily I could affect so many outcomes—at work or home, among strangers or friends—simply by acting in the ways that make people likable. In each instance, the snowball effects were remarkable. Every compliment bolstered my mood and confidence in successive interactions, and the cycle could last for hours or days.

In our daily lives we are involved in a constant, complex series of transactions that involve rapid social give-and-take. We offer something to the world around us—a social behavior, an attitude, a desire for connection—and the world usually offers something back in kind. It's an ongoing exchange that happens so quickly, and seems so automatic, that we often don't even realize it's happening. We simply think of it as life, rarely realizing how we have been contributing to its direction the entire time.

Sometimes acting likably is not so easy, however. That's because sometimes we don't realize how much our behavior turns others off, and we never understand how we ultimately contributed to a self-fulfilling fate brought about by our desire to be popular.

Pam is a successful immunologist and a close friend of mine in her mid-thirties, with a vibrant social life and an upbeat disposition. Her calendar is booked with creative outings and activities. She is funny, attractive, and highly accomplished. She has many friends and always seems to be hosting offbeat parties, like costume-themed get-togethers and whodunit murder-mystery dinners.

But despite her busy social life, Pam is lonely and often unhappy.

She would love to get married and have a family someday, but she doesn't think she has met the right man yet. That may well be the case, but it also might be a function of the fact that Pam is a generally likable person who occasionally engages in unlikable behavior. It doesn't affect her in every relationship, but it could account for her dissatisfaction with her romantic life.

When she meets new men, it's typically all fun, spontaneity, and affection. She and her dates go to art galleries, concerts, new restaurants. She is charmingly flirtatious, a master at witty banter, and the guys fall for her quickly. Inevitably, though, Pam begins to notice something they do, or neglect to do, that convinces her they might be losing interest. He might show up late for a date or pay more attention to his buddies than to her while at a party. He might stop holding the door open for her as often as he used to. At that point, Pam begins engaging in a type of behavior that is especially powerful in creating a negative transactional pattern.

It starts innocently enough. "Are we OK?" she'll ask her boyfriend. "I've just been noticing that something feels different between us." Occasionally Pam's instincts are correct: sometimes the men she dates have lost interest or even feel intimidated by her overt confidence. But more often than not everything is fine, and her boyfriend will affirm that that is the case. It's here that the problem begins.

Pam doesn't trust that others will like her as much as she hopes they will, so she simply doesn't believe their assurances. "I know in my head that he said everything is OK, but I just get scared that maybe it's not. What if he loses interest?" she explains. This is usually when she asks her boyfriend again for reassurance. Once again, she receives it, but once again she is doubtful, and a self-defeating pattern begins. Sometimes this cycle develops over a period of weeks or months, but it can even arise within the span of a single conversation. In either case, Pam's previous experiences with rejection cast a shadow over any potential relationship, triggering transactions that become very predictable.

Psychologists refer to this pattern as "excessive reassurance-seeking." It often takes place in the context of a romantic relationship but can also occur in friendships or even between employee and supervisor. Experts in excessive reassurance-seeking, like Jim Coyne and Thomas Joiner, have proposed that this behavior sets up a self-fulfilling prophecy of failure. The constant questioning and doubting of a reassurance-seeker can make an individual from whom reassurance is sought feel distrusted, stressed, and ineffective, wondering, "Why can't I help this person that I care so much about? Why doesn't he or she believe me?" Eventually, the pressure to continually reassure causes them to withdraw. They become slow to return messages, less convincing in their declarations of love. They become less comforting, and of course, this is exactly what the reassurance-seeker is hypervigilant to detect.

"I knew it! I knew he was pulling away!" is Pam's typical reaction when her boyfriends dump her. But in her furious righteousness and validation, she doesn't perceive that this outcome may have been the result of a transactional process that she initiated. It was her own behavior that elicited the rejection, and it is that rejection that makes her feel justified seeking constant reassurance in successive relationships. Each failed romance seems to doom the next one.

Research from my own lab has demonstrated just how powerfully excessive reassurance-seeking can undermine relationships and just how early this transactional pattern starts. In one study, we recruited 520 adolescents and asked them to tell us about their reassurance-seeking behavior. We also asked them to name their very best friend and how they thought that relationship was going. We then approached the friends and asked for their own feelings about the friendships. We followed up with our subjects and their friends twice more annually to see how their relationships evolved. We also measured how much each teen was liked or disliked using peer nominations.

Our results revealed that excessive reassurance-seeking can lead to negative transactions, starting in adolescence, and predicts which teens are disliked. In fact, adolescents who engaged in excessive reassurance-seeking told us that their friends had started to become angry with them for their behavior, even telling them to stop. But the adolescents who sought reassurance just couldn't understand how this was negatively affecting their relationships. While they still enjoyed their friendships, their friends had a different perspective. Specifically, the more frequently adolescents sought reassurance in the first year of our study, the more often their friends reported in year two that their relationship was troubled. They had less fun when they were together. Many friends had begun to withdraw, and some ended their friendships altogether. Not surprisingly, by the end of our study, excessive reassurance-seekers had grown significantly more depressed than others.

Understanding the transactional nature of relationships teaches us that popularity is a reflection of how others regard us, but it is, in some part, also a product of how we treat others. This cyclical give-and-take between our social interactions and others' reactions doesn't merely influence our day-to-day experiences. It truly can alter our life course, and it is for this reason that popularity is such a remarkably powerful predictor of so many life outcomes. Beyond all of the factors that we already know to be important predictors of our success, our mood, and even our physical health is one that we didn't really think mattered much after high school.

When I speak about popularity, I invariably hear from two different groups of people. The first are those who as children fit the standard categories—Accepted, Rejected, Neglected, Controversial, or Average. They tell me, for instance, that they were rejected on the day they started kindergarten, and they have felt that way in every school, relationship, and job ever since. They are convinced they are doomed to be rejected their whole lives.

Individuals in the other group tell me that their childhood popularity was transformed. They used to be liked, or disliked, they explain, but somehow, something changed. The process started with how they interacted with those around them. Now they look back on their childhoods and barely recognize the person they used to be. It is as if their memory stars a character they watch empathically, but one who has long since ceased to exist. This is the group that believes there's a way to break the pattern of popularity.

They are correct.

PART III

So What Do We Do Now?

CHAPTER 6

Our High School Legacy

How We Can Conquer the Prom Queen Today

If you're like most people, then high school may seem like a distant memory. Even if not many years have passed since you attended, it still *feels* like ancient history. We can't go back and change how popular we were back then, so what's the point in even thinking about it now?

But what if I told you that those teenage experiences are still affecting you today? Not through just occasional memories, but thousands of times each day. Arguably, those old confrontations with popularity are the very basis for your adult personality.

Fortunately, even just being aware how this dynamic works can be remarkably powerful in helping to keep the prom queen or locker room bully from affecting your life today.

A few weeks ago, I stumbled across my high school yearbook and, against my better judgment, decided to flip through the pages. There I was—tinted glasses, wide-collared shirt, and a wannabe mullet.

Who was that? Was I really the same person today as that boy in the yearbook? I recognized him—he was like a long-lost little brother—but I've now lived more years *since* that photo than I had when it was taken. My tastes have changed, and my hopes and dreams have evolved. I'm not that person anymore, am I?

Many of us feel this sense of distance when we think about ourselves over the course of time. Sometimes it occurs when we see an old photograph that seems like an abandoned version of who we once were. At other times, we may look in the mirror and be surprised to see someone so old staring back at us. It's amazing how detached we can feel from who we once were or even who we are now.

Of course, that really *was* me—I am the same person. Or at least, there are plenty of through lines that connect that teenage boy to the man I am now. For instance, the boy in that yearbook was very late to mature—even as a teenager, I was a pip-squeak. Today, I still religiously lift weights, which is probably not a coincidence. And surely my tendency to behave and dress like a young, cool professor is just an evolution of my mouthing off in high school advanced placement classes—both good strategies to avoid seeming like a total nerd.

These are the kind of continuities that are easy to recognize—the traces of our adolescent selves we see in the people we are today. Perhaps you like the same music. Maybe you still have the same core group of friends, or still wear your hair in the same way (thankfully, I do not). These are the superficial vestiges of our past that we feel we can control.

But what if the legacy of our adolescence extends deeper than that? What if it still marks us today in ways we don't even realize? And what if it is affecting us in ways that undermine our lives?

However alarming that is to imagine, accumulating evidence suggests that this is indeed the case. In fact, who we were as teenagers may influence our lives even more than who we are today.

For instance, in one recent study, a group of economics professors from the Universities of Michigan and Pennsylvania examined earning potential among men. Using large national databases in the United States and Great Britain, they looked at factors that predicted the salaries of over twenty thousand men at age thirty-three. One of the items they considered was each man's current height and how tall these same men were when they were sixteen years old. Was height related to how much money each subject made?

Yes, it was—tall men earn more money. But perhaps especially surprising was that it wasn't how tall these men were at their current age that was most closely related to their salary, but rather their height at age sixteen. Something about having reached that height in adolescence had an effect on these men for the rest of their lives. It changed something in them—how they felt about themselves, how they acted, or maybe what experiences they'd had since. Whatever it was, it remained with them for decades.

Studies show that it's not just our physical appearance in adolescence that marks our adult lives. There are other characteristics that matter, and some probably even more so, because as compared to how we feel about our changing looks, which are obvious to us, there are some things that occur during our teenage years that affect us in ways that we don't see.

In fact, recent research suggests that the aspect of our teen years that may have one of the most powerful influences on who we are today is that one thing that mattered to us so much back then—our popularity. And popularity didn't just change us superficially—it altered our brain wiring, and consequently, it has changed what we see, what we think, and how we act.

Luckily, the extent to which we let our teenage experiences dictate our lives today is well within our control. But we must first stop to consider what popularity meant to us when we were young.

In my own suburban hometown on Long Island, as in many hometowns, popularity was strongly linked to money, in the form of fancy houses, jewelry, and the "right" clothes. All the popular kids had Members Only jackets and designer acid-wash jeans. They were the first to get an Atari, and they spent the entire fall talking about their summers at expensive sleepaway camps in upstate New York.

But I was neither wealthy nor cool. I was raised by a single mother who worked as a secretary for a group of accountants. I worked, too, part-time at the local grocery store, and saved my paychecks to buy a Members Only look-alike jacket at a flea market. I even tried to make my own acid-wash jeans with a bottle of Clorox and a fresh pair of pants from Sears. (It didn't work.)

I tried hard to fit in, and that meant faking it. At lunch, I held my money in a clenched fist so no one could see that I was paying a reduced price. I pretended I'd watched music videos that in reality I never saw because we couldn't afford MTV.

Overall, when it came to popularity, my anxiety that I was too blue collar to fit in was a feeling that stuck with me. This doubtless accounts for the special kinship I feel with first-generation college students at the university where I teach.

So how does my background affect me today? Have I grown up desperate for wealth and materialistic excess, whether in the form of luxury cars or expensive watches? No, it's not that simple. Our adolescent hopes play out in our adult lives more imperceptibly and more pervasively. The power of popularity comes from the subtle, almost invisible ways it continues to define us—in what psychologists call our "automatic" reactions.

Although we don't talk much about antiquated psychological concepts like the id, ego, superego, and unconscious anymore, we do know that there are plenty of actions we take without thinking—feelings that seem to bubble up from nowhere and ways that we react to life that just seem to be part of our "personality." Today, we understand that all of these automatic behaviors, feelings, and thoughts are related to specific activity in our brains. Recent research suggests that, in a very literal sense, our brains were built on a foundation of popularity.

It's during adolescence—or at the start of puberty, to be more precise—that our brains develop more dramatically than at any other point in our lives after the age of one. As we enter our teens, our brains grow far more new neurons, allowing us to store substantially more information. Adolescence also results in more substantial neural coating with myelin, the fatty substance that makes our brains work faster, enabling more efficient and sophisticated thought. In short, our brains evolve from the way that children think (spontaneously, in the moment, and without self-consciousness) to the way adults do (more ruminative, autobiographical, and attuned to others' perceptions of us).

The experiences we have in those critical years have the potential to affect the brain we will live with for the rest of our lives, which gives our teenage experiences with popularity such immense power. They are among the first thoughts that seem especially important to us at the very time that our brains are evolving so substantially. It is in these newly maturing brains that popularity moments and encounters will be encoded and that all subsequent experiences will be compared to and built upon.

Did popularity play a big role in how *your* brain developed? Try testing yourself. What's easier to remember, the name of your ninth-grade social studies teacher or the prom king and queen in your high school? If you're like most people (who didn't major in history), then you probably have far richer memories of the popular kids in your school than anything else in adolescence. You can probably even recall the feelings you had about the cool kids—and maybe even relive some of those feelings all over again as you remember them. It's not just a matter of nostalgia—it's as if those teenage experiences seem far more recent than they actually are, and far more salient and impactful today than they should be.

This is no accident, as has been established by recent studies in psychology and neuroscience. Scientists used to think that different parts of our brain were autonomously responsible for what our senses perceived, how we behaved, and each of our emotions. But we now know that this isn't quite right. Functional MRI scans conducted with adults while they are asked to look, smell, hear, or feel what the researchers present to them tells us that it's actually a collection of interconnected brain regions that are at play—a neural network. The same thing happens when we experience emotions, solve problems, or make decisions. And findings have revealed that our hippocampus, the part of the brain responsible for so much of our autobiographical memory, is in on the action far more than was ever realized. This means that our past is continually called forth and used as a template for us to evaluate, compare, and respond to what we experience today. In other words, at some level, without our being aware of it, our brains spend all day, every day, drawing upon those initial, formative high school memories.

Adolescent memories can affect us in many powerful ways—specifically by creating biases in what we see, what we think, and what we do. Psychologists refer to these as several of the steps of "social information processing," which is a complex way of saying that if we were to review any social interaction in our lives in super–slow motion, we would discover that the thousands of reactions involved in it are actually the result of a series of discrete automatic decisions. We don't experience these as discrete steps, of course, but rather as instinctive behavior, because this all takes place in literally a fraction of a millisecond.

For instance, I recently ran an errand at the grocery store, and as I entered, a large man was hurrying out. As he passed by me, our shoulders bumped, and I was nudged a bit to the side. I instantaneously said, "Oops, sorry." That was an automatic reaction.

This kind of trivial incident happens so often that we never bother to think about it. But this time I asked myself: why did I apologize? The slight collision wasn't my fault, so my response seemed a bit foolish. A split second later, I saw another customer being brushed aside by the same man in the same way. His automatic reaction was different, shouting something that isn't fit to print. Neither one of us planned our responses to getting pushed—they just happened. The millisecond decisions we make in such reactions reveal some form of bias that can be traced back to our past. Individually, each of them may not always have significant consequences. But collectively, they define who we are and how our lives unfold.

Psychological science has now demonstrated exactly how these biases are shaped by our memories—referred to collectively as our "social database." In many ways, this process can be quite useful. It helps us efficiently scan all of the social information we confront, make decisions about how to respond, and execute satisfactory behaviors that maintain our survival. After all, we can't stop and seriously reflect on every single social interaction we have in a day. Our sophisticated and efficient adult brains simply rely on whatever has worked for us before. Someone walks by and says hello? Nodding back seemed to be successful previously, so we do so again. Someone bumps into you? Being polite, getting out of the way, and avoiding conflict has always proven to be the path of least resistance, so we'll go with that.

But remember: these biases are all skewed toward initial formative memories from our adolescence. Our adult brains began to form to help us survive in the hallways of high school. The problem is, we left high school long ago—and our brains never got the memo. This is probably why, every once in a while, something atypical happens, whether a miscommunication, a mental hiccup, or an embarrassing moment. It's in moments like these when our background biases get thrust to the fore and exposed, and the legacy of our experiences with adolescent popularity makes itself known.

Many years ago, I was attempting to hang Sheetrock to create an extra room in my small condo in New Haven. After a few hours, I realized that I have no aptitude for construction work and found myself covered in drywall dust, feeling stressed and exhausted. As it happened, I had just come back from a consulting job, during which I had discovered the joys of all-expenses-paid travel at a luxury hotel and spa, and it struck me that a massage—something I would never previously have considered—sounded like the perfect way to unwind.

I found a place calling itself a "health studio" that offered massages only a few miles away, in a tony Connecticut suburb. I scheduled an appointment and, at four o'clock, pulled into the parking lot of what looked like a high-end strip mall. You can probably see where this is headed, and by now you may be thinking that you would never make the mistake I was about to make. Surely no biases could possibly be so powerful that they would render you oblivious to such clear signals. But on that Friday afternoon, I was mostly concerned about appearing able to navigate fancy massage places and enjoy high-end indulgences. I wanted to fit in by not seeming too blue collar.

After spending some time searching for the place, I was told to walk to the back of the row of shops, where I finally found the entrance. It stood next to a Dumpster under a neon sign—a critical cue, had I been in the proper frame of mind to notice.

I stepped inside, took a look around, and with some confusion asked the receptionist, "Do you take credit cards?"

"No," she replied, "you need to give us cash. For thirty minutes, it will be forty dollars. And remember to bring your gratuity into the room with you."

That seemed odd, but again, I was new to the experience. I passed another man in the locker room who was wearing an expensive suit. He seemed extremely happy and had just begun loosening his tie. He looked up and offered me a quick nod. I felt calm again—after all, he seemed well adjusted and wealthy, so of course *he* would know what he was doing.

Gina, the massage therapist, was young, attractive, and glad to see me. She immediately asked for her tip.

"What? Oh, I'm sorry," I asked as I raised a ten-dollar bill clenched in my fist. "Did you want this now?"

Gina looked at the money, then looked at me, and then looked back at the bill. Speaking far more bluntly now, she asked, "Uhhh . . . what exactly is it that you want?"

Oh! I finally realized. *Is this one of* those *kind of places?* Immediately panicking, I wondered, *How do I get out of here quickly and politely?* and began looking for an escape route. I lied about having an injured shoulder that needed medical attention and bolted.

No one has ever gotten dressed faster. I was out of the locker room, down the stairs, past the Dumpster, and into my car before I was able to laugh at myself.

I began to take account of what had just happened. How did I miss the neon sign directly in front of me? Why did I think the presence of a well-dressed man automatically signaled a legitimate therapeutic massage, and why did I lie about my shoulder? Each of these automatic reactions revealed my own biases.

My visit to the "health studio" was humiliating, to say the least, and it's still embarrassing to recall. But this anecdote offers two important lessons. First, and perhaps most important, when booking a massage, be sure to carefully review the list of available spa services before confirming your appointment. Second, we all have substantial biases that have deep roots in popularity. And these biases are responsible for far more of our automatic actions, and our mistakes, than we ever may have considered before.

We would all like to think that we are highly skilled observers of the world around us, so it can be unsettling to consider that we may miss signals as obvious as a neon sign directly in front of us. But in fact, we misperceive cues all the time. This is due to the first step of social information processing, referred to as "cue encoding."

Cue-encoding biases can be remarkably powerful. Consider for a moment the huge amount of complex social information your brain must encode every day. Like a giant filter, it must sift through all the stimuli around you, make sense of them, and then decide what deserves your attention. Consider the few moments it takes to enter your workplace. As you pass dozens of people—in a big city it might be hundreds or thousands—your brain automatically reads each of their facial expressions, postures, fragments of speech, and spatial relationships to you, all to determine what social cues are present and require action. If someone nods at the very edge of your peripheral vision, you respond immediately by nodding back and smiling without even thinking. If someone with a worried expression is gazing past you, you turn and look over your shoulder almost instinctively. But if something no less noteworthy takes place—say, a plane flying overhead—only young children will notice and react. The rest of us know that such an event is rarely relevant to us, so we screen it out. We don't only ignore it; research reveals that if asked later, we would be quite certain that there had never been a plane at all.

What else are we missing? Or just the opposite: what information may we be overly attuned to? To examine this, a team of British psychologists conducted a study to see just how much cue-encoding biases can change what we observe, and the degree to which popularity is related to those biases. They asked adults to watch eight short movies and pay careful attention to every detail they could. Each movie depicted a typical adolescent school scene, such as teens standing near their lockers, in the cafeteria, or outdoors. Each scene also included a range of social cues. Some suggested that adolescents liked each other, depicted by smiling, nodding, laughing between peers. Other cues included scenes of peers interrupting or ignoring one another, arguing, or using closed body posture—all indicators of rejection. The researchers were interested in learning what the study participants would be most likely to notice, and so had each of the subjects wear a special device over their eyes that measured exactly where their pupils were directed and for how long they remained focused on specific images on the screen.

The results suggested that even when we are asked to watch something quite simple, we don't take everything in. Our eyes remain focused on small subsets of action that align with our own past social experiences. People in the study with prior histories of social success, for example, remained focused predominantly on the positive interactions in the videos. For 60 percent to 70 percent of the time, their gaze remained fixed on the people who were smiling, nodding, or including one another. They looked at the people engaged in negative social interactions less frequently, and when they did, they maintained their gaze briefly.

In contrast, those with histories of social isolation and loneliness scarcely looked at the positive scenes at all. For about 80 percent of the time, however, their pupils remained fixed on the actions that depicted social exclusion and negativity. It was as if they had watched a completely different movie altogether—focusing far more intently on cues that were barely noticed by others at all.

These findings have been replicated in many studies. When children are asked to watch cartoons that include hostile content, those who have been rejected by their peers take much longer than others to look away. When reading stories about social interactions, those who have had difficulties with popularity are more likely to recall the hostile moments in the narratives, while those who were popular remember the friendly and supportive exchanges between the characters.

> We do not see things as they are, we see them as we are.
>
> —*Anaïs Nin*

Does this mean that unpopular people are at risk for reliving their awkward high school days forever after, screening out all the positive social cues they witness? And are popular men and women always observing the world through "popularity-colored" glasses? To some extent, the answer is yes.

Consider your own biases. When speaking to a group, do you

look at the audience members making eye contact and nodding, or the ones staring at their phones and paying no attention to you? When you leave a party, do you recall all of the guests who spoke with you, or the one who didn't even say hello? Has your current desire for popularity led you to encode only the information that reinforces your happiness, or is it the data that remind you of a thwarted adolescent desire to belong?

Encoding negative social information is not necessarily a bad thing. For instance, imagine taking part in a meeting in which your firm is pitching its services to a potential client. Your teammates are friendly, charismatic, and project a sense of high status, and are all likely to encode social cues indicating that the client likes them. They notice that the client smiles often, nods in agreement, and shakes hands enthusiastically. After such a pitch meeting, research findings suggest that these employees will rate their own performance as outstanding and predict a high likelihood of landing the client.

However, in this situation, previously unpopular individuals might ultimately be more useful. They will be more likely to notice, for instance, if the potential client breaks eye contact or alters body posture whenever the presenter talks about the future. They might be especially attuned to signals indicating which of the firm's ideas are well received and which are falling flat. When asked later to reflect upon the pitch meeting, those who were less than popular as teenagers will offer a mixed review of how the gathering went. This phenomenon, referred to as "depressive realism," suggests that vigilance toward negative cues actually can lead to a more objective and clearer view of social information, undistorted by a positive bias. For this reason, some research has shown that previously unpopular people are perceived by others as more empathetic and more sensitive in social situations.

One study asked those high in power, prestige, and influence to draw an uppercase *E* on their foreheads as fast as they could, so that others would be able to read it. High-status people were far less likely than those low in status to draw the letter in its correct orientation and sketched a mirror image instead, leading the researchers to conclude that those high in status had a poorer ability to consider others' perspective. Participants high in social status also score more poorly than those low in status on tests of emotional intelligence, empathy, the ability to detect sarcasm, and correctly noticing a variety of emotional expressions.

In another study, researchers used an experimental manipulation to make their participants feel temporarily higher or lower in status and then tested whether there were differences between the groups in social information processing. They presented all participants with photos that only featured people's eyes while they made a variety of facial expressions. Results suggested that as compared to those who were made to feel high in status, those who were made to feel lower in status were suddenly better at identifying others' feelings. Even this artificial simulation of low status was sufficient to improve cue encoding. The benefits of unpopularity may even go deeper. Research using fMRI scans has demonstrated that while reading stories about others, those low in social status actually have more activation in the dorsomedial prefrontal cortex, the medial prefrontal cortex, and the precuneus/posterior cingulate cortex—regions associated with our ability to understand what others think, feel, and want.

Our adolescent experiences with popularity affect not just *what* we see, but also how we *interpret* these observations. Psychologists call this the "cue interpretation" step to social information processing.

For some, this is a concept hard to fathom. Wouldn't everyone, when presented with the same information, reach the same logical conclusion about it? Don't we all interpret data in similar ways?

I decided to test this myself in one of my classes by conducting a quick experiment. Participants were asked to watch a short video and describe what they saw. The video was simple and easy to absorb: at the center of a plain white screen was a box, while three colored circles—one blue, one green, one red—each moved around it. At one point two circles enter the box, and then leave, while the third circle trails behind. At another point, one of the circles bounces against the sides of the box, which then appears to break. As soon as the video ended, the students were asked for a written description of what they had observed.

The simplicity of the video was deliberate, designed to ensure that everyone watching was likely to have encoded the same information. In fact, the participants were shown it twice, so it would have been hard for any of them to have missed any of the objects in it. The task given to the students to write down what they had seen was likewise intentional, as it did not ask them to interpret the video's cues but rather to merely recount what they had observed. A reasonable response, therefore, would be to describe the action of the piece as three circles moving around a box, with two entering, and so on. But no one depicts it that way. Because cue interpretation is an automatic process, we ascribe meaning and intent even to fictional objects. And our descriptions of the same event can vary substantially.

Here are a few of the more colorful descriptions my students offered. Notice how they all interpret the video differently, ranging from neutral to far more aggressive takes:

> **Student 1:** "Red and Green were originally in the lead and Blue followed. Blue was very far behind and was left out of entering the square because the door closed before he got there."
>
> **Student 2:** "The Blue circle was mad at the other two circles for locking him out, so he broke into the box and was like, 'Hey, Green, why did you do that to me?!' Then the Red and Green circles were like 'whatever' and they deserted the Blue circle and left him altogether."
>
> **Student 3:** "OK . . . the Red and Green circles are chilling in the room (I think Red is a female). Blue is angry and feels left out—clearly blames Green circle for excluding it. Blue banged on the door and forced it open. Blue was very mad and was bouncing all over the place. Looks like there is violence. Green faced up to Blue and then left the room with Red and closed the door on Blue."
>
> **Student 4:** "Blue is a crazed lover, blinded by jealousy, who is furious and anxious. In a violent narcissistic rage, Blue blows down the door of Green (the man in the relationship) and Red, and provoked Green into a fight. Green was not in the mood for fighting because he was happy with Red. Red chilled in the corner, scared of Blue. Green and Blue duked it out and the

> Green circle, who appears the victor, took Red out of the box."

What led to such dramatically different interpretations of such simple cues? The answer, again, has everything to do with popularity. These same students had already reported their high school popularity to me using confidential ID numbers earlier in the semester. When I matched their accounts of the video to these data, I discovered that it was the students who were unpopular as teens, like Students 3 and 4, who interpreted the circles as fighting. The formerly popular students, like Student 1, were far more likely to see them as playful.

We all have biases in how we interpret social cues. Since we all have unique pasts, these biases are unique to each of us. For instance, some may see a well-dressed man loosening his tie, smiling giddily, and wonder what mischief he is up to and perhaps suspect their surroundings. Others would interpret the same information differently. Admittedly, our cue-interpretation biases don't typically land us in a den of iniquity, as they did to me, but if they are extreme, and left unchecked, they can affect our lives substantially nevertheless.

Research has revealed a few common themes in cue-interpretation biases that may be especially troublesome, especially when they begin to color the way we interpret the world around us on a regular basis. In long-term studies, these have been shown to be strong predictors of significant relationship problems and even psychological symptoms like depression, anxiety, or addiction years later. Most of us know someone whose behavior reveals these tendencies.

Imagine that you have plans to meet a friend, or maybe a first date, at a coffee shop at 6 p.m. By 6:30, you start to feel awkward sitting alone. You check your phone, but there is no email, text, or voice mail. What's the problem? You encode all of the available information: the person you planned to meet has not arrived, and you haven't heard a word. Now it's time to interpret the data. What's your gut response? Do you worry that something bad happened? Do you assume the friend is running late, or has forgotten your plans for reasons that have little to do directly with you?

Perhaps. But if you have ever felt slighted and left out, or longed to be more popular at some point in your life, you may begin to wonder—perhaps even assume—you've been stood up. Now you feel a little angry. Even if your friend does show up with a reasonable explanation, those feelings may persist. This is a sign of what psychologist Geraldine Downey calls a "rejection sensitivity" bias, a tendency to expect and emotionally react to rejection that creates a cycle of lifelong unpopularity: we wish to be popular, assume we are not, and then in turn yearn for it all the more. Not surprisingly, this type of bias also predicts a host of related negative outcomes throughout our lives, including body dissatisfaction, burnout at work, depression, and loneliness. Adults with high levels of rejection sensitivity are even more likely to contract infectious illnesses and to develop heart disease.

But can't rejection-sensitive people just *choose* to make another interpretation? Can't they just recognize that they are overly pessimistic and start making mental corrections for their self-critical biases? In other words, can't they just snap out of it?

It's not quite that easy. Prior social standing and resulting biases may cause changes in brain wiring that take some effort to override.

Harvard psychologist Leah Somerville asked subjects to complete a standard measure of rejection sensitivity involving a set of hypothetical social situations in which a number of individuals report that they strongly anticipate they will be hurt or abandoned by others. She then asked her subjects, who were either high or low in rejection sensitivity, to look at pictures of a new set of people and guess whether they would be liked or disliked by each of the individuals anticipating being hurt or abandoned. While they waited to hear the outcome, each participant's brain activity was measured using an fMRI scanner to reveal neural responses to social evaluation. Somerville's results are especially interesting because they revealed not how people's brains activated when they found out whether they were rejected or accepted; rather, the study focused simply on how brains responded when *anticipating* rejection or acceptance. People low in rejection sensitivity had fairly mild neural responses in a region of the brain that led Somerville to conclude that they didn't particularly care whether the strangers liked them or not. It did not seem relevant to their view of themselves.

But for the subjects with high rejection sensitivity, neural activity in this same region was quite strong when anticipating acceptance or rejection, suggesting that they placed high value on this type of social judgment. In other words, highly rejection-sensitive individuals feel that social feedback is very important, and it is strongly associated with how they feel about themselves.

A second common interpretation bias may also seem familiar: the tendency to assume that others are being hostile in an emotionally equivocal situation. Remember your tardy friend at the coffee shop? A person with a hostile attribution bias might feel intentionally stood up because their friend was being cruel. This type of bias is common among those who were unpopular adolescents. Psychologists uncover hostile attribution biases in children by asking them to interpret ambiguous stories. For instance, "You lend another child your favorite toy, and when she returns it, it is broken." Or, "You are sitting at lunch when someone walks behind you holding his drink. The next thing you realize is that there's milk all over your back." For each story, children are asked to report what they think happened and why.

After hearing these narratives, most kids report that the events were accidental. But some children, especially those who have been rejected by peers, consistently believe the slights involved were intentional acts of mean children. Experiences with unpopularity actually strengthen this bias over time. Being rejected at the start of the school term predicts who will exhibit hostile attribution bias by the end of the year, even after controlling for who may initially have had this type of bias. This probably occurs because for some children, a hostile attribution bias offers an adaptive way to interpret life experiences. For those who were treated poorly by their peers, it is reasonable to grow up protecting oneself from social unpleasantness. Unfortunately, some children never outgrow this bias, even years after the cruelty of adolescence fades away.

When they mature, children with hostile attribution bias turn into our paranoid neighbors and cynical coworkers, people who are at greater risk for problems at home and work. Mothers with this bias are more likely to assume that people are antagonistic toward their children and to assume that their own children are being purposefully hostile; their children are even more likely to become aggressive themselves. Parents with hostile attribution bias also are more likely to display aggressive behavior toward their romantic partners.

According to research from occupational psychologists, people with hostile attribution bias are more likely to engage in workplace aggression. They arrive late, skip meetings, waste supplies, antagonize coworkers, and bad-mouth the office to others who work elsewhere. When they are interrupted, their advice is ignored, or their contributions go unacknowledged, they are also much more likely than others to become angry or anxious, or even quit.

Our adolescent experiences don't only influence our cue encoding or our cue interpretations. They also influence how we act in the millisecond moments of social information processing. These "response biases" also have a lot to do with popularity. A bias toward wanting to fit in by seeming savvy and sophisticated may lead us to unnecessarily lie to a health studio employee just to save face, for instance.

In one recent study, a team of developmental psychologists showed a series of videos to over four hundred youth and asked each to imagine that they were a person depicted as the victim of bullying. In some videos, they watched peers spill water on a victim; in others, peers either called them names or damaged their toys or got them dirty. After each video, children were asked to discuss how they would respond to such treatment. The subjects discussed the video with the researchers, who were thus able to ensure that the children had encoded and interpreted the scene in the same way. But the results showed that those who were popular chose to behave in ways that would allow them to mend relationships and even build friendships with the bully. In contrast, those who were unpopular were more interested in revenge, in appearing dominant, or in avoiding the situation entirely. In other words, unpopular children's impulses were to be aggressive, rude, or passive. This, too, is a bias, but not in cue encoding or cue interpretations. It is a bias in how we choose to act in the span of a millisecond.

Related research indicates the same biases affect adults based on whether they used to be popular or not, and these biases are particularly evident when they are feeling very emotional or are intoxicated.

We have thousands of social interactions every day. For each event, we encode information from the world around us and interpret it. Finally, if the situation calls for a response, we act. While psychologists understand this reaction as a series of social information processing steps, we experience it in less than a millisecond, without contemplation or deliberation. Those milliseconds combine to fill our days, influence our relationships, define our identities, and ultimately determine our lives—who we are. These automatic reactions can make us seem as if we have terrific instincts or can get us into trouble. And the basis for what we see, how we act, and what we do all day every day is in large part a function of our high school popularity. Those old foundational memories are referenced again and again as our brain helps us get through the day.

If you were popular in high school, and your adult brain initially archived memories of inclusion, acceptance, and admiration, this may all seem like great news. You've been endowed with a set of favorable biases that research suggests will contribute to your optimism, self-confidence, and trusting nature today. But be warned:

they may also lead you to an unrealistic sense of the world around you and can result in overconfidence and naiveté.

If you were not popular, those old desires to fit in, or those old wounds of rejection, may feel as if they will never heal. Because the power of popularity is strongest when left unchecked and unchallenged, it's worth the effort to attempt to reduce how much our past affects how we experience the present. While it may seem depressing or fatalistic to discover that our high school experiences are working behind the scenes to make us repeat our adolescence over and over again, it is very important to remember that we don't have to become victims of our past. We now know that within each of the milliseconds of our social lives, we are presented with opportunities to make new choices. By understanding how our high school popularity affects us now, we are not doomed to be dominated by our past. We are freed to overwrite it! Eventually, we can fill our social databases with new memories to replace the damaging ones.

It's been a while since I browsed the pages of my high school yearbook, but in that time, I've done a fair amount of thinking about that period of my life. I recently had a dream that I was at a faculty meeting, but the other professors were all kids from my graduating class, and they weren't paying attention to what I had to say. I remember that during the dream I felt confused. *Why are they here? I don't work with any of these people. I'm a grown-up. They're not even part of my life anymore!*

But maybe they are, in ways I never imagined.

CHAPTER 7

Clicks and Cliques

What's Not to "Like"?

It was not long ago—the year 2000 to be exact—that two Silicon Valley engineers, James Hong and Jim Young, had a difference in opinion about the appearance of a woman walking by. Their disagreement may have started as a calm (albeit sexist) discussion, but it arguably launched a worldwide phenomenon that changed our entire society, perhaps as substantially and pervasively as any other innovation in the twentieth century, including the automobile, the telephone, or the microchip.

It was this conversation that Hong and Young say led to the development of a website they called Hot or Not. You may remember having heard about this site back in the day. You may have even visited it or sent in your photo. It probably didn't seem paradigmatic at the time, but then you may not remember what the world was like when this site first launched.

In 2000, the web was not too crowded. It was only four years earlier that Google had been conceived in a research lab a few miles away. Hot or Not wasn't the first website of its kind. But it was that site that hit a nerve and became one of the most popular internet destinations of its time by far. Within just one week, it reached over two million hits per day. A few weeks later, it was ranked by the Nielsen Company as one of the top twenty-five sites worldwide for internet advertising. But perhaps the most significant effect of this site actually had more to do with how it inspired others—and one man in particular. Hot or Not was reportedly an inspiration for Mark Zuckerberg's own Harvard-based Facemash. And we all know what happened after that.

At its simplest conceptualization, Hot or Not offered a public service for anyone who was insecure about his or her looks. Just minutes after posting their photos, users would receive objective feedback from thousands of people around the world enabling them to learn just how they were perceived by others.

But the site also offered something much more important that changed our relationship with popularity forever. Recall that this was the same year in which reality competition shows first appeared on prime-time TV in countries all over the world. In the United States, *Survivor* and *Big Brother* appeared, soon followed by *American Idol.* It wasn't long before versions of each would launch in over forty different countries. This was the era in which we were first introduced to the idea that anyone could achieve national fame, visibility, and positive regard from others, and in which the public could decide who was popular and who was not without ever leaving their living room couches.

That was likewise possible on Hot or Not. Its developers didn't merely make attractiveness ratings of each picture confidentially available to the visitor who had submitted his or her photo. It posted those ratings publicly. Moreover, average ratings were rank-ordered and viewable on the site as a list of who received the most favorable votes. Suddenly we could reach an unfathomable number of people with the simple click of a button, and they could approve of us, or at least of our appearance, just as easily.

This opportunity for instant worldwide popularity is fundamental to all social media platforms today. Whether it's Facebook, Twitter, Instagram, or Snapchat, the common goals are to get "likes," or even to go "viral"—in other words, to become highly popular. What makes this so appealing?

Throughout this book, I have discussed factors that motivate us to care about what others think of us, both the forces that we're conscious of and those well outside our awareness. Recall that one of these factors involves the unique way that our brains are organized, with the more primitive regions, in our limbic system, being especially sensitive to social rewards. In those moments in which we feel we are getting attention and approval from peers, fMRI studies reveal activation in the anterior cingulate cortex, which reflects the presence of neurotransmitters that make us feel good, giving us some of the same pleasure that we obtain from recreational drugs. And remember that the activation of these brain regions is important not only because it is pleasurable but also because it powerfully affects nearby brain regions that influence our feelings, motivate us to change our behavior, and even make us crave whatever we indirectly linked to the source of that pleasure.

In 2016, researchers at UCLA decided to investigate the extent to which social media may have the same effects on us. They did so by developing a clever approach to determine what happens in our brains at the very moments that we are viewing and "liking" what we see. They decided to conduct this study with adolescents aged thirteen to eighteen, which is the period during which the anterior cingulate cortex has just developed the advanced brain circuitry of adulthood.

The participants were asked to enter an fMRI scanner and interact with a platform that was designed to be similar to Instagram, the popular photo-sharing social media site. They had earlier asked each participant to submit his or her own Instagram photos, which they claimed would be viewed by fifty other teens who also were part of the study. This wasn't true, but it enabled the experimenters to manipulate how many times each of the participant's own photos had been "liked," ostensibly by peers. Half of the subjects' photos were randomly chosen to be popular among the peers, with a high number of "likes" recorded under each one. The other half were made to look as if they had gotten few "likes."

Not surprisingly, they found that social media can provide a big boost of social rewards, which was reflected by dramatic effects in the brain. When participants viewed their own pictures and saw that they had been "liked" by many others, it was accompanied by significant activation in the anterior cingulate cortex, suggesting that the subjects experienced pleasure in a way that could be hard to resist—and even become addicting. The effects were surprisingly comparable to the rewards we receive when engaging in off-line interaction.

This may explain some of the reasons why social media has become so popular. In 2015, the Pew Research Center reported that 76 percent of adolescents and 65 percent of adults in the United States use social media, the vast majority of whom report that they are online several times a day. In fact, most Americans are on multiple social media sites, with 71 percent of all teens on Facebook, 52 percent on Instagram, 41 percent on Snapchat, 33 percent on Twitter, 33 percent on Google+, and 14 percent on Tumblr. Among adults, some of the most visited platforms may be different but the proportion of those active on these sites is fairly similar. Interestingly, there are only minimal to modest differences by gender, ethnicity, or economic status. Today, most youth and many adults report that they have more social interaction each day through social media than they do face-to-face or voice-to-voice—a finding that should be alarming now that we know how much social media encourages status-seeking, and how powerfully status can lead to a lifetime of despair!

Much has been written about social media in the past two decades—some critics warn that it marks the end of society as we know it, with adverse effects on children's development, adults' productivity, and, through its natural cliquish segmentation of the world into those we follow and those we don't, the degeneration of our unified global community. Others have extolled the virtues of social media and its unprecedented opportunity to provide social connections and viral information exchange.

Scientists have debated these points as well, with studies appearing more slowly than many would like, probably because the online world changes far too quickly for science to keep up. Initially data suggested that those who use social media extensively may be at risk for psychopathology, a concept that had begun to be known in the psychological literature as "Facebook depression." Excessive use of the internet was even considered as a possible psychiatric diagnosis in the newest version of the *Diagnostic and Statistical Manual of Mental Disorders* (*DSM*).

But research has come a long way since then, and we are now beginning to understand a bit more about how social media is changing our relationships. The effects of social media have less to do with whether we use it than *when* we use it, *how* we use it, and *who we were* before we ever logged in.

My own lab has conducted a few studies to determine exactly what may go wrong, or right, when we use social media. For instance, following the lead of my graduate student Jackie Nesi, we have been able to demonstrate that excessive use of online communication during key life periods may have implications for the social proficiencies that are supposed to be developed in adolescence. Our results revealed that for young adolescent boys in particular, those who communicated with their romantic partners over the computer more than they did in person grew up to be a bit worse than others at basic romantic relationship skills, such as how to resolve arguments or express relationship needs.

In other work, we have learned that social media use also may be detrimental if we use it for the "wrong" reasons. In another study with about eight hundred teenagers, Jackie and I found that while many used social media to connect with old friends and make new ones, some lurkers were more interested in going online just to observe others. When they did, they were especially likely to compare themselves to their peers to determine whether they were as attractive, popular, and active as them. This may sound like something that characterizes teenagers, like the girls Ira Glass featured in his story on NPR's *This American Life* who reported pressure to immediately offer exaggerated compliments on their friends' posts for fear of relationship sanctions.

Adults use social media this way as well. Our findings revealed that this use of online platforms to engage in "social comparison" and "feedback-seeking" was linked with later depression, especially for those who were unpopular and made "upward comparisons" while viewing peer profiles.

Social media is not inherently bad. There may be some ill-advised ways of interacting on it and opportunities for abuse, but that is true of almost any social activity. In fact, some suggest that social media may provide rapid coping support for those who have suffered adversity. It may help to establish social connections among those who may not have access to similar peers in their community. Social media may even help teens develop impression management skills or efficient communication patterns that may prove beneficial years later. Social media is not a problem. But it may be worth considering how it has begun to change our societal values at a much broader level. A world overly dependent on social media is one where we care about the popularity of a message (or messenger) more than its veracity. It's a world in which we express even insincere ideas to gain visibility or power, and one where our "friends" are no longer sources of companionship or support, but an audience for our posts and dopamine-boosting agents. Perhaps most concerning, our casual use of social media also can affect our deepest held values and opinions, but this is an issue we can address, because if we don't, we may find ourselves surprised at what has become hot, and what is not.

My wife and I recently attended a dinner party. It was a great event. The food was delicious, the wine was flowing, and our laughter became so loud that we woke up our hosts' kids. None of us knew more than a few of the other guests before we arrived, but we were all close friends by time dessert was served. It was around that time that a man sitting across the table from us remarked that he was disappointed that his wife had decided to stay home.

"Is she OK?" we asked.

"Oh no, sorry," he explained. "She's not home sick. She's at home live-tweeting a TV show so she can get more followers on her Twitter."

This incident reminded me of another occasion when I was at a restaurant with friends and observed nearby diners waiting to see how many "likes" they got on a photo of their dinner plate rather than talking to one another.

Or the time I was standing in front of the Sydney Opera House in Australia and overheard a group of friends debating which selfies would be best to post on their Facebook profiles rather than pictures of one another.

For me, each case highlighted the differences between the two types of popularity and made me wonder whether we had begun to lose sight of the one that really matters. In each of these instances, and in so many others that we all surely can recall, it seemed that people were choosing to invest in visibility, prominence, and immediate social rewards rather than in more meaningful social connections. People were, in short, choosing to pursue status over likability.

Some aspects of social media offer an excellent way to make friends, share mutual interests, and build relationships. Social media also provides an easily accessible platform where we can celebrate our achievements with peers and elicit social support when we feel down. It offers a route to track down old acquaintances and coworkers with whom we hope to reconnect, and a chance to get more detail about others' lives than we might have time to share over a quick phone call or lunch. With every click that enables us to truly invest in others, express positive affect, or share a sentiment that helps our peers more than ourselves, we are also engaging in an activity that will make us more likable.

But we all know that that's not the only kind of popularity that social media promotes, nor is it the only kind that people log in to obtain. Our online "friends" are not always people we are actually friends with or people we even know. On some platforms, there's no attempt to even pretend that friendship is involved at all—the goal is simply to collect as many "followers" as possible, hundreds or even thousands of people who we know we will never meet and who will never know much of any substance about us. The goals are simply to be as visible as possible, to have as many people listen to us as possible, and to be as influential as possible. These are all classic markers of status.

"Like" buttons are also something of a misnomer, depending on the context. To those who click them, they can be a way of expressing heartfelt support or genuine emotional connection. But for those who obsessively seek "likes" (or "favorites" or "notes"), they are often just an attempt to get the rush that comes from seeing that we were seen and approved of by as many people as possible. Those who use social media extensively will acknowledge that, as exciting as it may be to see that a specific friend may have "liked" a post, it can be just as rewarding, if not much more so, to learn that hundreds of unknown people "liked" a post as well.

Ultimately our concern over living so much of our lives online should be less about how it affects us as individuals than its general repercussions on our culture. Although one can imagine an overdependency on seeking status online as eventually becoming problematic—

and you probably know someone for whom this is true—for most of us, social media is used to feel a small status boost every now and then. That's not so bad, particularly if we leverage our use of social media in ways that would make us likable at least as often as we seek recognition. Far more worrying is when the distinction between these two types of popularity gets lost among us as a society more generally. Whether you participate in social media or not, you know that rapid adoption of these platforms has had a profound effect on the world we live in and the kind of popularity that is valued.

In May 2015, *Tiger Beat* magazine featured a cover story for its teen audience titled "How to Be Social Media Famous!" Inside was a six-page spread detailing exactly how readers could achieve the kind of popularity that was positioned as the ultimate success for a teen today.

It began with an article on the band 5 Seconds of Summer, revealing how fame, fortune, and millions of fans were the means by which each member "bounced back from unpopularity." At first, they were all "loners," "geeks," and "invisible," the article noted, but now "a whole lot of people like [them]."

The feature went on to explain how to get as many followers as possible on social media. It urged readers to post as often as possible, take their phones everywhere they went, stay engaged with whatever is already big and popular, and so on.

There were interviews with "teen celebrities," each defined by the number of his or her followers. Many of their stories were the same: They were once sad and lonely, but now, with so many followers, they had found happiness. A sidebar encouraged kids to hire a social media manager if they wanted to find similar happiness. "This isn't a casual hobby," one manager advised. "It's a career."

Adults get the same messages in their own media consumption. "Blow Up Your Feed: The 10 Commandments of Taking Instagram Food Pics," the foodie magazine *Bon Appétit* advised its readers. The article in question offered tips designed to help Instagram users get the most "likes" as possible with their pictures of food. One came from a user highlighted as having 264,000 followers: "Foods that are universally popular and that people really want to eat always do well." Another suggested, "Sweets and little treats appeal to the widest audience. Who doesn't get excited when they see ice cream?" For its part, *Forbes* encouraged its readers to use "known hashtags" and to "like hundreds of random pictures from people in your target audience."

If we look away from the magazine rack, it may not surprise anyone that YouTube now includes over thirteen thousand different video tutorials on topics like "How to Take the Perfect Selfie." In fact, the "selfie stick" market has become a multimillion-dollar industry worldwide. So many people take photos of themselves, and occasionally do so in dangerous situations, that the Russian government has released guidelines to reduce selfie-taking-related deaths. Cover Girl cosmetics has even released a line of makeup designed specifically to look good in selfie shots.

In contrast, YouTube offers only about four hundred videos on "How to Be More Likable." I watched a few, and ironically, most are actually about gaining status as well.

Why should this trouble us? The answer lies in what we have learned from neuroscience. For instance, in the same UCLA study mentioned earlier, the researchers decided to examine their participants' neural responses not only to their own photos they had posted on Instagram but also to a series of photos that the investigators had acquired. They included some images that depicted provocative subjects (aggressive gestures, inappropriately dressed teens, illegal substances) while others were of neutral ones (household objects, coffee, unfamiliar peers). Again, they randomly selected half of these pictures to ostensibly have been judged to be popular, with many "likes," and half to have only a few "likes."

The results suggested that our interest in what is popular may be so strong that it can begin to undermine our values. When the participants viewed the provocative pictures that had gotten only a few "likes," they responded in much the way you might hope or expect: they were unlikely to "like" the photos themselves, and the responses in their brains reflected activity in the prefrontal cortex, a region that activates when we hit the brakes and stop ourselves from engaging in impulsive acts. But when provocative photos were made to look popular, the response was just the opposite—adolescents were dramatically more likely to "like" the picture themselves. Moreover, simply seeing that the picture had many "likes" on social media reduced their prefrontal cortex activity, releasing the brain's brakes. In other words, just by associating pictures with the number of "likes" they had ostensibly obtained, social media suddenly had made provocative acts "hot," while neutral acts were "not."

This finding has serious implications. It suggests that the more we value status, the more our ability to distinguish between good and bad may be compromised. Popularity can become the only value that matters, and we will begin to confuse status for quality in ways that do not bode well for the century to come.

CHAPTER 8

Parenting for Popularity

Can Mom and Dad Make a Difference, and Should They?

Just outside Portland, Oregon, around the start of June each year, two hundred townsfolk gather in the local school auditorium for the kindergarten student showcase. The event is a time-honored tradition—a rite of passage for every resident who has ever attended elementary school there.

It is an event that Peggy remembers vividly. About thirty years ago, she was standing onstage in that auditorium behind two rows of classmates as they took turns singing a verse from *The Sound of Music* songbook. But while her classmates smiled and waved to their families from the stage, Peggy hid in the back, emerging only when cued by the start of the melody to "My Favorite Things." Suddenly Peggy's palms became slick and warm. She walked slowly toward center stage as the children ahead of her sang their parts. By the time they had reached the "warm woolen mittens," Peggy's heart already was beating twice as fast as the music. She finally reached the front of the stage and looked out at the crowd of parents, teachers, and schoolmates all staring up at her. The lights were hot, she could hear her own breath, and it seemed as if the music slowed just as it came her turn to sing. Finally, she opened her mouth . . .

Peggy did not enjoy her kindergarten year. Born to immigrant parents, she looked a little different from her classmates. Her body was noticeably rounder. Her hair was darker, and her clothes came from a secondhand store. Her parents didn't know many others in their community, so Peggy usually played alone on the weekends. On occasions when she was able to convince her mother to take her to the neighborhood park, the visit always seemed to end in despair. While her mom read a book, some issue inevitably led to a shouting match between Peggy and the other kids.

On that June morning of the school assembly, the choice of verse for Peggy was particularly unfortunate. As she began to sing she could hear snickers from her schoolmates in the front rows. Her voice quivered just as she reached the part about crisp apple strudel and schnitzel with noodles.

"Piggy!" one child screamed.

"She's even bigger than Captain von Trapp!" shouted another.

The whole first row laughed. The adults tried to hush the children, but they continued to taunt her. By the time the verse was over, Peggy's cheeks were covered with tears, and she ran off the stage into the arms of her teacher.

In the decades since the kindergarten showcase, Peggy hadn't thought much about it, but as her daughter stood on that same stage, and the accompaniment to *The Sound of Music* began, the pain of that experience came flooding back. There stood her own child, dressed as an Austrian schoolgirl, and her turn to sing was approaching. Peggy could feel her own hands beginning to perspire.

Do you remember kindergarten? Can you picture the details of your classroom or your teacher? What were the other kids in your class like? Did you play with them or watch them from afar? Were they kind to you?

Is there a particular incident or scene that stands out in your mind from back then? Why do you think this remains your clearest memory after so many years? What does that event mean to you?

These questions were posed to a group of mothers by Duke professor Martha Putallaz as part of a study she conducted on children's popularity. Each mother had a child in kindergarten at the time she was asked to participate. I once conducted a similar study, and like Putallaz, I found that mothers' recollections of their own childhood peer experiences varied quite dramatically.

"It reminds me of how important it is to have strong bonds with friends . . . it was a great time," one participant wrote.

"It reminds me how cruel and mean kids can be, and I always pray my own kids' feelings don't get hurt like that," said another.

A third replied, "I was somewhat insecure, cared what others thought, felt isolated."

Studies that ask mothers to recall their early experiences with peers reliably find that, based on their most salient memories, they fall into one of three categories. Putallaz found that one group of mothers had positive memories. When these women remembered kindergarten, they recalled their peers as a source of fun, happiness, and excitement. Over half of her respondents relayed stories with joyous, positive themes, with scarcely any trace of regret, fear, or sadness.

As one woman wrote, "I had happy times with my friends . . . I felt confident and comfortable with myself when I was with them."

Other mothers' memories were less pleasant. Putallaz divided these subjects into two groups. One included women whose recollections were of aggression, hostility, and meanness. In their accounts, their childhood peers were a source of ridicule and cruelty. Sometimes these themes were recalled in the context of an otherwise positive memory, but they were notable nevertheless when compared to those women whose recollections were completely positive.

"It hurt so much," one woman remembered. "The teasing was so antagonizing to me . . . it represents the pain we suffer as children to try to fit in, belong, and have people like us."

The third group of mothers had recollections that were characterized by anxiety or loneliness. The stories offered by these women involved unrequited longing for peers, feeling left out, and watching from the sidelines. These were experiences that many believed left them damaged years later.

As one said, "It set a pattern for me that made me uncomfortable in groups of strangers."

After this group of mothers offered their own childhood peer memories, Putallaz then studied how their children fared in their own social lives at school. She asked their kindergarten classmates to nominate which children they liked most and which they liked least. She used this information to derive a score of each child's popularity—the type of popularity based on likability. The results revealed that even with the small amount of information she had about each mother, Putallaz was able to predict which children would be most or least popular.

Popularity was remarkably consistent across generations. Mothers who recalled their own peer experiences as positive had children who were above average in popularity. Mothers with memories of hostile experiences had unpopular children. But unexpectedly, the women with anxious or lonely memories had children who did not appear to be at all unpopular. In fact, children with anxious/lonely mothers were either of average popularity or, in some cases, just as well liked as the kids with positive moms.

Putallaz's results raise two interesting questions.

Can popularity be inherited? If so, why do children of mothers with happy memories and those of mothers with anxious/lonely kindergarten recollections both do equally well with their peers?

Of course, it's impossible to ascertain whether the mothers accurately recalled their childhood experiences. Memories are not always reliable, and in this particular study, the recollections offered by mothers could have been as much a reflection of their children's lives today as anything that occurred to them decades earlier. For this reason, Putallaz referred to the mothers' recollections as "social frames"—lenses through which they view past, current, and future social experiences. What Putallaz found was that moms with positive social frames and those with anxious/lonely social frames were much more similar than might be expected in at least one important respect: both cared deeply about how their children interacted with peers. Specifically, both reported much stronger intentions to help their children become likable than the mothers with hostile social frames. And this seemed to make all of the difference.

This leads to the two questions I am often asked by concerned parents: First, can they help make their children more popular? And second, should they?

The short answer to the first question is yes: parents *can* affect their children's popularity in several ways. Some of these are well within our control—others are not.

For instance, parents influence their kids' popularity through genetics. No single gene can make a person popular, as far as we know, but a group of them seem to give some kids an edge and others a lifelong disadvantage.

Physical appearance is one example of an inherited trait. We usually think of beauty as being a contributing factor to the type of popularity that emerges in adolescence and is based on status and dominance. But physical attractiveness is a predictor of likability too, and attractive parents tend to have attractive children.

Countless studies have demonstrated the powerful effect of physical beauty on popularity. Some of this work has focused on body attractiveness. Obese children, for example, are more likely to be teased by others than are those with average body shapes, even as early as preschool. But most research has focused specifically on facial features, suggesting that looks play an important role in determining whom we like and whom we don't—even well before sexual attraction per se is a factor.

In a typical study, a group of adults is asked to review a series of photos of children's faces and rate each on attractiveness. To make sure these ratings are not influenced by how wealthy or happy each child may appear, photos are cropped so that the raters cannot see the children's hair or clothes, and all the faces have a neutral expression. These attractiveness ratings are then compared to children's likability, as reported by their peers. Findings from investigations like these reveal that the most attractive children are also the most popular. The children rated least attractive are the most strongly rejected, even among children as young as five years old.

How can this be? Have kindergarteners already absorbed the standards by which our society values beauty? Have they developed biases against less attractive peers?

It seems to go deeper than that. Research conducted by psychologist Judith Langlois at the University of Texas at Austin finds that even infants at three months old stare longer at attractive faces than unattractive ones. It doesn't matter whether the faces belong to adults or other infants, or whether they are from the same or different ethnic groups. Infants are also more likely to be fussy around unattractive strangers.

Why, starting at birth, are we hardwired to prefer attractiveness? Some think it's because we are programmed to propagate, and attractive faces signal good genetic health, increasing the chances for successful reproduction. Others suggest that attractive faces are favored by babies because they best represent the prototype of what a face is supposed to look like. Langlois has demonstrated that attractive people have faces that are more symmetrical than others, and more "typical" as well. When she digitally combined photographs of a number of different faces to create a composite, the result always appeared more attractive than the individual faces used to make it—even if all of the faces were already very attractive. Our idea of attractiveness is based in large part on facial "averageness." As infants, we are drawn toward the average or typical because it helps us contextualize all of the new things we are exposed to. It is an instinct we are born with to help us understand what is prototypical, and then we can understand everything else as deviating from that average template.

Because our predilection for attractive people is present from birth, our good-looking peers have a head start on becoming the most likable people in our social circle. Research shows that teachers pay greater attention to the better-looking children in their classrooms. Even parents, in subtle ways, tend to offer greater comfort and support to their more handsome offspring.

Note that beauty is not the only inheritable trait that contributes to popularity, however. There also is a genetic basis for our general comfort level when we interact with others. This is not extroversion per se but rather an attribute that is referred to as "behavioral inhibition," which is more broadly associated with an interest in what is new and different versus a preference for what is comfortable and familiar. As one might imagine, babies who are genetically disposed to be socially inhibited are less interested in interacting with others, which has a direct effect on popularity. Each avoided social interaction is another lost opportunity to develop social skills that will be needed to become accepted, likable children years later.

But genes do not always control our destiny, especially in our social lives. Just as those of us who don't have the genetic foundation to be models or movie stars may still be considered beautiful, research has found that inherited predispositions toward popularity or unpopularity are also substantially influenced by powerful environmental factors.

It's noon and I am near my hometown on Long Island, in New York. It has been years since I lived here, so I feel like a tourist, watching the people around me like a foreigner would gape at the natives. As I sit in the cafeteria of the local Ikea, I watch the crowd of kids screaming in every direction while their parents bicker over the decision between a Duken and a Fjell. Suddenly a tray of food falls to the floor just behind me, but before I can turn around to help clean up the mess, I hear a woman, presumably a mother, whispering so loudly, and so tensely, that she might as well be yelling.

"What. Are. You. *Doing?*" she asks. "Get your hands in your lap right now. You think this is funny? If you drop one more thing, I promise you won't be laughing anymore!"

Too stunned to turn around, I sit very still, not meaning to eavesdrop but unable to help hearing the argument that has erupted just inches behind my head.

"Honey, let it go," a man's voice says. "She doesn't know what she's doing."

"I'm sick of it," the woman replies. "She does it on purpose. She just loves to aggravate me." She sighs and then exasperatedly snaps at the child, "Why won't you *listen*?"

At this point, I lean over to pick up a sippy cup that has landed at my feet and turn to hand it to the woman. She takes it from me, rolls her eyes while nodding to her child, and offers her thanks. I catch a glimpse of the cup-thrower: she is only about eighteen months old and giggling in her high chair. She has no idea why it's not permissible to push a tray onto the floor.

I don't know anything about this woman or her child, but anyone can tell that this mother is overstressed, and research suggests that adults like her may not have been very well liked when they were younger. Studies have also indicated that children like that little girl might grow up to have problems with popularity, too. The same will be true of *her* children, because popularity is related not only to the kind of parents we had but also to the kind of parents we become.

One of the factors that most strongly predicts who will be popular and who will be rejected is whether they are raised in an aggressive social environment, an atmosphere that tends to persist across generations of a family. Psychologists can measure a child's social environment fairly easily. In fact, the way parents complete just one simple task can offer remarkable insight into their own past and their children's future.

The assignment is easy: talk about your child for five minutes. Parents effectively practice this all the time. After running into an old friend they haven't seen for years or a colleague on an elevator, they are typically asked, "So, how are the kids?" Almost all parents can go on at great length in response, but their answers differ greatly.

Psychologists Terrie Moffitt and Avshalom Caspi asked almost six hundred mothers from England and Wales to complete this task with respect to their five-year-old children. The researchers were interested in learning how warm or critical the children's social environments were, and after only five minutes of conversation with their parent, they discovered a world of differences. They also wanted to investigate how this social environment may be related to children's aggressive and unpopular behavior. Interestingly, they chose to include only monozygotic twins in their study, which enabled them to ensure that any differences they identified in children's behavior could not be explained by genetic variation, since each pair of twins had identical DNA.

They found that even though they were born at the same time, to the same parents, in the same household, and with the same genetic makeup, each twin grew up in seemingly very different social environments. This was evident from the ways that their mother spoke about them. Some of the women offered descriptions and details about their children that communicated warmth and affection ("She is so funny—the other day she made up a song and she was dancing and singing in the garden") while others were far more critical ("She is horrible" or "He is so lazy").

Moffitt and Caspi returned to their subjects two years later to see how the children were growing up. Now, at seven years old, some were highly aggressive, while others were well behaved. These outcomes were strongly predicted by the social environments in which they grew up. The results are especially notable given that the researchers even saw differences between identical twins. The more warmly mothers spoke of their children at age five, the less aggressive their children were at age seven. The more critical the mother, the more her child's aggression increased over the two-year period. Subsequent research has confirmed the link: mothers (as well as fathers) who are critical when discussing their children, even for as short a time as five minutes, tend to create more hostile social environments for their children, who subsequently grow up to be unpopular.

It's not just aggression—there are plenty of other qualities in a child's social environment that also predict his or her popularity. For instance, research has revealed a long list of ways in which depressed mothers may differ from other moms, and many of these have a direct impact on their children's eventual popularity, too. Compared to other mothers, depressed women discipline their children less effectively. They spend less time with their children and smile less often. Depressed moms and dads also may pass along genes that predispose their kids to be sad or withdrawn. Probably for these reasons, these kids are much more likely to have social difficulties years later.

When it comes to the factors that set children on a path toward popularity or rejection, even seemingly trivial interactions can make a difference. Picture a baby lying in her or his crib, looking up at a dangling mobile. If its mother is feeling playful, her smiling face may suddenly appear—she may even tickle her baby—causing the infant to laugh and kick with glee. The laughter is so infectious that mom turns the moment into a little game. She again makes a surprise appearance over the crib, the baby laughs in return, and the process continues, over and over. After a few giggling exchanges, the mom may turn on the mobile to help soothe her baby, who falls peacefully asleep.

This sounds pretty normal, but can such a brief episode really affect a baby's eventual popularity? Can it influence his or her entire life?

It can. Those few moments during which the infant had a chance to see Mom smiling produced a biological reaction in the baby's brain. Research suggests that this reaction will help the child cope with stress more productively for decades to come. This will help her remain calm when a peer makes her angry at school years later, or even decades after that, when she becomes a mom and her own baby cries. The game of peekaboo also taught the baby the concept of turn taking, which is a fundamental social skill we use in every successful conversation. Watching her mom smile got her excited, and that, too, is critical for teaching children how to experience strong emotions and how to regulate them. Mothers who are depressed may deprive their children of some of these opportunities, and consequently, research studies find, these children are far less capable of managing their emotional outbursts.

As that baby drifts off to sleep watching her mobile, she is also learning how to calm herself—a skill that never would have been acquirable had her mother not approached her crib in the first place. Of course, this small episode had transactional effects, too, as described in Chapter 5. The more fun that Mom had playing this game, the more likely she will be to play it again, giving that baby even more opportunities to practice all of the same social skills.

If you weren't very popular when you were a child, the results of the studies cited above may have tempted you to draft an angry email to your parents right about now. It would be easy to blame them for all of the ways that they compromised the development of your social skills and your opportunities for social success.

And if you are a parent, you may be feeling a little pressured or guilty based on this research. Believe me, I understand. When my own kids were born, I felt bombarded by a barrage of information on how I was supposed to raise them and what kinds of things I could do to help my kids reach their full potential. It was all very helpful, but ultimately exhausting, and seemed to set a virtually impossible standard. After all, what parent hasn't lost patience, felt hopeless, or said something critical to a child that they later regretted? At times, we all feel frustrated with our kids. And with one out of every five women and one out of every ten men in the United States experiencing a clinically significant depressive episode by age twenty-five, it's worrisome to think that any time we express a sad mood we might be damaging a child's long-term success with peers. It's simply impractical to expect that we can play peekaboo with a baby twenty-four hours a day.

But we can let ourselves off the hook, at least a little, because a child's popularity isn't completely within her parents' control. The key factor is the nature of the relationship *between* parent and child, and this has as much to do with how parents behave as with what children bring into each social interaction. It is the back-and-forth, the constant give-and-take, that shapes both parents and children, and that also strongly influences a child's social development. Psychologists refer to this as the parent-child "attachment."

Parent-child attachments come in two types: secure or insecure. It takes only about twenty minutes to identify which version describes a particular family unit. A parent brings his or her nine- to eighteen-month-old baby to an unfamiliar room. After playing together, a friendly adult stranger joins them, and over the next few minutes, the baby stays alternatively in the room either with his parent, with the stranger, or with both. Psychologists measure whether the child seems more likely to explore and play with the parent, the stranger, or with neither in the room. The baby's reaction to the inconspicuous disappearance of his parent also is noted, as well as how he reacts when the parent returns.

About two-thirds of parent-child pairings prove to be securely attached, which is established by the fact that the child is most likely to play when his parent is nearby. Securely attached children become mildly distressed when their parent steps out, are a little skittish around the stranger, and then are quickly soothed when the parent returns. Parents in securely attached relationships respond in ways that show that they are highly attuned to their child's distress, able to help their baby calm down, and attentive to what their child needs.

But in insecurely attached relationships, any number of things can go wrong. Some babies don't appear to be entirely comfortable with their parents and even seem to avoid them altogether. Others are overly clingy. Some are inconsolable when their parents leave the room; others don't even seem to notice. Parents, for their part, may be overly responsive or seemingly unconcerned about their child's behavior.

Research has demonstrated that infants in secure attachments grow up to have far more interpersonal success. Not only are they more popular but they also are happier in their romantic relationships and are more likely to form secure attachments with their own children. In one study, a team of Dutch researchers led by Marinus van IJzendoorn measured parent-child attachment in twelve-month-olds who were adopted; thus any connection between their outcomes and their parents' behavior could not be attributed to shared genes. They found that at age seven, children who had been securely attached as infants were far more likely to be popular, according to their schoolmates, than those who were insecurely attached, even after accounting for socioeconomic status and individual temperament. Studies that looked at the effects of attachment with a father have found the exact same effects.

It also may be comforting to learn that parents can easily change the family's social environment. In fact, one way they can affect their children's later popularity is by playing games with them. But it depends on *how* they play.

When psychologists Ross Parke, Gregory Pettit, and Jackie Mize observed parents playing with their children, they noticed differences that help set the stage for how children learn to behave socially. Some parents, Mize and Pettit found, play with their children as equals. They let their kids decide what game to play, make up the rules for original games, and decide when to switch to another. They talk a lot to their kids while playing, and they express a range of emotions. Their children grow up much more likely to be accepted by their peers. Through these moments of parent-child interaction, kids learn how to share and cooperate, be creative and explorative, and empathize with others. In other words, these moments of play are rich opportunities to learn emotional intelligence.

But not all parents play in this manner. Some dominate, set stern limits, and remain reserved, even stoic while playing with their children. Not surprisingly, their children behave in the same way when playing with others their own age. The more that mothers asserted their own power when interacting with their children, especially when they displayed an absence of warmth or responsiveness to children's needs, the more aggressive their children were with peers even years later, and ultimately they became very unpopular.

The way that fathers play is also important. Compared to mothers, dads are more likely to be rough-and-tumble with their kids. Children typically laugh much harder and get more excited when wrestling with a parent than when, say, putting a puzzle together. These highly physical play sessions are valuable for teaching children how to regulate strong emotions. Moms and dads who express their own emotions freely while playing, and demonstrate how to safely control those feelings, also have children who grow up to be more popular. That's likely due to the fact that children learn from their parents how to express themselves, cope, and get support when they need it.

Of course, being responsive to children's needs and involved in their play can go too far. If you've ever been to a playground, you have seen what this looks like. When kids are playing, swinging, sliding, and climbing, eventually someone falls. It's the shock of the fall that is more upsetting than any actual injury, and the child looks as if he may start to cry. But he doesn't—at least not immediately. The first thing he does is look up at Mom or Dad. If the parent remains calm, the child might brush himself off and return to playing. But if the parent looks worried or upset, the tears begin.

Some parents may even overreact. They run to their child and coddle them, remaining very close by—closer than is needed for their child's age—to make sure he doesn't fall again. Or they may get themselves so stressed over the possibility of a future fall that they decide to take the child and leave the playground altogether. Research suggests that these children are much more likely to be victimized by their peers when they are older. Having parents who are hypersensitive to their children's emotions and overly protective is a strong predictor of unpopularity.

Parents can also influence their offspring's future popularity by directly intervening in their social lives. Consider Sam, who is a proud dad. His son, Joey, looks exactly like him, with the same curly hair, lanky frame, and freckles running up his arms. Sam loves watching Joey grow up. In the afternoons, he stands proudly in the ballpark as Joey runs the bases. On Saturdays, he likes to be nearby while Joey jokes around with his friends. Wherever Joey goes, Sam is not far behind.

When Joey's school hosted a party, Sam called another parent to see if his son could attend it with her daughter. In the gym, Sam looked on while Joey and the girl got punch together, made their way around the dance floor, and sat at a table together. "Don't forget to share!" Sam called out. When Joey started to lean very close to his date, Sam admonished, "Use your words. Keep your hands to yourself!"

Joey turned around, red-faced, glared at his father, and ran out of the party.

Sam was doing what any good parent might do—a parent of a preschooler, that is. But Joey was seventeen years old, and the occasion was his high school's homecoming dance. In that context, Sam seems far too involved in his child's peer relationships.

Do you know parents who effectively become personal assistants to their kids? They set up playdates for their one-year-olds and later enroll their kids in music or gymnastics classes to play with other toddlers. It seems they spend much of the day driving their little ones to activities and appointments.

Don't scoff—these are precisely the steps parents can take to help make their children become more likable among their peers, and indeed these are very appropriate ways to parent a toddler. But the effectiveness of this approach depends on when and how parents manage their children's social lives, according to Arizona State University psychologist Gary Ladd. Ladd suggests three specific ways that parents can increase their child's likability.

The first has to do with setting up playdates. While it is important for children to have the chance to play with others, it's not merely creating the opportunities for play that matters most. Rather, it's how that parent sets up these encounters that makes the biggest difference. When their children are two, Ladd says, some parents already contact others, coordinate get-togethers, and select friends. While these companions and playdates help children develop a broader social network, parents should change the way they intervene as their kids get older. By three, children should be able to pick which peers they are most interested in seeing. By four, they should be able to choose the activities they will engage in during the playdate, and by five or six, children should start taking the lead in initiating meet-ups.

Developmental psychologists call this "scaffolding," and the metaphor is apt. At each stage of his or her development, it's important to provide only as much support as a child needs, but no more. Structure can be withdrawn as the child is able to stand well on their own. Ladd found that by kindergarten the children who grew up to be most popular were those whose parents taught them how to identify compatible playmates, ask them if they wanted to meet outside of school, and suggest activities. Soon they are able to do so independently, which helps accelerate the learning curve for future social interactions.

As kids get older, this translates into learning how to introduce oneself to new groups and eventually how to trust others in close relationships. These skills continue to grow more complex, of course, and soon children have to learn how to think of others first, balancing their own preferences with what is best for the group. They learn how to respect differences between themselves and others. Even in middle school, parents can help scaffold more intricate social negotiations, such as whom to invite to a birthday celebration when seats are limited, or how to decline an invitation when two or more events are occurring simultaneously. Each of these tasks is a chance for kids to learn how to live in an increasingly sophisticated social world. Research suggests that children who learn these skills in childhood are better able to transition into romantic relationships later in life.

A second way that parents can affect their child's popularity has to do with the way they get involved in their kids' playdates. The more that parents monitor their children while they play during their very early years, the better. In one study, parents and their one- to two-year-old children attended a play session with other toddlers. At first, the parents were instructed to either join their children as they played or remain uninvolved. The parents then left, leaving the kids to play on their own for a few minutes longer. Those whose parents had been instructed to get involved were more likely to remain happy and play amicably with their peers after the parents departed. Those whose parents had been uninvolved fell apart more quickly. When the same experiment was conducted with kids just a few years older, however, the results were the opposite. For preschoolers, heavy parent involvement was no longer as helpful.

By preschool and kindergarten, parents monitor from afar, which offers them an important opportunity to ask children later what they did with their friends, whether they had any disagreements, and how they helped resolve those problems. These are rich conversations that help kids understand how to identify their emotions, what they were thinking about a given situation, and how they behaved. So, if a kid comes home and says, "When Johnny grabbed my truck to play with it himself, I punched him in the face," it is a good teachable moment to explore alternative solutions. "How did you feel when he did that?" a parent might ask. "Did he ask you first whether you would share?" "Had you been playing with it for very long?" "What are other things you could have done when he took the truck?" "How does it make you feel when someone punches you?" and so on.

Not only does this help children in the short term, but it also sets the stage for how they will think about social experiences, manage their feelings, consider various solutions, and evaluate how those solutions worked—a nice framework that many wish adults drew upon more often. These are skills that predict not only which kids will become more popular, but also those who will have higher levels of academic achievement.

A third tip has to do with how parents coach their children when they have experienced a problem. This is a matter of more than simply listening to children recount what they did during an afternoon with their peers. It involves, rather, a parent's offering specific instruction and practice regarding the management of peer relationships. Of course, most parents will offer such basic guidelines as "Don't hit others," "Share your toys," and "Say please and thank you." But the type of coaching that is especially important is the advice adults offer regarding the event in question and the way they model how to act in social situations.

Typically, parents coach their children to behave like they do. It's quite remarkable the degree to which children model themselves on their parents. It's not just the little things, either, like the way my own daughter has my facial expressions or how my son uses his hands when he talks, just like I do. Such behavior is also reflected in how kids decide to interact with one another.

In another one of her studies on intergenerational similarities in popularity, Martha Putallaz asked mothers to bring their children to her lab at Duke to play together. Using a one-way mirror, Putallaz and her research assistants were able to watch the children play and record the extent to which each was agreeable and cooperative, or aggressive. Meanwhile, each child's mom was observed talking with the mothers of the other children being studied. The children of the women who conversed amicably in one room behaved in the same companionable way with their peers just down the hall. Moms who tried to dominate their conversations tended to have children who were also excessively self-focused in their interactions.

Preschool children rely on their parents to be coaches—studies have shown that parents talk to their children about how to interact with peers at least once every other day, and this predicts children's popularity. Of course, some don't simply coach but insert themselves into their children's social interactions to help kids negotiate their way into a game or out of a fight. By middle school, such parental behaviors are considered intrusive and remarkably damaging to kids' popularity. Older children and adolescents still need their parents to guide them, but they like to believe that they didn't ask for help. Nevertheless, in one study examining how coaching helped teenagers interact with peers they had not met before, findings revealed that parental involvement made a difference. Those parents who spoke with their children about peers, reviewed the best qualities to look for in a friend, or discussed the best ways to act with others had kids who developed closer relationships within just a few months.

For all of the speculation on how parents' own popularity might affect their parenting years later, and all of the research on how moms and dads can affect how well their children do with peers, one question has gone unexplored: *should* parents try to affect their children's popularity at all?

The answer is both yes and no.

I say yes, because as a clinical child psychologist, I strongly recommend that parents be alert to those kids who are having issues with likability. Sometimes it's clear that there are problems afoot.

I remember one five-year-old boy who was so rambunctious and energetic that he never stopped to play with other kids at school. He just ran by as they called out for him to join their games. When it came time for him to pick a partner on a school trip, he didn't have anyone who wanted to sit with him.

Then there was the short-tempered girl who only talked to her peers aggressively in an impatient tone. You could almost hear the echo of her parents yelling at her every time she told her classmates that they were being "bad, bad children." It didn't take long for her to be rejected by all of her classmates—a status she reinforced every day when she would scream at anyone who dared to try to play with her.

Another girl was so painfully skittish that just being at school was a difficult experience for her. She clung to her father's leg until she was forcibly detached, and then she never ventured more than a few feet from her teacher. She cried all day, even when the other kids seemed to have sympathy for her and kindly asked her to join them on the swings.

It's these kids—the ones who before first grade already seem to be shunned by peers, those who have more tears than laughs with others, or those who just don't seem that interested in joining in—who may benefit from some degree of intervention. Because it is these kids who will suffer from the worst manifestation of unpopularity, bullying—a crisis finally getting attention from a worldwide audience.

Psychologists have been interested in understanding the causes and consequences of bullying for many years, but it was only after the massacre in Columbine that the rest of the world began to take serious notice of this problem. On April 20, 1999, two teens who had purportedly been victimized by their peers brought guns and bombs to their Colorado high school, viciously killing twelve fellow students and one teacher, wounding twenty-one others, and ultimately turning their weapons on themselves to end their own lives. Americans stood in shock as the details came to light of how these seemingly typical teens had suddenly turned to rage and murder. It was not the first mass killing to take place in a school and sadly not the last. School shootings in the years since have become so disturbingly frequent that most of us can't help but simply hope that such tragedies never come to our own community.

In their wake, however, came a renewed interest in peer victimization. When federal anti-bullying legislation was proposed, but failed, states enacted their own laws, proposing severe sanctions on any student who bullied another on school grounds. These laws and the rise of public attention to the issue have helped. Overt forms of bullying no longer occur quite as frequently in those schools that have imposed severe penalties. But the popularity dynamics that underlie bullying haven't gone away, and of course kids have found plenty of ways to bully one another more covertly, whether anonymously, away from school, or even online.

There is now evidence that some anti-bullying measures are effective at reducing instances of peer victimization, but it would be wishful thinking to believe that all bullying will stop, as kids have been victimized by other children since the beginning of time. What's needed is an equal focus on helping children cope with those moments when they will be teased, excluded, tormented, or even derisively talked about by their peers. And psychologists know exactly how parents can help.

Have you and a friend ever experienced a stressful event and both walked away with a completely different reaction to it? That happens all the time, and it's due to the fact that what we *feel* about a given situation has much less to do with what actually happens to us than it does with what we *think* about what took place.

Imagine two children who fail a history exam. One blames herself, regrets the decisions she made the night before the test, and begins to feel hopeless that she will ever do well in school. The other blames the teacher, decides the test was unfair, and remains emotionally unscathed.

The difference between how these two students responded to a stressful incident is what psychologists call "attributional style." Do you attribute negative life events to your own characteristics ("I'm stupid") that are both global ("I can't do anything right") and stable ("I will never do well at school")? This kind of attributional style is a fast track to depression. Ascribing all negative events to ourselves, leaving no room for improvements or alternative explanations, enables stressors to have their worst impact on us psychologically—particularly if this is the way we habitually react.

Or do you attribute such experiences to things that have nothing to do with you ("The test was poorly constructed"), are specific ("I don't do well when tests use multiple choice"), or are unstable ("I would probably do better if I had more time to study")? This is the healthier response, though it does not imply that people shouldn't also take responsibility for their actions.

In 1998, Sandra Graham and Jaana Juvonen did a study in which they asked 418 sixth- and seventh-grade children to talk about how they would respond if they were victimized by peers. The group had widely different responses. Some said that if they were teased it would be due to their own failings or self-deficits. ("This will happen to me again." "If I were a cooler kid, I wouldn't get picked on." "It's my fault, I shouldn't have been in the restroom/locker room.") Graham and Juvonen found that it was these kids who were at greatest risk for depression, anxiety, and low levels of self-esteem. They were also most likely to be rejected by peers and at risk for further victimization.

But others had a more adaptive response that recognized that being bullied may not have had as much to do with them specifically. ("These kids pick on everybody." "It was my bad luck to be in the wrong place at the wrong time.") These kids were fine in the long run.

Parents have a very significant influence on the kind of attributional style their children develop, and again, the similarities across generations are remarkable. Attributional style is also a characteristic that is relatively easy to modify.

Imagine a world where we cast the bullies not as those with the power to intimidate others but as those who likely are experiencing the most profound psychological difficulties. They may seem cool, and they may get lots of attention when they successfully victimize others. But this is only a sign of the kind of popularity we recognize as based on status, which ultimately leads to bad outcomes, like loneliness, addiction, and an ongoing preoccupation with social standing. Bullies often have the harshest upbringings, having watched their parents fight and intimidate one another. They have often been victims themselves, and their aggressive ways may be cries for attention, in the form of status-seeking.

In some ways, it is troubling that new zero-tolerance legislation immediately expels bullies. While it is an effective way to protect their victims and sends a strong warning to other aggressors, these are the kids who may be in most desperate need of help. Expelling them from school offers a good short-term solution, but it may be sending those who are highly vulnerable directly back to where they learned to become so aggressive.

While no one expects victims to easily or suddenly sympathize with their tormentors, parents can help in a way that few others can by teaching their children to understand why other kids behave this way. When victims realize that they have a choice about how to interpret why they have been bullied, they are more likely to emerge from victimization bruised, perhaps, but psychologically unharmed.

Earlier, I suggested that there are cases, such as those described above, when it makes sense for parents to try to influence their child's popularity. But does it follow that parents should always try to make their children more popular?

Some parents feel inclined to do so. They want their child to be the one with the most friends, invited to the most parties, and the one picked first for every team or class project. They speak proudly when they relate how all the other kids look up to their own son or daughter.

Here, I would say no—this is not a great idea, because encouraging popularity of this type is a hairsbreadth away from encouraging kids to value status instead of likability. It's the tactic of a desperate stage parent, trying to have his child live out his own popularity fantasies.

In 1991, Texas mother Wanda Holloway was so desperate for her daughter to become a popular cheerleader that she conspired to murder the mother of her daughter's chief competitor, hoping it would lead to an open spot on the squad. There are two aspects of this story that are distasteful. One is the homicidal behavior, naturally. But the other was that a parent became so focused on her child's status. Less extreme but equally concerning examples abound: I have heard countless stories of parents who orchestrate friendships with peers they perceive as most powerful, buy their children expensive clothing, phones, or jewelry, and even allow their teenagers to engage in risky behavior, all to help them achieve the highest levels of status in their school. Yet, research suggests such status-seeking is only advisable if you want that child to ultimately be at greater risk for overdependency on others, risky behavior, relationship problems, and unhappiness.

Perhaps the best parents can do is simply to teach their children about the two types of popularity. My own kids are only just starting school, so we'll see how I feel when they get closer to adolescence. But for now, I'm doing my best to make sure that, at the very least, they understand that it's fine to be popular, as long as it's the type of popularity that will make them happy.

Almost every night, at least one of them asks me to read them the story of a race car named Lightning McQueen, who seeks fame and fortune in a championship race. Lightning has spent his entire life working to win the prized Piston Cup, and there is nothing he wants more than to come in first place and reap the many benefits of a champion: a new paint job, fancy sponsorships, and most of all hordes of fans that idolize him. But before he can pursue this dream, Lightning gets detoured to a small town called Radiator Springs, where he is forced to stay and work with its residents, a bunch of cars who are far more interested in having fun with Lightning and becoming his friends. By the end of the story, after he leaves the town, Lightning finally competes in the race he has dreamed about for so long, but he is surprised to discover that he really misses the cars in Radiator Springs. Just inches from the finish line, he decides to give up the championship and offer a selfless act of kindness to a fellow racer instead.

This is usually the part when my son asks, "Daddy, why didn't Lightning finish the race?"

"Because no matter how long you have been racing," I tell him, "winning will never make you happier than having good friends."

CHAPTER 9

Most Likely to Succeed

Choosing the Type of Popularity We Want

Late one night at Foodtown, a local supermarket in the suburban town of Plainview, a sixteen-year-old boy who looked and sounded as if he was eleven picked up the store's microphone.

"Attention, shoppers," he announced. "The time is now 9:45, and Foodtown will be closing in just fifteen minutes." As his high-pitched voice echoed down the aisles, customers looked over their carts. One approached the courtesy desk where the boy was placing the microphone back in its holder.

"Do you work here?" she asked, grinning. "How old are you?"

"Sixteen," he said, pushing his glasses up.

Her expression changed. "You're sixteen!" she shouted. "Oh, I thought you were gifted, like Doogie Howser or something."

The boy's announcement also served as the signal for all the teen employees of Foodtown to start making their plans for the night. It was Friday, and as was the custom, whichever stock boy whose parents were away would invite everyone over to hang out and drink cheap beer.

On this particular night it was Jason, a congenial high school senior, who walked the aisles to let everyone know the party would be at his house. Of course, he told Tony first. Tony was the quiet junior whom all of the girls working the cash registers would find excuses to talk to. If Tony wasn't able to make it, it was hardly worth having the party at all. Jason next invited Sean, the kid who seemed to have made it through adolescence without a single sign of acne. By the time of the final announcement that the supermarket was closed, Jason had invited just about everyone. As they all quickly worked to clean up the store and get ready for the night ahead, a cashier named Sandra approached the young boy at the courtesy counter and asked him to the party, an invitation that left him speechless. Sandra, as it happened, was his first crush.

Jason seemed especially excited that the young boy would be attending. "Guess who's coming tonight!" he called out to Sean while pointing and smiling.

That young boy, in fact, was me, and I still remember vividly that moment when the cool kids—the Jasons, the Tonys, and the Seans—wanted me to be a part of their group. I felt that at long last, despite how different I looked from the others, I would now be one of them. In my own high school, on the other side of town, the popular kids never invited me to hang out with them, much as I wished they would. They all knew me, of course: I was the guy who was still four-foot-seven in ninth grade, barely reaching five feet tall when I turned sixteen, and I wouldn't weigh more than a hundred pounds until my sophomore year of college. I had worn bifocals since the age of five, and while everyone else was ditching school to go hang out at the beach, I dutifully attended class every day, ultimately earning the decidedly uncool Perfect Attendance Award at high school graduation for never missing a class since kindergarten. At the time, it never made sense to me why I was left out when the popular kids hung out together. I was just as cool as them, I thought.

And now, at last, I was. Sean, Tony, and Sandra left the store a few minutes later, walking through the inner set of heavy doors that normally opened automatically but now had been deactivated for closing. Then they made their way through the outer set and stood outside. Jason waited to hold the inner door open for me, and after we both walked through, he turned to lock it for the night. But then, just as I started to head outside, I felt a tug on the hood of my winter jacket. Before I realized what was happening, Jason had pushed me against the inner wall of the vestibule. Stunned, I watched him run through the second set of doors without me, and as it slammed shut, he locked the outer doors as well.

I was now trapped, unable to get back into the dark store behind me or outside, where Sean, Tony, and Jason had started banging against the door and laughing.

Of course, for a few seconds I tried to affect nonchalance and make it seem like I was in on the joke. "OK, haha. You got me."

But as seconds turned to minutes, a pit in my stomach grew. The guys crouched down so their heads were level with my own. They yelled and pointed at me. They used singsongy voices to tease and mock me, and as my expression began to wilt, from feigned amusement to misery, they began to hold their sides from laughing so hard. I remember looking into Jason's eyes as he made taunting faces at me through the glass. *I thought you were my friend.*

Sandra, who was standing quietly outside a few yards away, wasn't doing anything to help. In fact, she even seemed to be giggling a little at the sight of me pushing at the doors. It was at that moment that I remember looking through the glass, thinking that life must be so much better and so much easier for those who are popular.

Why am I sharing this story? It's because I know my experience was hardly unique. We have all had our moments of humiliation, times when we felt as if we were left out or even bullied. Studies confirm that over 80 percent of us have been victimized by our peers at some point in our childhoods. Whether it was because we were too small or too big, too smart or not clever enough, too loud or too quiet, we have all been there.

But we didn't leave these injuries safely back in adolescence—we carry those memories with us for the rest of our lives. We may keep them private or deny their significance. But they remain with us tenaciously, sometimes as raw and sensitive as they were when we experienced them as teens. They are part of who we are, and we continue to believe, at least at some level, that being popular would make our lives better. If only we were popular, we would be more successful, wealthy, more confident, less stressed. If everyone else thought highly of us, we might feel that way about ourselves. Popular equals happy, at least in our minds.

For many, being unpopular is among the darkest of fears. Aaron Beck, the father of cognitive therapy and the recipient of the first Community Mental Health Award from the Kennedy Forum, suggested that almost every moment of anger, depression, addiction, worry, or despair we experience can be traced to what Beck called our "core beliefs" or "schema." Beck's former student Jeff Young discovered that there are only a dozen or so of these schema that people in every culture have in common, and many of them ultimately have some relation to popularity. We fear ending up alone, being excluded, losing the attention or support of others, or becoming unlovable. At some level, it's these concerns about popularity that underlie so many moments when we excessively worry, overreact, or turn toward maladaptive means to make ourselves happy. If you think hard enough about the most recent occasion in which you felt particularly upset, and dig deeply enough to discern what about it made it so distressing, there's a good chance you'll find that it was due to some core belief that you might become unpopular.

Throughout this book, I have argued that the desire to be popular is a quintessential human experience. Whether it's the evolutionary by-product of our ancestors' herding instincts, now reflected in the social sensitivity of our DNA, a function of adolescent memories that have become a template for all our subsequent social interactions, or at the root of our collective psychological schema, we all share a universal desire to be regarded positively by others. Our minds, our bodies, our health, and our emotions are linked to popularity in ways that only the most current and sophisticated methods in psychology and neuroscience are now beginning to reveal.

But you have a choice: you can allow these instincts to direct you toward status or toward likability. Choosing likability is not always an easy option in a world so obsessed with status. We're constantly invited to idolize those with status, we determine quality based on status, and we even pay attention to those with status with whom we may disagree, as if being visible, dominant, powerful, or cool are admirable qualities in their own right. We're so tempted to obtain status for ourselves that we have invented ways that enable us to simply press buttons and strive for it on a round-the-clock basis.

Yet decades of accumulated research reviewed in this book have established that the relentless pursuit of status puts us at risk for a wide range of serious life problems, including addiction, loneliness, and depression. The efforts required to obtain status—behaviors such as aggressiveness, disregarding the feelings of others, and selfishness—should not be what we esteem for ourselves or for our society.

It turns out that the answer we are looking for is what we have known all along: the thing that will make us happiest is if we are likable. For some, likability comes easily. Their natural tendency to attract others will help them effortlessly establish new relationships, and their likability will pay dividends for years to come. But for others, being likable requires more of an effort, and after an adolescence of ostracism or exclusion, it can seem impossible. In fact, it may be these individuals who are the most heavily invested in status-seeking.

I hope this book has been successful in demonstrating that regardless of our pasts, we all have an opportunity to become more likable—maybe hundreds of opportunities each day, in fact. Doing so requires us to shed our adolescent conceptions of what's "most popular" and return to what we learned as children. Prioritizing likability over status means choosing to help our peers rather than exclusively satisfying our own needs, showing more interest in others rather than vying for more attention and power, and cultivating relationships more than "likes." It's making the choice to help others feel included and welcome rather than making ourselves feel superior. Attaining the most gratifying form of popularity comes from making the effort to fit in more than trying to stand out, and from doing what we can to promote harmony rather than focusing on how to dominate others.

Over the past two decades, I have been approached by hundreds, perhaps thousands of people who have asked me how to benefit from the lessons gleaned from research on popularity. Many want to know how we can we become more likable today, especially when popularity eluded us in our youth. Others wonder how best to advise their children, particularly the parents of tweens and teens who are beginning to succumb to their biological attraction to status. Still others are interested in learning how best to make use of popularity dynamics at work, leveraging our bosses' natural tendencies to hire and promote those most likable, and avoiding the traps that come from status-seeking among our coworkers. Below, I offer my responses to each, with hopes that this advice will help everyone achieve the kind of popularity that is worth pursuing. Also included is a brief letter to a teen that may be of use not only for today's younger generation, which is growing up in a status-obsessed world, but also for anyone who still remembers their own adolescence and recognizes some part of their teenage self in the adult they have become today.

Becoming More Likable

I have probably heard hundreds of objections to becoming more likable. Among the most common: "I don't care what other people think of me," "If someone doesn't like me, it's their problem—not mine," "I wasn't likable as a child and I can't do anything about it now." I hope this book has successfully demonstrated that each of these objections deserves to be challenged. In fact, we all do care what others think about us, whether we care to admit it or not. Our standing among others powerfully affects our behavior every day, our physical and mental health, our DNA, and our lifetime happiness and success. Caring about what others think of us may be one of our most human qualities, and most who deny they care about feeling included do so with such emotional conviction that it almost undermines their point.

I hope this book also has successfully illustrated that being disliked is worthy of our attention and certainly within our power to change. In fact, as compared to the abundant resources our society has dedicated to other powerful predictors of health, wealth, safety, productivity, contentment, and harmonious citizenship, it seems a bit foolish that there has been far less attention to likability—one of the most powerful factors that dramatically affects each and every one of these outcomes.

Luckily, it's not hard to become more likable. We like those who make us feel (1) happy, (2) included, and/or (3) valued, and those who are most likable seem to be able to accomplish all three in roughly equal measure. There are countless ways to do so. You don't have to be an extrovert, a comedian, or the life of the party. Nor are likable people submissive, passive, and ingratiating. Rather, there are at least a dozen ways to enhance one's likability that don't require a personality overhaul at all but instead just a few minor adaptations to try out what has been correlated with popularity in scientific studies.

For instance, we can make others feel happy just by being positive around people who are down, upbeat in a bored crowd, calm within an angry group, or serene while others are stressed. Recall that findings on social mimicry suggest that others will emulate your behavior without even realizing they have been susceptible to contagion and will begin to associate you with someone whom they like to have around. Of course, this doesn't suggest that likable people have to be saccharine cheerleaders all the time. In fact, those who are overly energetic and ebullient are often disliked, precisely for the reason that their hyperpositivity makes others feel bad about themselves in comparison, and they are deemed annoying and unrealistic. What likable people do so well is to understand how others feel—they know how to "read the room"—and complement their surroundings without going overboard. They are the mood managers of the group who everyone likes because their presence truly changes the dynamic of the communities they join. When I think of the most likable people I know, I rarely choose the sad sacks who are cynical, complaining, or pessimistic. Instead, I pick those people who make me feel validated. They make me laugh harder at what I find funny, more excited when I am enthusiastic, and justified when I feel irritated. We all tend to feel happier when we believe that someone "gets us" and agrees with us.

A second reliable way to increase likability is to make others feel included. This remarkably effective tip is powerful because it acts on our instinctual need to feel a part of the herd, and it's not at all difficult to execute. Of course, I'm not talking about simply assembling a large guest list for every social event, or cc'ing all of your acquaintances on every email. Instead, by included I mean the ways that we make special efforts to help others feel as if they are welcome members of a group. They can be as simple as the non-verbal signal we offer by widening a conversation circle when someone new approaches, or a more concerted effort to fight for someone who may feel abandoned or victimized. The key to each approach is to make others feel as if they were enthusiastically selected, and thus they like us in return.

When speaking about popularity research with groups of people who know one another, I often ask them who in their circle is most well-liked, and why they think that person is so universally admired. It is this ability to make others feel included that is cited again and again, whatever the makeup of the group. In one middle school, parents told me how much they loved the president of their PTA specifically because of the ways that she made every parent feel as if he or she was the most special guest in attendance. They spoke of her tireless efforts to find meeting times that would leave no one out; her brief but heartfelt notes to those who were absent to let them know they were missed, or were referenced fondly by those in attendance; and her unique way of greeting everyone as if she was especially excited to see them. One parent said, "I like feeling that I am one of 'her' people, that she cares about me—she cares about all of us—and that just makes me kind of trust her, root for her, and want to be even closer with her."

Equally important to becoming more likable is developing the ability to make others feel valued. We communicate value through validation and inclusion, but truly valuing others establishes a social connection that goes beyond what might be possible between strangers. Valuing each other is the essential ingredient that makes an acquaintanceship start to become a deeper relationship.

I have found that people often mistakenly believe that valuing a person, his opinions, or his contributions means that they must become unquestioningly agreeable, or perhaps even submissive, but that is not the case. Recall that research on even young children who became most likable, and retained that status for almost a decade, revealed that they are the best leaders precisely because they offer novel, innovative, and even sometimes controversial ideas, but in a way that allows all the members of the group to feel as if their input was valued. One way they do so is simply to reflect what someone else has proposed before offering a new contribution or idea. Psychologists use this same principle to quickly establish therapeutic rapport, paraphrasing what a client has said and repeating it back to him before expounding, elaborating, or disagreeing with it. You might think that offering someone a summary of what she has just told you will elicit an odd or annoyed response ("Uh, yeah, didn't I just say that?!"). In fact, upon hearing their own contributions paraphrased or reflected back to them, people feel remarkably gratified and instantly more connected to the person to whom they are talking. Most important, they feel instantly valued.

Of course, it's also possible to make others feel valued by directly expressing praise and gratitude. It's a simple point, but one that increasingly bears reminding as our society becomes more anonymous and depersonalized. When is the last time a stranger looked you in the eye and genuinely offered you thanks? How recently has one of your neighbors, friends, or even your partner given you earnest, unsolicited, selfless praise? I suspect the answers from people in the early twenty-first century might be different from those of people a half-century ago for reasons described earlier in this book. It has become far too easy to hide behind our electronic barriers and self-reliant systems. Consequently, members of our society—each and every one of us—feels less and less valued.

In the spirit of practicing what I preach, I decided to try this by offering more praise and gratitude myself when I was faced with the annual Facebook birthday ritual that we now all know too well. Remember the days when we received cards or phone calls to wish us a happy birthday? Each expression served as a sign that someone had remembered us, taken time out of her or his day to dedicate to us—to value us. With each call, we were also offered an opportunity to personally express our thanks. Today, of course, we may receive dozens or even hundreds of messages on our Facebook feeds. But these represent a "value mirage," because in our hearts we know that most of those who have posted did not remember the date of our birthday, but were prompted by Facebook itself to send a greeting—sometimes by people we haven't actually spoken with in decades. In fact, in recent years the platform has dispensed with the illusion of intimacy altogether by simply altering us to the *number* of people who posted a birthday greeting—it requires several clicks to even learn the identity of the sender of each message. Is it any wonder we feel less valued and connected when even our friendships have become a depersonalized, practically automated digital exercise?

One year—while working on this book, in fact—I decided to bring humanity back to the experience by letting my social media friends know that I valued them. Bucking the recent trend to simply post a "thanks to everyone for the birthday wishes" on my feed, I wrote back to each and every well-wisher individually to thank them and to offer a comment about how their message, and consequently my memory of them, had made my day a little brighter.

The notes were a very brief—sometimes just a single line to re-establish a genuine connection on a human level and to avoid the status-marking tallies that could have otherwise become so easy to focus on in this yearly social media exercise. The result was remarkable. Over the next few days, I was flooded with replies, private messages, and yes, actual phone calls that enabled me to rekindle so many relationships that had become digital ghosts of relationships past. These conversations continued not just over the next week, but in many cases, the entire year. Soon I noticed a spillover effect, changing the way I used social media more generally, and how people used it with me—not to seek status, but to cultivate human connections again. Had my brief notes letting others know how much I valued them made me more likable? It's hard to know, of course. But they did lead to a year filled with far more fun interactions with friends, more warmth, more support, and more contentment than likely would have occurred otherwise, and that is something I valued tremendously.

Feeling Popular After High School

Of course, another attribute we typically associate with likability is confidence. By confidence I do not mean the bravado or immodesty that is associated with narcissism, but the laid-back, easygoing, and perhaps even self-effacing demeanor of someone who genuinely feels comfortable in his or her own skin.

Confidence is not something we can learn. We are born feeling good about ourselves, and it is our experiences with others that introduce insecurity, perhaps especially our experiences with popularity in our youth. That's why increasing one's confidence, or even faking it, can be especially difficult when we feel we have not always been accepted by others. Before working to become more likable, therefore, a critical first step is to actually feel more liked, secure, and accepted.

Increasing confidence in social interactions involves three straightforward steps. If these steps seem academic it's because psychological research overwhelmingly supports the idea that if we want to change how we feel and act we first have to change how we think. It is the single most effective way to stop a pattern of dislikability that can plague some for their entire lives.

First, we must accept the premise that our past experiences with popularity still matter. Despite how much we would like to sweep them under the rug, or pretend that we no longer care about them, the simple truth is that our self-image sometimes has less to do with who we are today and more with who we were when we were fifteen. Research on the predictors of our success in adulthood and findings in neuroscience regarding the enduring power of our adolescent memories confirm that who you were is still affecting who you are now. Own that. And revisit those painful memories of adolescent angst, longing, and exclusion to understand what forces are still influencing your goals, your desires, and your insecurities now.

Earlier in this book, I spoke of how our adolescent experiences create powerful biases or filters that affect the way we see, interpret, and respond to social interactions, all outside of our conscious awareness. A second step for building confidence is to examine what kind of bias you are most likely to have. Some have too rosy a view of the world, always assuming that others are accepting, and resist constructive feedback. Others have a hostile perspective, or a rejecting one, or one characterized by fear and worry—perhaps persistently perceiving threats or anger, even when others see a given situation differently. Everyone has a bias of some sort, and research suggests that it is in moments when our emotions are strong, or when we are intoxicated, that our biases will affect us most deeply.

A third step toward feeling more confident is to recognize when your filters are working overtime and to challenge what may feel like your most basic assumptions, no matter how threatening it may seem to do so. Question whether your spouse is truly being critical of you, even when what you perceive in your gut is surely hostility. Consider that maybe your coworker did not intentionally ignore your email, and challenge your assumption that your neighbor has slighted you. In instances like these, your first instinct may be right. But it also may be the case that you have come to expect criticism, neglect, or offense because at some point in your past you felt that way before. In at least some cases, it is important to test this possibility.

Challenging ourselves, and revealing our biases, can be accomplished by simply examining the evidence that supports an assumption and any clues that might suggest an alternate explanation. This exercise may seem mundane, but it is fascinating to witness how often people find themselves smiling knowingly with self-recognition when they realize that, in fact, their automatic assumptions were probably irrational, and they have ignored a far simpler and less threatening interpretation of others' behavior.

I remember when Tovah, one of my closest friends, called me immediately after a staff meeting to say that she was about to send a blistering email to a colleague. "I can't believe her!" Tovah told me. "I just finished presenting my projections for the next quarter—I worked on it for days—and the senior vice president was at the meeting to hear my forecasts. As soon as I stop talking, this new woman from sales started challenging me right in front of everyone! I held it together long enough to get back to my desk, but this was completely over the line! She has been trying to get on the bosses' good side since she transferred here, and she needs to know that no one is going to stand for her undermining, passive-aggressive. . . . ," Tovah continued, using a variety of colorful words at this point.

Tovah asked for my advice on a draft of her email, which would have resulted in a full-throttle conflict with this new employee, most assuredly making her far less likable. I asked her whether there might be an alternate interpretation for this woman's behavior. First, we discussed everything that supported the assumption that her remarks constituted a hostile attack. Tovah constructed this list easily and fervently. Then, we talked about other possibilities. "Well, I guess she is new, so maybe her questions were just meant as clarifications," Tovah acknowledged. "I did hear her say last week that her boss wants her to speak up more in meetings." Tovah confessed that she was so nervous about presenting in front of her superiors that she may in fact have been reading motives into her colleague's behavior and instead decided to construct a far more balanced email suggesting a drink after work to talk about the meeting. Ironically the two have become close confidants today. Tovah now feels like she has a trusted ally at work, and she feels more confident during each presentation.

Should we challenge every gut instinct and engage in such mental exercises following every social interaction? Of course not. But many whose natural biases have left them feeling insecure now and again can try these steps a few times, and if they are useful, this technique can become quickly become a valuable habit. By explicitly overriding these subconscious patterns, and by intentionally examining our reflexive responses, we can stop ourselves from a remarkably damaging cycle and become more likable.

Popularity for Parents

Almost twenty years into the new millennium, parents are faced with the unenviable task of raising a new generation in a world that is foreign to them. Youth today interact with their peers in a way that none of us have experienced, and the medium with which they do so offers opportunities for profoundly new kinds of social relations and expectations. In the 1980s, we learned to cope with the possibility that we might not always be able to contact our closest friends—our efforts stymied by a now ancient busy signal or perhaps an answering machine. Yet today's youth expect, and often demand, constant access to one another, with severe relationship sanctions levied against friends who postpone a reply text for longer than ten minutes. Cyberbullying didn't exist when most of today's parents were raised either. In the past, the worst that most unpopular youth might experience was humiliation in front of only a small group of peers. We also didn't have selfies in the twentieth century, or followers, or "likes," and consequently, we didn't expect constant reinforcement, reassurance, or reminders of our standing among others. Instead, we were required to feel good about ourselves on our own and focus exclusively on relationships with those who were physically near us. Try explaining this to adolescents today, and you will be met with a bewildered eyeroll. They live in a status-oriented world, and it is our job as parents to play catch-up.

Yet it is critical that we do so. As noted in earlier chapters, adolescents' online interactions are literally changing how their brains respond to dangerous, illegal, and destructive imagery, undoing the values we have instilled and all we have taught them to remain safe. The online world—and so many offline cues urging adolescents to log in—also have the potential to turn our children into chronic status-seekers.

As a child psychologist and a parent, this scares me deeply. Our children are literally being lured toward something that we know will harm them and will ultimately make them unhappy, unsuccessful, and lonely. Fortunately, parents can make a difference. Despite everything that teens do to convince us that they don't care what we have to say, research suggests that parents do, in fact, continue to have substantial influence over their children, perhaps especially when it comes to the way their teens navigate complex social interactions. In particular, parents may want to offer four clear messages when the opportunities arise.

First, although it may seem as if teens understand their electronically mediated worlds more than we do, we must remember that they still require education about how best to process what they view online. Schools teach media literacy, but children also need *social media* literacy. Parents can work to remind their kids that most people post carefully curated images and selected life updates that offer the best possible self-portrayal. Teens should be reminded that there's no point in comparing themselves with what they see their popular peers post online, because what they are viewing may not actually be authentic. Selfies can be Photoshopped or filtered, and full-body pics (posted remarkably frequently among girls) that have many "likes" can often have been manufactured by demanding one's friends respond favorably to each and every post immediately. It is important for parents to pull back the curtain on social media profiles and reveal the genuine, flawed, and honest human beings behind them.

I am often reminded of the couple I overheard fighting incessantly on the beach, until the moment they posted for a selfie with a caption about their "awesome vacation," followed by continued arguments the moment they logged off. Parents can help teens recognize the potential artificiality of their peers' posts by asking them to talk about what they see online versus what they think their peers really feel, do, or look like. There's some evidence that teens themselves may be beginning to identify the "fronting" that many on social media engage in, with some now creating two profiles online—one representing their public persona, and another sharing more candid images and more vulnerable emotional disclosures.

It may also be useful for parents to help teens understand that they should not regard their offline experiences as mere fodder for enhancing their online profiles. This is something I consistently observe when my family and I visit a local frozen yogurt shop that is a popular hangout for local teens. The round tables throughout the store typically are occupied by high school students who are not looking at one another but at their phones, and the conversation rarely strays from a discussion of the number of "likes" their yogurt-eating selfies have received. While this can be fun, it's a missed opportunity for teens to talk to one another in ways that will enhance their likability. Parents might remind their kids about significant events going on in their friends' lives, or upcoming experiences they will both share in a perhaps not-so-subtle attempt to seed a conversation between teens about something other than Snapchat.

Third, note that teens are not the only group likely to become engaged in seeking online status. National data suggests that adults are now on social media almost as much as youth. Parents therefore want to be especially careful about messages they may inadvertently be conveying about status. How often do teens overhear their parents talking about how many people "liked" their own Facebook posts? Or celebrating the number of their Twitter followers? Parents' unintentional reinforcement of status also might come from conversations in which they ask their children to compare themselves to their peers on the number of their invitations to parties, dates, or even when they simply talk to others about their children's social standing. Children are listening, and these messages may be suggesting to them that status is worth vying for.

Fourth, recall that teens are less capable than adults of understanding long-term consequences, so it is critical that parents explain to their children that status increases risk for lifelong difficulties, no matter how enviable it may seem when we are fourteen years old. Much as we might warn them about the dangers of teen substance use, or risky driving, we should also offer our strongest cautionary messages to teens about the perils that come with excessively pursuing status in high school. When the possible outcomes are explained to them, many teens can understand the pitfalls. The most popular might enjoy power and influence in high school but quickly face an adult world when their aggressive tactics, their use of others to elevate their own standing, and their incessant focus on their own popularity ultimately leads to a lifetime of unsuccessful relationships. The social struggle that many teens experience in high school does offer lifelong advantages, as we need adversity to grow and to deal with hardship in order to learn new skills. Because popular teens escape so many of the normal travails of adolescence, they pay the price in adulthood.

Perhaps most important is that parents teach their children empathy—the antidote to aggression and thus a surefire way to help youth embrace likability instead of, or in addition, to status. Teaching moments can present themselves routinely by asking teens each day how they made others feel welcome, happy, or valued. Talking with kids about the way you felt when you were a child also can help them understand the emotions of others, as well as how short-term experiences can evolve over a lifetime. Parents have great potential to shape their children's social behavior from when they begin spending significant time with peers in daycare or preschool and well into late adolescence.

Popularity at Work

For all of our modern innovations, management principles, and team-building strategies, one simple fact holds true: businesses are run by human beings. And humans want to feel liked. This is why popularity still continues to play such an important role in the workplace. Many companies are just like high school, whether we care to admit it or not. We may refer to our adult social interactions as *networking* or *interfacing*, but in truth, every office is the school cafeteria all over again, filled with Accepteds, Rejecteds, Neglecteds, and Controversials. Today's businesses would benefit from leveraging the popularity principles discussed in this book to better enhance productivity, loyalty, marketing/sales, and leadership. For instance, a smart company knows how to focus human resource management not on individuals but on relationships because it is the transactions between people that make businesses successful. Modern companies could also benefit from understanding who among their employees fits each sociometric group and aligning job responsibilities with the social styles that were embedded so deeply in our adolescence. Sales organizations have long known that people don't invest in ideas as much as in the likable people who communicate them, and marketers should consider how different campaigns may need to appeal to the human desire for status versus likability when selling products, ideologies, or even political candidates.

Yet for many, the application of the research discussed in this book may be far more straightforward, perhaps especially for those who hope to eventually get promoted: how do we become more likable at work? Doing so is not quite the same as seeking likability in our personal lives. Within our communities, we foster relationships among one another as equals. But at work, particularly for leaders, the goal is to cultivate a HIVE—a group that feels Happy, Included, Valued, and Engaged toward achieving a common productive goal. Below are the most effective tips to help leaders increase their workplace likability, as well as some general suggestions that can help everyone make best use of popularity principles at the office.

1) **Know your employees and coworkers.** No matter how busy they are, likable leaders make time to connect with members of their team at a deeper level. What are their hopes and goals? What are their pressures and joys outside of work? What do they do on vacation, and who are their loved ones? Employees work hard to impress a manager, but work harder for someone who truly cares about them. Try to remember one specific detail about each coworker, and ask her about it from time to time. Nothing makes people feel more connected than when someone takes time out of her busy schedule to inquire about their life and ask them how they are feeling. This one simple compassionate and genuine act is remarkably powerful in gaining trust, building camaraderie, and helping others feel that they are an important member of the group.
2) **Don't rush to take credit for successes.** Take every opportunity to praise your team. Likable leaders know that when their team succeeds, they will gain recognition for their leadership. There's no need to explain how you made up for others' shortcomings or to undermine your employees' contributions. Your team will appreciate how you had its back and will step forward to have yours when you need it the most.
3) **Move your team from within.** When it's time for a team-based decision, it's easy for busy leaders to dictate objectives and the best path to reach them. When a leader uses his or her authority to overturn a discussion headed in a counterproductive direction, it's demoralizing to all who had invested in being innovative themselves. In contrast, likable leaders have exceptional skill in taking the temperature of the room and moving their team one degree at a time. They listen more than talk,

and offer input that challenges team members to come up with their own decisions. Employees ultimately feel ownership of the strategy and more invested to make their own ideas work.

4) **Attend to the team's social dynamics.** Pay particular attention to your most rejection-sensitive employee who is most likely to undermine a team's morale, and even bad-mouth your business to competitors. Notice how members of your team get along with one another, and help foster better social relations among them.
5) **Assign employees based on their strengths.** Recall that we all fit within one of five different sociometric groups based on the popularity experiences we had as a youth. These popularity profiles offer a unique set of skills that can be leveraged to meet different needs on your team. Those who were Accepted may be best at management, sales, or anything else that requires them to communicate likability. Rejecteds likely excel at evaluating risk scenarios and being most empathic toward others. Employees who were neglected are likely to be the most adaptable to new settings and will work especially well across different teams, given their inherent abilities to listen and modify their behavior to the norms of multiple groups. Controversials are most likely to be motivated by the promise of status and may be productive if they feel they have control and power over their subordinates.
6) **Praise, praise, praise.** A high-status leader dispenses with pleasantries, favoring power-assertion as a way to motivate others. But a likable leader praises direct reports for each of their contributions, increasing their investment, loyalty, and persistence to succeed.
7) **Don't speak first.** In meetings, be among the last to voice your

opinions, and reflect upon what others have contributed. Simply letting others know they were heard, that their comments shaped your own thinking, and their contributions taken seriously makes others feel valued. Ideas expressed toward the end of a meeting are also more likely to get pick-up and buy-in than the suggestions made early in a discussion because they are regarded as the result of a collaboration rather than a command by a superior.

Who do you feel has been your most valued coworker? Who is the leader that you were willing to follow off a cliff if they asked? Who has been promoted faster than others, and who seems happiest in their job? Odds are the answer to all of these questions is someone who followed these seven simple popularity principles.

A Letter to a Teen

Dear Teenager,

Hey, I'm a child psychologist who studies popularity. For about twenty years now, I—and so many other psychologists like me—have researched why some kids are more popular than others and how popularity affects our lives when we grow up.

Someone may have just handed you this book and suggested you read this letter, which may seem a little random, so let me just cut to the chase.

Popularity is not what you think it is. And you may be getting manipulated without you realizing it.

Remember back in elementary school when kids ran around the playground and went to each other's houses to play? Some kids were everyone's favorites, and others had a hard time finding playmates. It may have seemed like popularity was an important thing even when you were as young as three years old.

That's true—there is one kind of popularity that even very young kids are tuned in to. But that's not the same kind of popularity that everyone talks about in high school. Childhood popularity is referred to as "likability." The kids who make others feel good, and included, and valued are the ones who are the most likable, and being likable leads to all kinds of benefits in life. It affects your friendships, your dating life, what kind of job you get, how happy you are as an adult, and even how long you will live.

But when you reach high school, everyone begins talking about who is most popular, or cool, or who seems to have the most followers on Instagram or whatever. This is referred to as "status," and it's not the same as likability at all. In fact, in most high schools the kids who are most popular (i.e., have the highest status) aren't actually very well liked. Among girls especially, the high-status crowd is disliked by many of their peers.

The reason status is a big deal starting when kids are around eleven or twelve has something to do with how your body starts to change in middle school. Scientific studies are now revealing that part of maturing affects how your brain responds to people around you, and right now it is kind of supercharged to care about your social relationships. Specifically, adolescent brains start to become really tuned in to who is getting the most attention, who seems most powerful, influential, and who everyone else wants to look at the most.

That's fine, but it's important to understand that the kind of popularity that teens care about—the status kind—can actually be bad for you if you are not also likable. You know how some of the high-status kids are mean to others by being bullies or gossips, or making other people feel bad about themselves? That kind of behavior will only come back to haunt them later. Research studies have been done to see what happens to the coolest kids in high school once they grow up, and the findings are not pretty. They are at much greater risk for being lonely, getting fired, having their boyfriends and girlfriends break up with them, and suffering from addictions.

If you are one of these high-status kids, make sure you are likable, too. Be kind to others, and spend as much time having really honest relationships with others as you do maintaining your reputation.

If you are not popular, I am happy to tell you that you will be OK. I know school can feel awful now, and every day might be a challenge. But as long as you are liked by even just one or two friends, you will not suffer the same consequences that bullies will experience years from now. Most every adult remembers their high school years when they grow up, and most of us recall that we wished we were more popular than we were. It's normal to feel that way. The good news is that the struggle you are experiencing will turn out to be good for you in the long run.

Oh yeah, about that manipulation bit. I need to tell you about that too. You know how everyone is online all the time now? Most of your friends are probably on Instagram or Snapchat, or whatever else seems cool at the moment? I know it's fun. In fact, it probably feels like it's impossible to keep up with kids at school these days unless you are constantly on your feed.

There's been some interesting research done recently to see what happens to teens' brains when they're on Instagram. Researchers looked at what parts of the brain are activated when teens look at Instagram posts. First, they looked at what the normal response would be when looking at different kinds of pictures. They found that when kids look at fun, positive, cute, and prosocial material, a part of the brain is activated that is related to wanting more of whatever we saw. When we look at pictures of things that are illegal, immoral, dangerous, or risky, a different part of the brain is activated, telling us to stop. So far, so good.

Here's the catch: When these same pictures are shown on an Instagram-like platform, with markers that suggest that the dangerous pictures have been "liked" a lot, suddenly things change. Our brains' brakes seem to get released. In other words, we start to lose our inhibitions toward dangerous and illegal stuff just because the picture was popular on social media.

All of this is taking place in the parts of the brain that we are not consciously aware of—somewhat like the parts that tell our heart to keep beating and our lungs to keep taking in air. This is important because it means that what you see on social media is influencing your values and behaviors without your even realizing it. You better believe that this is being used by people, companies, and even politicians to try and change your preferences, attitudes, and even thinking.

I'm not saying you should avoid social media altogether. It's fine to use once in a while and may even be good for you in some ways. Just be careful with it. You already know that much of what you see there is faked by people to make themselves seem cool or to gain status. So just give it a rest once in a while. Don't worry about what you are missing. Research says that lots of teens are starting to get tired of social media and feel burdened by how much pressure there is to be online all the time. So take a smartphone holiday once in a while and just hang out with your friends face-to-face instead. It's actually a great way to become more likeable anyway!

Here's the bottom line: If you sometimes feel like being more popular would make your life much easier, and you wish that everyone would treat you a little more like they do the cool, high status kids, then you are in great company. No matter what they may tell you, most of your peers feel the exact same way. Also, almost every single adult felt that way when they were kids, and many probably continue to feel a version of that now in their adult relationships.

But that's a whole lot of angst, worrying, longing, and regret for nothing. All you need is just a few good people to like you, and everything will turn out okay.

—Mitch

ACKNOWLEDGMENTS

Through writing *Popular*, I now know what it feels like to be pregnant. It wasn't long after this book was conceived that I began to feel nauseous. Within a few weeks, I was exhausted, and the more the Word files within my computer began to divide and grow, the more it became clear to me that I was in for a ride like none I had previously experienced. Writing a book on popularity was the fulfillment of a dream—a chance to celebrate psychological science and potentially help people all over the world live happier lives. I had no idea how much I would grow as a result of this experience, however. As the weeks turned to months, and my draft slowly expanded, I noticed that I started to see everything around me through the lens of the hypotheses I was putting forth in each chapter. The text itself encroached on my daily existence, spilling into conversations, and eventually overcoming what had been the comfortable waistband of my daily routines. By the end, I couldn't wait to have it all finally out of my system. Now, as these words are about to be launched into the world, I must wrestle between my protective instincts and my hope that this book will survive on its own, perhaps fulfilling some of the dreams I wished for it.

I am grateful for the enormous support of three midwives who each served extraordinary roles in the delivery of my manuscript. The first is Richard Pine, who wasn't only an outstanding agent—he also was a mentor, a colleague, a confidant, and a friend through this entire process. Richard believed in this project, and in me as an author, long before I did. As he shepherded me through each of the tasks involved in trade publishing, I was consistently struck by his actions and his character. In his role as an agent, Richard had an unwavering commitment to excellence. At every turn, I was convinced that his desire for *Popular* to help others lead happy lives was equal to mine, and he remained committed to every last detail to make this the best book it was meant to be. He was with me for every single step with remarkable patience, limitless energy, and impeccable judgment. I can't imagine anyone being as dedicated and supportive as Richard was throughout this process. But perhaps even more notably, working with Richard offered me a life class in confidence, kindness, and consistency. Perhaps because he himself is enormously popular, I experienced vicarious benefits simply by standing alongside Richard. He is a powerful mensch, a benevolent force of nature, and one of the most effective people I ever have met. *Popular* would not exist without him. Special thanks also to all of Richard's colleagues at Inkwell Management, especially Eliza Rothstein, Lyndsey Blessing, and Nathaniel Jacks, for taking me by the hand throughout this process and being so thoroughly likable.

Bill Tonelli is the guy you want to have yelling "Push!" when you feel like you may give up. His uncensored feedback on draft after draft and his unique ability to offer an honest, grounded perspective on every idea were very much appreciated. Modest, candid, and as "real" as they get, Bill was there for me whenever I needed him, and I am thankful for his guidance.

Third, I am enormously indebted to Rick Kot at Viking, who is as brilliant, thoughtful, and astute as he is gentle, amiable, and kind. Rick didn't just edit *Popular*; he was an inspiration. It was his curiosity and encouragement on the day I met him that I drew upon each day as I wrote. His supportive, constructive, and enthusiastic feedback is reflected on every page. Most important, Rick nurtured me as well. I cannot imagine a better experience and I am honored that Rick was with me as *Popular* was born. Special thanks to the whole Viking team, including Brian Tart, Andrea Schulz, Lindsay Prevette, Mary Stone, and Diego Nunez. Their collective energy has been infectious, and their expertise impressive. A very special thanks to Carolyn Coleburn for her passion, her professionalism, and her love of popularity! I am equally indebted to Whitney Peeling at Broadside for her energy, humor, and optimism.

There are so many others who also deserve credit for *Popular*, and for the journey I experienced while writing it. First and foremost, I am consistently inspired by the amazing scientific discoveries of my colleagues, role models, and friends in the field, including Amanda Rose, Karen Rudolph, Julie Hubbard, Jaana Juvonen, Mara Brendgen, Joe Allen, Toon Cillessen, George Slavich, Paul Hastings, Ben Hankin, David Schwartz, Ernest Hodges, Bill Bukowski, Brad Brown, Jamie Ostrov, Wendy Troop-Gordon, Ron Scholte, Rutger Engles, Noel Card, Audrey Zakriski, Janis Kupersmidt, Jeff Parker,

Ken Dodge, John Coie, Bill Hartup, Ken Rubin, Steve Asher, Tom Dishion, Wyndol Furman, Gary Ladd, Geertjan Overbeek, Marlene Sandstrom, Catherine Bagwell, Adrienne Nishina, Amori Mikami, Amy Bellmore, Andy Collins, Dianna Murray-Close, Doran French, Lawrence Steinberg, Jennifer Lansford, John Lochman, Barry Schneider, Dorothy Espelage, Frank Vitaro, Heidi Gazelle, Hongling Xie, Becky Kochenderfer-Ladd, Brett Laursen, Carolyn Barry, Cathryn Booth-Laforce, Sandra Graham, Scott Gest, Shelley Hymel, Marian Underwood, Martha Putallaz, Michel Boivin, Rene Veenstra, Richard Fabes, Robert Coplan, Ryan Adams, Stacey Horn, Thomas Berndt, Thomas Kindermann, Wendy Craig, Christina Salmivalli, Craig Hart, David Nelson, David Perry, Debra Peplar, Julie Bowker, Karen Bierman, Kristina McDonald, and Lara Mayeux. Nicki Crick, Phil Rodkin, and Duane Buhrmester, you left us too soon, but your legacies lives on. Steve Hinshaw, special thanks for your terrific support. To all these colleagues, and so many others I fear I may have missed: thank you. I attempted to highlight research conducted by each of you so others might be inspired by your work as much as I have.

Thank you to current and former graduate students, who always serve as my greatest source of professional joy. I continue to learn from you every day, and your encouragement as I have embarked on this crazy adventure has meant the world to me. Thanks to Sophie Choukas-Bradley, Jackie Nesi, Matteo Giletta, Laura Widman, Casey Calhoun, Adam Miller, Sarah Helms, Maya Massing-Schaffer, Sarah Owens, John Guerry, Whitney Brechwald, Caroline Adelman, Joe Franklin, Shelley Gallagher, Leigh Spivey, Chris Sheppard, Diana Rancourt, and Matt Nock for being so excited with me! A huge debt of gratitude also is due to Sam Sifrar, Ryn Linthicum, Blaire Lee-

Nakayama, Matt Clayton, and Jeff Parlin for all the support and incredibly hard work with the Peer Relations Lab, so we may learn more about peer relationships. Thank you to Emmy Mallasch and her always-smiling face for making my day job so fun. And of course, thanks to all of my undergraduate students in Popularity class at Yale and at UNC. Your enthusiastic participation, incisive comments, and keen insights help me rediscover my passion for this subject matter all over again every Tuesday and Thursday.

Special thanks to my mentors, Annette La Greca and Tony Spirito. You invested in me so many years ago, and have remained dedicated advisors for decades since. The lessons you taught me extend well beyond a clinical psychology curriculum. Through your examples, you have taught me how to be a better human being.

Popular was a labor of love, and it would not have been written without the love and support of so many friends who were with me throughout this journey. Jack Harari, this was your dream more than mine, but you helped me selflessly through every step. Thanks to Adam and Jackie Golden, Vicki DiLillo, Barbara Kamholz, Mike Friedman, Erika Lawrence, Doug Mennin, and Lindsey Cohen for your sage advice, perspective, and companionship. Thanks to Lois and Bobby Suruki, Jen Rutan, and Zach Purser for the Tuesday night check-ins at Moe's. Ilene and Gabe Farkas, Anna Gassman-Pines, David Halpern, Mo Pleil, and Ryan Williams also deserve thanks for their input and encouragement. Thanks to my friends in Davie Hall, particularly Eric Youngstrom, Jon Abramowitz, Deborah Jones, Anna Bardone-Cone, Don Baucom, Don Lysle, and Kristen Lindquist for their support. Steve Reznick, I miss you. Special thanks to the growing UNC group of trade book authors who offered extremely valuable advice along the way: Barb Fredrickson, Kurt Gray, and especially my book-twin Keith Payne. Adam Grant, thanks for your willing advice and terrific publishing resources, and for serving as a role model. Gary Sosinsky, David Kraut, Alan Calderon, and Michael Cohen are owed a debt of gratitude for making my high school experience so fun; thanks also to Jami and Andrew Huber and Steve and Melissa Brooks, who have been with me through every chapter since.

Of course, I could not have written this book without my family. My mother, Judy, and my brother, Rich, as well as Dick and Etta Reigel, offered me a foundation without which nothing would have been possible. But there is one member of my family who deserves my gratitude most of all. And to her, I will forever be in awe and debt.

It's a miracle I ever met her. In a tiny, bucolic corner of West Virginia, nestled in a valley between Cheat Mountain and the Allegheny foothills, is a tiny town called Arbovale. Just two miles from the National Radio Astronomy Observatory, it has been dubbed the nation's "quiet zone," where radio transmissions are strictly limited to preserve the integrity of astronomers' work. While the rest of the world has become increasingly dependent on 24/7 access to the internet, rapid texts, and social media, the residents of Arbovale are not permitted to use cell phones, wireless internet, high-frequency radio stations, or even overpowered microwave ovens. It is a town that remains sheltered from the rest of the chattering world—about seventy-five minutes from the nearest movie theater or grocery store—and it is certainly the last place where one might go to promote their own status. Perhaps it is no coincidence that Arbovale was the home of the most likable woman whom I have ever met. Her name is Tina, and I married her. And in far more ways than I can articulate, the lessons in *Popular* were inspired by her. She is a social phenomenon in every context—the most likable at work, in our community, no matter where we go. She brightens the day of everyone she meets, and because of her popularity, she is remarkably effective at everything she attempts. Tina embodies the power of likability. As with many authors' spouses, Tina offered feedback on dozens of ideas and listened to countless drafts as I wrote this book. She rearranged her life to make it possible for me to begin this new adventure in mine. But most important, just by being herself, Tina made *Popular* possible, and for me, her love became the only kind of popularity that mattered.

NOTES

INTRODUCTION

2. **one or two in every classroom:** John D. Coie and Kenneth A. Dodge. "Continuities and Changes in Children's Social Status: A Five-Year Longitudinal Study." *Merrill-Palmer Quarterly* 29, no. 3 (1983): 261–82.

5. **mental health initiatives as never before:** Mitchell J. Prinstein and Michael C. Roberts. "The Professional Adolescence of Clinical Child and Adolescent Psychology and Pediatric Psychology: Grown Up and Striving for Autonomy." *Clinical Psychology: Science and Practice* 13, no. 3 (2006): 263–68.

6. **childhood popularity predicted soldiers' behavior:** M. Roff. "Relation Between Certain Preservice Factors and Psychoneurosis During Military Duty." *United States Armed Forces Medical Journal* 11 (1960): 152.

6. **other studies in nonmilitary populations:** Emory L. Cowen et al. "Long-term Follow-up of Early Detected Vulnerable Children." *Journal of Consulting and Clinical Psychology* 41, no. 3 (1973): 438; Jeffrey

G. Parker and Steven R. Asher. "Peer Relations and Later Personal Adjustment: Are Low-Accepted Children at Risk?" *Psychological Bulletin* 102, no. 3 (1987): 357.

6. **worldwide study conducted in:** Mitchell J. Prinstein, Jacqueline Nesi, and Casey D. Calhoun. "Recollections of Childhood Peer Status and Adult Outcomes: A Global Study" (in preparation, University of North Carolina at Chapel Hill, 2016).

7. **to have greater academic success:** Sarah E. Nelson and Thomas J. Dishion. "From Boys to Men: Predicting Adult Adaptation from Middle Childhood Sociometric Status." *Development and Psychopathology* 6, no. 2 (2004): 441–59; Ylva B. Almquist and Lars Brännström. "Childhood Peer Status and the Clustering of Social, Economic, and Health-Related Circumstances in Adulthood." *Social Science & Medicine* 105 (2014): 67–75; Bonnie L. Barber, Jacquelynne S. Eccles, and Margaret R. Stone. "Whatever Happened to the Jock, the Brain, and the Princess? Young Adult Pathways Linked to Adolescent Activity Involvement and Social Identity." *Journal of Adolescent Research* 16, no. 5 (2001): 429–55.

7. **stronger interpersonal relationships, and to make:** Amanda M. Jantzer, John H. Hoover, and Rodger Narloch. "The Relationship Between School-aged Bullying and Trust, Shyness and Quality of Friendships in Young Adulthood: A Preliminary Research Note." *School Psychology International* 27, no. 2 (2006): 146–56; Joseph P. Allen, Megan M. Schad, Barbara Oudekerk, and Joanna Chango. "Whatever Happened to the 'Cool' Kids? Long-term Sequelae of Early Adolescent Pseudomature Behavior." *Child Development* 85, no. 5 (2014): 1866–80.

7. **money in their jobs years later:** Gabriella Conti, Andrea Galeotti, Gerrit Mueller, and Stephen Pudney. "Popularity." *Journal of Human Resources* 48, no. 4 (2013): 1072–94.

7. **greater risk for substance abuse:** Alexa Martin-Storey et al. "Self and Peer Perceptions of Childhood Aggression, Social Withdrawal and Likeability Predict Adult Substance Abuse and Dependence in Men and Women: A 30-Year Prospective Longitudinal Study." *Addictive Be-*

haviors 36, no. 12 (2011): 1267–74; Marlene J. Sandstrom and Antonius H. N. Cillessen. "Life After High School: Adjustment of Popular Teens in Emerging Adulthood." *Merrill-Palmer Quarterly* 56, no. 4 (2010): 474–99.

7. **were not popular . . . obesity:** A. A. Mamun, Michael J. O'Callaghan, G. M. Williams, and J. M. Najman. "Adolescents Bullying and Young Adults Body Mass Index and Obesity: A Longitudinal Study." *International Journal of Obesity* 37, no. 8 (2013): 1140–46.

7. **were not popular . . . anxiety, depression:** Jenny Isaacs, Ernest V. E. Hodges, and Christina Salmivalli. "Long-term Consequences of Victimization by Peers: A Follow-up from Adolescence to Young Adulthood." *International Journal of Developmental Science* 2, no. 4 (2008): 387–97; Bitte Modin, Viveca Östberg, and Ylva Almquist. "Childhood Peer Status and Adult Susceptibility to Anxiety and Depression. A 30-Year Hospital Follow-up." *Journal of Abnormal Child Psychology* 39, no. 2 (2011): 187–99; Sandstrom and Cillessen. "Life After High School." 474–99; Lexine A. Stapinski et al. "Peer Victimization During Adolescence and Risk for Anxiety Disorders in Adulthood: A Prospective Cohort Study." *Depression and Anxiety* 31, no. 7 (2014): 574–82.

7. **were not popular . . . problems at work:** Nelson and Dishion. "From Boys to Men." 441–59; Sandstrom and Cillessen. "Life After High School." 474–99.

7. **were not popular . . . criminal behavior:** Nelson and Dishion. "From Boys to Men." 441–59.

7. **were not popular . . . injury, illness:** Per E. Gustafsson et al. "Do Peer Relations in Adolescence Influence Health in Adulthood? Peer Problems in the School Setting and the Metabolic Syndrome in Middle-Age." *PLoS One* 7, no. 6 (2012): e39385; Lisa Dawn Hamilton, Matthew L. Newman, Carol L. Delville, and Yvon Delville. "Physiological Stress Response of Young Adults Exposed to Bullying During Adolescence." *Physiology & Behavior* 95, no. 5 (2008): 617–24; Caroline E. Temcheff et al. "Predicting Adult Physical Health Outcomes from Childhood Aggression, Social Withdrawal and Likeability: A 30-Year

Prospective, Longitudinal Study." *International Journal of Behavioral Medicine* 18, no. 1 (2011): 5–12.

7. **were not popular . . . suicide:** William E. Copeland, Dieter Wolke, Adrian Angold, and E. Jane Costello. "Adult Psychiatric Outcomes of Bullying and Being Bullied by Peers in Childhood and Adolescence." *JAMA Psychiatry* 70, no. 4 (2013): 419–26; Barber, Eccles, and Stone. "Whatever Happened to the Jock, the Brain, and the Princess?" 429–55.

7. **more than one type of popularity:** Philip C. Rodkin, Thomas W. Farmer, Ruth Pearl, and Richard Van Acker. "Heterogeneity of Popular Boys: Antisocial and Prosocial Configurations." *Developmental Psychology* 36, no. 1 (2000): 14; Antonius H. N. Cillessen and Amanda J. Rose. "Understanding Popularity in the Peer System." *Current Directions in Psychological Science* 14, no. 2 (2005): 102–5; Mitchell J. Prinstein and Antonius H. N. Cillessen. "Forms and Functions of Adolescent Peer Aggression Associated with High Levels of Peer Status." *Merrill-Palmer Quarterly* 49, no. 3 (2003): 310–42.

CHAPTER 1. The Adult Playground: Where Popularity Still Matters

18. **Chapel Hill called Southern Village:** Lee S. Sobel, William Anderson, and Jade Shipman. *Market Acceptance of Smart Growth*. Washington, DC: U.S. Environmental Protection Agency, 2011.

18. **scene from *The Truman Show*:** *The Truman Show*. Directed by Peter Weir. Los Angeles: Paramount, 1998.

24. **Daniel has founded and sold:** Personal interview with Daniel Clemens, May 10, 2016.

CHAPTER 2. Boorish Bully or Likable Leader: There's More Than One Type of Popularity

28. **Ignaz Semmelweis began working:** Ahmet Doğan Ataman, Emine Elif Vatanoğlu-Lutz, and Gazi Yıldırım. "Medicine in Stamps-Ignaz

Semmelweis and Puerperal Fever." *Journal of the Turkish German Gynecological Association* 14, no. 1 (2013): 35; also see Sherwin B. Nuland. *The Doctors' Plague: Germs, Childbed Fever, and the Strange Story of Ignác Semmelweis* (Great Discoveries). New York: W. W. Norton, 2004.

28. **was caused by "cadaver particles":** Ignaz Semmelweis. *Etiology, Concept and Prophylaxis of Childbed Fever*. Translated by K. Codell Carter. Madison: University of Wisconsin Press, 1983.

29. **"hurled outrageously rude insults":** Howard Markel. "In 1850, Ignaz Semmelweis Saved Lives with Three Words: 'Wash Your Hands.' " PBS *Newshour*, May 15, 2015, retrieved from http://www.pbs.org/newshour/updates/ignaz-semmelweis-doctor-prescribed-hand-washing.

29. **"publicly berated people":** Rebecca Davis. "The Doctor Who Championed Hand Washing and Briefly Saved Lives." NPR *Morning Edition*, January 12, 2015, retrieved from http://www.npr.org/sections/health-shots/2015/01/12/375663920/the-doctor-who-championed-hand-washing-and-saved-women-s-lives.

29. **"not even understand the limited truth":** Semmelweis. *Etiology, Concept and Prophylaxis of Childbed Fever*.

29. **as "wretched observers":** Ibid.

29. **"obstetrical training in Berlin":** Ibid.

31. **"Anyone who is popular":** Perhaps erroneously attributed to Yogi Berra. Hugh Rawson and Margaret Miner. "Yogi Berra 1925–," *Oxford Dictionary of American Quotations*, 2nd ed. New York: Oxford University Press, 2006.

32. **etymology of the word "popular":** William M. Bukowski. "Popularity as a Social Concept." *Popularity in the Peer System* (2011): 3–24. Retrieved from http://www.etymonline.com.

33. **now-seminal series of experimental studies:** John D. Coie, Kenneth A. Dodge, and Heide Coppotelli. "Dimensions and Types of Social Status: A Cross-Age Perspective." *Developmental Psychology* 18, no. 4 (1982): 557.

36. **designed a follow-up study:** John D. Coie and Janis B. Kupersmidt. "A Behavioral Analysis of Emerging Social Status in Boys' Groups." *Child Development* (1983): 1400–16; also see Kenneth A. Dodge. "Behavioral Antecedents of Peer Social Status." *Child Development* 54, no. 6 (1983): 1386–99.

39. **same group over five years later:** Coie and Dodge. "Continuities and Changes in Children's Social Status." 261–82.

43. **ask many questions of each other:** Dorothy Miell and Steve Duck. "Strategies in Developing Friendships." In *Friendship and Social Interaction*. Eds. Valerian J. Derlega and Barbara A. Winstead. New York: Springer, 1986, 129–43.

43. **associated with the release of dopamine:** R. I. M. Dunbar. "Bridging the Bonding Gap: The Transition from Primates to Humans." *Philosophical Transactions of the Royal Society B: Biological Sciences* 367, no. 1597 (2012): 1837–46; Alan W. Gray, Brian Parkinson, and Robin I. Dunbar. "Laughter's Influence on the Intimacy of Self-Disclosure." *Human Nature* 26, no. 1 (2015): 28–43.

44. **Billy is described by others:** Coie and Kupersmidt. "A Behavioral Analysis of Emerging Social Status in Boys' Groups." 1400–16; also see Andrew F. Newcomb, William M. Bukowski, and Linda Pattee. "Children's Peer Relations: A Meta-analytic Review of Popular, Rejected, Neglected, Controversial, and Average Sociometric Status." *Psychological Bulletin* 113, no. 1 (1993): 99.

44. **when Accepted children become adults:** See, for example, Almquist and Brännström. "Childhood Peer Status and the Clustering of Social, Economic, and Health-Related Circumstances in Adulthood." 67–75; also see Ylva B. Almquist and Viveca Östberg. "Social Relationships and Subsequent Health-Related Behaviours: Linkages Between Adolescent Peer Status and Levels of Adult Smoking in a Stockholm Cohort." *Addiction* 108, no. 3 (2013): 629–37; also Isaacs, Hodges, and Salmivalli. "Long-term Consequences of Victimization by Peers." 387–97.

44. **Some Neglecteds are anxious:** Robert J. Coplan and Julie C. Bowker, eds. *The Handbook of Solitude: Psychological Perspectives on Social Isolation,*

Social Withdrawal, and Being Alone. New York: John Wiley & Sons, 2013; Kenneth H. Rubin, Robert J. Coplan, and Julie C. Bowker. "Social Withdrawal in Childhood." *Annual Review of Psychology* 60 (2009): 141.

44. **Neglected people are a bit slower:** Jennifer Connolly, Wyndol Furman, and Roman Konarski. "The Role of Peers in the Emergence of Heterosexual Romantic Relationships in Adolescence." *Child Development* 71, no. 5 (2000): 1395–1408; Annette M. La Greca and Eleanor Race Mackey. "Adolescents' Anxiety in Dating Situations: The Potential Role of Friends and Romantic Partners." *Journal of Clinical Child and Adolescent Psychology* 36, no. 4 (2007): 522–33.

45. **though they almost never became Controversials:** Coie and Dodge. "Continuities and Changes in Children's Social Status." 261–82.

45. **Rejecteds can be divided:** Antonius H. N. Cillessen, Hendrik W. IJzendoorn, Cornelis F. M. van Lieshout, and Willard W. Hartup. "Heterogeneity Among Peer-Rejected Boys: Subtypes and Stabilities." *Child Development* 63, no. 4 (1992): 893–905.

45. **do not even know they are rejected:** Audrey L. Zakriski and John D. Coie. "A Comparison of Aggressive-Rejected and Nonaggressive-Rejected Children's Interpretations of Self-directed and Other-directed Rejection." *Child Development* 67, no. 3 (1996): 1048–70.

45. **Rejected-Aggressives have far worse outcomes:** Karen Linn Bierman and Julie B. Wargo. "Predicting the Longitudinal Course Associated with Aggressive-Rejected, Aggressive (Nonrejected), and Rejected (Nonaggressive) Status." *Development and Psychopathology* 7, no. 4 (1995): 669–82.

46. **declines in their emotional well-being:** Mitchell J. Prinstein and Annette M. La Greca. "Peer Crowd Affiliation and Internalizing Distress in Childhood and Adolescence: A Longitudinal Follow-Back Study." *Journal of Research on Adolescence* 12, no. 3 (2002): 325–51.

46. **peers' attitudes toward high achievement:** Jaana Juvonen and Tamera B. Murdock. "Grade-Level Differences in the Social Value of Effort: Implications for Self-Presentation Tactics of Early Adolescents." *Child*

Development 66, no. 6 (1995): 1694–1705; Margaret R. Stone and B. Bradford Brown. "Identity Claims and Projections: Descriptions of Self and Crowds in Secondary School." *New Directions for Child and Adolescent Development* 1999, no. 84 (1999): 7–20.

47. **more likable to the American people:** David W. Moore. "Instant Reaction: Bush Beats Gore in Second Debate." Gallup News Service, http://www.gallup.com/poll/2443/instant-reaction-bush-beats-gore-second-debate.aspx.

47. **range of later psychological symptoms:** Parker and Asher. "Peer Relations and Later Personal Adjustment." 357; Mitchell J. Prinstein and Annette M. La Greca. "Childhood Peer Rejection and Aggression as Predictors of Adolescent Girls' Externalizing and Health Risk Behaviors: A 6-Year Longitudinal Study." *Journal of Consulting and Clinical Psychology* 72, no. 1 (2004): 103; Mitchell J. Prinstein, Diana Rancourt, John D. Guerry, and Caroline B. Browne. "Peer Reputations and Psychological Adjustment." In *Handbook of Peer Interactions, Relationships, and Groups*, 548–67. New York: Guilford Press, 2009; Gustafsson et al. "Do Peer Relations in Adolescence Influence Health in Adulthood?" e39385.

48. **continual need for reassurance:** Mitchell J. Prinstein et al. "Adolescent Girls' Interpersonal Vulnerability to Depressive Symptoms: A Longitudinal Examination of Reassurance-Seeking and Peer Relationships." *Journal of Abnormal Psychology* 114, no. 4 (2005): 676.

48. **Many describe them as Machiavellian:** Patricia H. Hawley. "Prosocial and Coercive Configurations of Resource Control in Early Adolescence: A Case for the Well-Adapted Machiavellian." *Merrill-Palmer Quarterly* 49, no. 3 (2003): 279–309.

49. **most likely to become teen moms:** Marion K. Underwood, Janis B. Kupersmidt, and John D. Coie. "Childhood Peer Sociometric Status and Aggression as Predictors of Adolescent Childbearing." *Journal of Research on Adolescence* 6, no. 2 (1996).

49. **especially likely to have high *status*:** Jennifer T. Parkhurst and Andrea Hopmeyer. "Sociometric Popularity and Peer-Perceived Popularity,

Two Distinct Dimensions of Peer Status." *Journal of Early Adolescence* 18, no. 2 (1998): 125–44.

51. **high in status are also highly:** Ibid.

51. **to stop washing their hands:** Markel. "In 1850, Ignaz Semmelweis Saved Lives with Three Words: 'Wash Your Hands.' "

51. **purportedly from an infection:** K. Codell Carter and Barbara R. Carter. *Childbed Fever: A Scientific Biography of Ignaz Semmelweis.* New Brunswick, NJ: Transaction Publishers, 2005.

CHAPTER 3. The Problems with Popularity: What's Wrong with What We Want?

53. **sits the Trevi Fountain:** "Your Resourceful Site on the Trevi Fountain in Roma," http://www.trevifountain.net/description.htm; "Trevi Coins to Fund Food for Poor." BBC News, November 26, 2006, http://news.bbc.co.uk/2/hi/6188052.stm.

54. **report their "fundamental motives":** Kenneth R. Olson and Dale A. Weber. "Relations Between Big Five Traits and Fundamental Motives." *Psychological Reports* 95, no. 3 (2004): 795–802.

54. **what Germans call *Sehnsucht*:** Susanne Scheibe, Alexandra M. Freund, and Paul B. Baltes. "Toward a Developmental Psychology of *Sehnsucht* (Life Longings): The Optimal (Utopian) Life." *Developmental Psychology* 43, no. 3 (2007): 778.

54. **most important "aspirational goals":** Tim Kasser and Richard M. Ryan. "Further Examining the American Dream: Differential Correlates of Intrinsic and Extrinsic Goals." *Personality and Social Psychology Bulletin* 22, no. 3 (1996): 280–87.

55. **"If you could have three wishes":** Laura A. King and Sheri J. Broyles. "Wishes, Gender, Personality, and Well-being." *Journal of Personality* 65, no. 1 (1997): 49–76.

55. **fewer intrinsic wishes than might be:** Tim Kasser. "Aspirations Index," http://faculty.knox.edu/tkasser/aspirations.html.

56. **still want this type of popularity:** Cameron Anderson, John Angus D. Hildreth, and Laura Howland. "Is the Desire for Status a Fundamental Human Motive? A Review of the Empirical Literature." *Psychological Bulletin* 141, no. 3 (2015): 574–601.

58. **first parts of the brain:** Leah H. Somerville, Rebecca M. Jones, and B. J. Casey. "A Time of Change: Behavioral and Neural Correlates of Adolescent Sensitivity to Appetitive and Aversive Environmental Cues." *Brain and Cognition* 72, no. 1 (2010): 124–33; Leah H. Somerville. "The Teenage Brain Sensitivity to Social Evaluation." *Current Directions in Psychological Science* 22, no. 2 (2013): 121–27; B. J. Casey. "The Teenage Brain: An Overview." *Current Directions in Psychological Science* 22, no. 2 (2013): 80–81.

59. **"motivational relevance network":** Kristen A. Lindquist et al. "The Brain Basis of Emotion: A Meta-analytic Review." *Behavioral and Brain Sciences* 35, no. 3 (2012): 121–43; Kristen A. Lindquist and Lisa Feldman Barrett. "A Functional Architecture of the Human Brain: Emerging Insights from the Science of Emotion." *Trends in Cognitive Sciences* 16, no. 11 (2012): 533–40; Robert P. Spunt and Matthew D. Lieberman. "An Integrative Model of the Neural Systems Supporting the Comprehension of Observed Emotional Behavior." *Neuroimage* 59, no. 3 (2012): 3050–59.

59. **the brain's likes and wants:** Kent C. Berridge, Terry E. Robinson, and J. Wayne Aldridge. "Dissecting Components of Reward: 'Liking,' 'Wanting,' and 'Learning.'" *Current Opinion in Pharmacology* 9, no. 1 (2009): 65–73.

59. **our brain has caught up:** Somerville, Jones, and Casey. "A Time of Change." 124–33; Laurence Steinberg. *Age of Opportunity: Lessons from the New Science of Adolescence*. New York: Houghton Mifflin Harcourt, 2014.

60. **refers to these links as:** Berridge, Robinson, and Aldridge. "Dissecting Components of Reward." 65–73.

62. **or even just look at them:** J. T. Klein, S. V. Shepherd, and M. L. Platt. "Social Attention and the Brain." *Current Biology* 19, no. 20 (2009): R958–62; Jessica E. Koski, Hongling Xie, and Ingrid R.

Olson. "Understanding Social Hierarchies: The Neural and Psychological Foundations of Status Perception." *Social Neuroscience* 10, no. 5 (2015): 527–50; Noam Zerubavel, Peter S. Bearman, Jochen Weber, and Kevin N. Ochsner. "Neural Mechanisms Tracking Popularity in Real-world Social Networks." *Proceedings of the National Academy of Sciences* 112, no. 49 (2015): 15072–77.

62. **longer than we look at others:** Tom Foulsham et al. "Gaze Allocation in a Dynamic Situation: Effects of Social Status and Speaking." *Cognition* 117, no. 3 (2010): 319–31.

62. **we admire likes us in return:** Christopher G. Davey et al. "Being Liked Activates Primary Reward and Midline Self-related Brain Regions." *Human Brain Mapping* 31, no. 4 (2010): 660–68.

63. **inhibitions when faced with social rewards:** Leah H. Somerville, Todd Hare, and B. J. Casey. "Frontostriatal Maturation Predicts Cognitive Control Failure to Appetitive Cues in Adolescents." *Journal of Cognitive Neuroscience* 23, no. 9 (2011): 2123–34.

63. **own most basic attitudes and preferences:** Erik C. Nook and Jamil Zaki. "Social Norms Shift Behavioral and Neural Responses to Foods." *Journal of Cognitive Neuroscience* 27, no. 7 (2015): 1412–26.

65. **psychologists call "reflected appraisal":** Susan Harter. "Developmental Processes in the Construction of the Self." In *Integrative Processes and Socialization: Early to Middle Childhood.* Eds. T. D. Yawkey and J. E. Johnson. Hillsdale, NJ: Lawrence Erlbaum Associates: 1988, 45–78.

65. **"emotional salience" network:** Lindquist et al. "The Brain Basis of Emotion." (2012): 121–43; Spunt and Lieberman. "An Integrative Model of the Neural Systems Supporting the Comprehension of Observed Emotional Behavior." 3050–59.

66. **"It's much safer to say popularity sucks":** Cameron Crowe. *Almost Famous*. Directed by Cameron Crowe. Los Angeles: DreamWorks, 2000.

67. **Valerie Jane disappeared:** Jane Goodall. *My Life with the Chimpanzees*. New York: Simon & Schuster, 1996.

67. **chimpanzees want to be popular:** "Chimpanzee Facts," http://www.janegoodall.org, accessed October 7, 2015; Peter Buirski, Robert Plutchik, and Henry Kellerman. "Sex Differences, Dominance, and Personality in the Chimpanzee." *Animal Behaviour* 26 (1978): 123–29; Stephanie F. Anestis. "Behavioral Style, Dominance Rank, and Urinary Cortisol in Young Chimpanzees (Pan Troglodytes)." *Behaviour* 142, no. 9–10 (2005): 1245–68.

68. **Goodall calls Silaho:** "Updates from the Islands—the Jane Goodall Institute," http://www.janegoodall.org, accessed October 7, 2015.

68. **observing a group of cheerleaders:** Don E. Merten. "Being There Awhile: An Ethnographic Perspective on Popularity." In *Popularity in the Peer System.* Eds. A. N. Cillessen, D. Schwartz, and L. Mayeux. New York: Guilford Press, 2011, 57–76.

69. **hostile behavior as "proactive aggression":** Willard W. Hartup. "Aggression in Childhood: Developmental Perspectives." *American Psychologist* 29, no. 5 (1974): 336; Konrad Lorenz. *On Aggression*. Trans. Marjorie Latzke. London: Methuen, 1966; Kenneth A. Dodge and John D. Coie. "Social-Information-Processing Factors in Reactive and Proactive Aggression in Children's Peer Groups." *Journal of Personality and Social Psychology* 53, no. 6 (1987): 1146.

69. **"I've made fun of people":** "Cliques: Behind the Labels." *In the Mix*. New York: Castleworks, 2000.

70. **for teens to increase their status:** Prinstein and Cillessen. "Forms and Functions of Adolescent Peer Aggression Associated with High Levels of Peer Status." 310–42; Cillessen and Rose. "Understanding Popularity in the Peer System." 102–5.

71. **Tom Cruise was known:** "In Tense Moment, Cruise Calls Lauer Glib," http://www.today.com/id/8344309#.WBuBSPorLa8, June 28, 2005.

72. **McCarthy never claimed:** Seth Mnookin. *The Panic Virus: A True Story of Medicine, Science, and Fear*. New York: Simon & Schuster, 2011.

74. **In 1975, 38 percent:** Robert D. Putnam. *Bowling Alone: The Collapse and Revival of American Community*. New York: Simon & Schuster, 2001.

75. **Similar results were obtained:** Joan Jacobs Brumberg. *The Body Project: An Intimate History of American Girls*. New York: Vintage, 2010.

75. **proposed a hierarchy of needs:** Abraham Harold Maslow. "A Theory of Human Motivation." *Psychological Review* 50, no. 4 (1943): 370.

78. **at least partially rooted in culture:** Christopher S. Sheppard et al. "Is Popularity Universal? A Cross-cultural Examination of Popularity Among Peers." Manuscript in preparation (2016); also see Li Niu, Shenghua Jin, Ling Li, and Doran C. French. "Popularity and Social Preference in Chinese Adolescents: Associations with Social and Behavioral Adjustment." *Social Development* 25, no. 4 (2016): 828–45.

78. **referred to as a "super-peer":** Jane D. Brown, Carolyn Tucker Halpern, and Kelly Ladin L'Engle. "Mass Media as a Sexual Super Peer for Early Maturing Girls." *Journal of Adolescent Health* 36, no. 5 (2005): 420–27; Victor C. Strasburger, Barbara J. Wilson, and Amy B. Jordan. *Children, Adolescents, and the Media*. Thousand Oaks, CA: Sage Publishing, 2009.

79. **Joshua Gamson and Denis McQuail observed:** Joshua Gamson. *Claims to Fame: Celebrity in Contemporary America*. Berkeley: University of California Press, 1994; Denis McQuail. *Mass Communication*. New York: John Wiley & Sons, 1983; Violina P. Rindova, Timothy G. Pollock, and Mathew L. A. Hayward. "Celebrity Firms: The Social Construction of Market Popularity." *Academy of Management Review* 31, no. 1 (2006): 50–71.

81. **outcomes like depression:** Marlene J. Sandstrom and Antonius H. N. Cillessen. "Likeable Versus Popular: Distinct Implications for Adolescent Adjustment." *International Journal of Behavioral Development* 30, no. 4 (2006): 305–14.

81. **interview over a dozen:** Donna Rockwell and David C. Giles. "Being a Celebrity: A Phenomenology of Fame." *Journal of Phenomenological Psychology* 40, no. 2 (2009): 178–210.

84. **"I estimate that 50 percent":** "Faces of Depression: Philip Burguières" in the series *Depression: Out of the Shadows + Take One Step: Caring for*

Depression, with Jane Pauley. PBS, http://www.pbs.org/wgbh/takeonestep/depression/faces.html.

84. **"[I've been] depressed":** "Imagine Dragons on Being 'Atypical' Rock Stars, and Singer Dan Reynolds on His Depression Struggles and Conflicts with His Mormon Faith." Billboard, February 13, 2015, http://www.billboard.com/articles/6472705/imagine-dragons-cover-smoke-and-mirrors-touring-grammys.

84. **"The cancer of attention":** "Ian Thorpe: 'I Was Surrounded by People but Had This Intense Loneliness.'" *The Guardian*, November 12, 2012, https://www.theguardian.com/sport/2012/nov/12/ian-thorpe-swimming-depression.

85. **Joe Allen and his colleagues:** Allen, Schad, Oudekerk, and Chango. "Whatever Happened to the 'Cool' Kids?" 1866–80.

87. **life satisfaction and well-being:** Kennon M. Sheldon, Richard M. Ryan, Edward L. Deci, and Tim Kasser. "The Independent Effects of Goal Contents and Motives on Well-being: It's Both What You Pursue and Why You Pursue It." *Personality and Social Psychology Bulletin* 30, no. 4 (2004): 475–86.

CHAPTER 4. Herds and Headaches: How Our Bodies Are Programmed to Care About Popularity

91. **An old house sits:** *Citizen Kane*. Directed by Orson Welles. Los Angeles: RKO Radio Pictures, 1941.

93. **largest global brands:** "Rankings," Interbrand, 2015, http://interbrand.com/best-brands/best-global-brands/2015/ranking.

93. **Salganik and his colleague at Yahoo!:** Matthew J. Salganik and Duncan J. Watts. "Leading the Herd Astray: An Experimental Study of Self-fulfilling Prophecies in an Artificial Cultural Market." *Social Psychology Quarterly* 71, no. 4 (2008): 338–55.

95. **Scottish journalist Charles MacKay:** Charles MacKay. *Memoirs of Ex-*

traordinary Popular Delusions and the Madness of Crowds. London: George Routledge and Sons, 1869.

96. **"Men . . . think in herds":** Ibid.

97. **Geoff Cohen and I examined:** Geoffrey L. Cohen and Mitchell J. Prinstein. "Peer Contagion of Aggression and Health Risk Behavior Among Adolescent Males: An Experimental Investigation of Effects on Public Conduct and Private Attitudes." *Child Development* 77, no. 4 (2006): 967–83.

97. **about one of every four adolescents:** Centers for Disease Control and Prevention. Youth Risk Behavior Survey Data (2015), retrieved from http://www.cdc.gov/yrbs.

99. **"You can't sit with us!":** *Mean Girls*. Directed by Mark Waters. Los Angeles: Paramount, 2004.

100. **not the only humanlike species:** Nathalie Wolchover. "Why Did Humans Prevail?" *Live Science*, June 6, 2012, http://www.livescience.com/20798-humans-prevailed-neanderthals.html; Robert Boyd and Joan B. Silk. *How Humans Evolved*. New York: W. W. Norton, 2012; Robert C. Berwick, Marc Hauser, and Ian Tattersall. "Neanderthal Language? Just-So Stories Take Center Stage." *Frontiers in Psychology* 4 (2013): 671.

102. **Julianne Holt-Lunstad, a psychologist:** Julianne Holt-Lunstad, Timothy B. Smith, and J. Bradley Layton. "Social Relationships and Mortality Risk: A Meta-analytic Review." *PLoS Med* 7, no. 7 (2010): e1000.316.

103. **top ten causes of death:** Centers for Disease Control and Prevention, National Center for Injury Prevention and Control. Web-Based Injury Statistics Query and Reporting System (WISQARS) (2005), accessed December 14, 2016, http://www.cdc.gov/injury/wisqars.

103. **ostracism from a peer group:** Nicole Heilbron and Mitchell J. Prinstein. "Adolescent Peer Victimization, Peer Status, Suicidal Ideation, and Nonsuicidal Self-injury: Examining Concurrent and Longitudinal Associations." *Merrill-Palmer Quarterly* 56, no. 3 (2010): 388–419;

Mitch Van Geel, Paul Vedder, and Jenny Tanilon. "Relationship Between Peer Victimization, Cyberbullying, and Suicide in Children and Adolescents: A Meta-analysis." *JAMA Pediatrics* 168, no. 5 (2014): 435–42.

103. **Kathleen Mullan Harris, a sociologist:** Yang Claire Yang et al. "Social Relationships and Physiological Determinants of Longevity Across the Human Life Span." *Proceedings of the National Academy of Sciences* 113, no. 3 (2016): 578–83.

104. **participating in a support group:** David Spiegel, Helena C. Kraemer, Joan R. Bloom, and Ellen Gottheil. "Effect of Psychosocial Treatment on Survival of Patients with Metastatic Breast Cancer." *Lancet* 334, no. 8668 (1989): 888–91; Bert N. Uchino, John T. Cacioppo, and Janice K. Kiecolt-Glaser. "The Relationship Between Social Support and Physiological Processes: A Review with Emphasis on Underlying Mechanisms and Implications for Health." *Psychological Bulletin* 119, no. 3 (1996): 488.

105. **cortisol has a Goldilocks-like quality:** Bruce S. McEwen. "Stress, Adaptation, and Disease: Allostasis and Allostatic Load." *Annals of the New York Academy of Sciences* 840, no. 1 (1998): 33–44; Anna C. Phillips, Annie T. Ginty, and Brian M. Hughes. "The Other Side of the Coin: Blunted Cardiovascular and Cortisol Reactivity Are Associated with Negative Health Outcomes." *International Journal of Psychophysiology* 90, no. 1 (2013): 1–7.

105. **Casey Calhoun and I set out:** Casey D. Calhoun et al. "Relational Victimization, Friendship, and Adolescents' Hypothalamic–Pituitary–Adrenal Axis Responses to an In Vivo Social Stressor." *Development and Psychopathology* 26, no. 3 (2014): 605–18; Ellen Peters, J. Marianne Riksen-Walraven, Antonius H. N. Cillessen, and Carolina de Weerth. "Peer Rejection and HPA Activity in Middle Childhood: Friendship Makes a Difference." *Child Development* 82, no. 6 (2011): 1906–20; Casey D. Calhoun. "Depressive Symptoms and Acute HPA Axis Stress Regulation in the Context of Adolescent Girls' Friendships." Dissertation Abstracts International, forthcoming.

108. **Neither Mary Sue nor her town:** *Pleasantville*. Directed by Gary Ross. Los Angeles: New Line Cinema, 1998.

108. **UCLA neuroscientist Naomi Eisenberger:** Naomi I. Eisenberger, Matthew D. Lieberman, and Kipling D. Williams. "Does Rejection Hurt? An fMRI Study of Social Exclusion." *Science* 302, no. 5643 (2003): 290–92; Naomi I. Eisenberger and Matthew D. Lieberman. "Why Rejection Hurts: A Common Neural Alarm System for Physical and Social Pain." *Trends in Cognitive Sciences* 8, no. 7 (2004): 294–300; Naomi I. Eisenberger. "Social Pain and the Brain: Controversies, Questions, and Where to Go from Here." *Annual Review of Psychology* 66 (2015): 601–29.

110. **implicate the same brain regions:** Helen E. Fisher et al. "Reward, Addiction, and Emotion Regulation Systems Associated with Rejection in Love." *Journal of Neurophysiology* 104, no. 1 (2010): 51–60; Ethan Kross et al. "Neural Dynamics of Rejection Sensitivity." *Journal of Cognitive Neuroscience* 19, no. 6 (2007): 945–56; Harald Gündel et al. "Functional Neuroanatomy of Grief: An fMRI Study." *American Journal of Psychiatry* 160, no. 11 (2003): 1946–53; Eisenberger. "Social Pain and the Brain." 601–29.

110. **taking a Tylenol:** C. Nathan DeWall et al. "Acetaminophen Reduces Social Pain—Behavioral and Neural Evidence." *Psychological Science* 21, no. 7 (2010): 931–37.

111. **Some of its genes are turned:** C. D. Allis, T. Jenuwein, D. Reinberg, and M. Caparros. *Epigenetics.* Cold Spring Harbor, NY: Cold Spring Harbor Laboratory Press, 2007.

111. **human social genomics:** George M. Slavich and Steven W. Cole. "The Emerging Field of Human Social Genomics." *Clinical Psychological Science* 1, no. 3 (2013): 331–48.

111. **"exquisitely sensitive to social rejection":** Personal interview with George Slavich, October 11, 2014.

112. **a wide range of diseases:** Christine Gorman and Alice Park. "Inflammation Is a Secret Killer: A Surprising Link Between Inflammation and

Asthma, Heart Attacks, Cancer, Alzheimer's and Other Diseases." *Time*, February 23, 2004.

113. **when we merely imagine being rejected:** George M. Slavich and Michael R. Irwin. "From Stress to Inflammation and Major Depressive Disorder: A Social Signal Transduction Theory of Depression." *Psychological Bulletin* 140, no. 3 (2014): 774; personal interview with George Slavich, October 11, 2014.

113. **trigger an entire "molecular remodeling":** Personal interview with George Slavich, October 11, 2014.

113. **have no close confidant has tripled:** Holt-Lunstad, Smith, and Layton. "Social Relationships and Mortality Risk." e1000.316.

114. **all networked within a matrix:** *The Matrix*. Directed by Lana and Lilly Wachowski. Los Angeles: Warner Brothers, 1999.

CHAPTER 5. The Popularity Boomerang: How We Create the World We Live In

119. **remarkably similar across the life span:** Willard W. Hartup and Nan Stevens. "Friendships and Adaptation in the Life Course." *Psychological Bulletin* 121, no. 3 (1997): 355.

120. **benefits enjoyed by Accepted people:** Parker and Asher. "Peer Relations and Later Personal Adjustment." 357; Scott D. Gest, Arturo Sesma Jr., Ann S. Masten, and Auke Tellegen. "Childhood Peer Reputation as a Predictor of Competence and Symptoms 10 Years Later." *Journal of Abnormal Child Psychology* 34, no. 4 (2006): 507–24; Xinyin Chen et al. "Sociability and Prosocial Orientation as Predictors of Youth Adjustment: A Seven-Year Longitudinal Study in a Chinese Sample." *International Journal of Behavioral Development* 26, no. 2 (2002): 128–36; also see Peter Zettergren, Lars R. Bergman, and Margit Wångby. "Girls' Stable Peer Status and Their Adulthood Adjustment: A Longitudinal Study from Age 10 to Age 43." *International Journal of Behavioral Development* 30, no. 4 (2006): 315–25; Jelena

Obradović, Keith B. Burt, and Ann S. Masten. "Testing a Dual Cascade Model Linking Competence and Symptoms over 20 Years from Childhood to Adulthood." *Journal of Clinical Child & Adolescent Psychology* 39, no. 1 (2009): 90–102; Michelle M. Englund et al. "Early Roots of Adult Competence: The Significance of Close Relationships from Infancy to Early Adulthood." *International Journal of Behavioral Development* 35, no. 6 (2011): 490–96; Ann S. Masten et al. "The Significance of Childhood Competence and Problems for Adult Success in Work: A Developmental Cascade Analysis." *Development and Psychopathology* 22, no. 3 (2010): 679–94.

120. **a specific set of traits:** Newcomb, Bukowski, and Pattee. "Children's Peer Relations." 99.

121. **"brown eyes, blue eyes" demonstration:** William Peters. *A Class Divided: Then and Now*, vol. 14021. New Haven, CT: Yale University Press, 1987.

123. **ice-cream sales and the growth:** Craig A. Anderson et al. "Temperature and Aggression." *Advances in Experimental Social Psychology* 32 (2000): 63–133.

123. **ten thousand Swedish youth:** Almquist and Brännström. "Childhood Peer Status and the Clustering of Social, Economic, and Health-Related Circumstances in Adulthood." 67–75; Gustafsson et al. "Do Peer Relations in Adolescence Influence Health in Adulthood?" e39385.

124. **over 150 tenth-grade students:** Mitchell J. Prinstein and Julie Wargo Aikins. "Cognitive Moderators of the Longitudinal Association Between Peer Rejection and Adolescent Depressive Symptoms." *Journal of Abnormal Child Psychology* 32, no. 2 (2004): 147–58.

128. **form emotionally intimate friendships:** Jeffrey G. Parker and Steven R. Asher. "Friendship and Friendship Quality in Middle Childhood: Links with Peer Group Acceptance and Feelings of Loneliness and Social Dissatisfaction." *Developmental Psychology* 29, no. 4 (1993): 611.

128. **participate in monogamous romantic partnerships:** W. Furman,

B. B. Feiring, and C. Feiring. *The Development of Romantic Relationships in Adolescence*. Cambridge, MA: Cambridge University Press, 1999.

128. **behaviors that lead to being disliked:** Newcomb, Bukowski, and Pattee. "Children's Peer Relations." 99.

129. **This cycle can start as early:** Jennifer E. Lansford et al. "Developmental Cascades of Peer Rejection, Social Information Processing Biases, and Aggression During Middle Childhood." *Development and Psychopathology* 22, no. 3 (2010): 593–602.

133. **Social mimicry has subtle yet pervasive:** Jessica L. Lakin, Valerie E. Jefferis, Clara Michelle Cheng, and Tanya L. Chartrand. "The Chameleon Effect as Social Glue: Evidence for the Evolutionary Significance of Nonconscious Mimicry." *Journal of Nonverbal Behavior* 27, no. 3 (2003): 145–62; Roland Neumann and Fritz Strack. "'Mood Contagion': The Automatic Transfer of Mood Between Persons." *Journal of Personality and Social Psychology* 79, no. 2 (2000): 211; John A. Bargh and Tanya L. Chartrand. "The Unbearable Automaticity of Being." *American Psychologist* 54, no. 7 (1999): 462.

134. **overlap in the parts:** Harald G. Wallbott. "Congruence, Contagion, and Motor Mimicry: Mutualities in Nonverbal Exchange." In *Mutualities in Dialogue*. Eds. I. Markova, C. F. Graumann, and K. Foppa. New York: Cambridge University Press, 1995, 82–98.

134. **walked more slowly afterward:** John A. Bargh, Mark Chen, and Lara Burrows. "Automaticity of Social Behavior: Direct Effects of Trait Construct and Stereotype Activation on Action." *Journal of Personality and Social Psychology* 71, no. 2 (1996): 230.

134. **speed-dating event in Belgium:** Madeline L. Pe, Ian H. Gotlib, Wim Van Den Noortgate, and Peter Kuppens. "Revisiting Depression Contagion as a Mediator of the Relation Between Depression and Rejection: A Speed-Dating Study." *Clinical Psychological Science* 4, no. 4 (2015): 675–82.

139. **pattern as "excessive reassurance-seeking":** Thomas E. Joiner and Gerald I. Metalsky. "Excessive Reassurance Seeking: Delineating a Risk

Factor Involved in the Development of Depressive Symptoms." *Psychological Science* 12, no. 5 (2001): 371–78; James C. Coyne. "Toward an Interactional Description of Depression." *Psychiatry* 39, no. 1 (1976): 28–40.

140. **negative transactions, starting in adolescence:** Prinstein et al. "Adolescent Girls' Interpersonal Vulnerability to Depressive Symptoms." 676.

CHAPTER 6. Our High School Legacy: How We Can Conquer the Prom Queen Today

147. **Was height related to how much:** Nicola Persico, Andrew Postlewaite, and Dan Silverman. *The Effect of Adolescent Experience on Labor Market Outcomes: The Case of Height*. No. w10522, Cambridge, MA: National Bureau of Economic Research, 2004.

149. **our brains were built:** Emerging evidence on the importance of autobiographical memory on present and future cognition comes from Donna Rose Addis et al. "Constructive Episodic Simulation of the Future and the Past: Distinct Subsystems of a Core Brain Network Mediate Imagining and Remembering." *Neuropsychologia* 47, no. 11 (2009): 2222–38; R. Nathan Spreng and Cheryl L. Grady. "Patterns of Brain Activity Supporting Autobiographical Memory, Prospection, and Theory of Mind, and Their Relationship to the Default Mode Network." *Journal of Cognitive Neuroscience* 22, no. 6 (2010): 1112–23; Mathieu Roy, Daphna Shohamy, and Tor D. Wager. "Ventromedial Prefrontal-Subcortical Systems and the Generation of Affective Meaning." *Trends in Cognitive Sciences* 16, no. 3 (2012): 147–56.

149. **our brains develop more dramatically:** Sarah-Jayne Blakemore and Suparna Choudhury. "Development of the Adolescent Brain: Implications for Executive Function and Social Cognition." *Journal of Child Psychology and Psychiatry* 47, no. 3–4 (2006): 296–312; Joan Stiles and Terry L. Jernigan. "The Basics of Brain Development." *Neuropsychology Review* 20, no. 4 (2010): 327–48; Rhoshel K. Lenroot and Jay N.

Giedd. "Brain Development in Children and Adolescents: Insights from Anatomical Magnetic Resonance Imaging." *Neuroscience & Biobehavioral Reviews* 30, no. 6 (2006): 718–29.

151. **more than was ever realized:** Lindquist et al. "The Brain Basis of Emotion." 121–43; Lindquist and Barrett. "A Functional Architecture of the Human Brain." 533–40.

151. **steps of "social information processing":** Nicki R. Crick and Kenneth A. Dodge. "A Review and Reformulation of Social Information-Processing Mechanisms in Children's Social Adjustment." *Psychological Bulletin* 115, no. 1 (1994): 74; Elizabeth A. Lemerise and William F. Arsenio. "An Integrated Model of Emotion Processes and Cognition in Social Information Processing." *Child Development* 71, no. 1 (2000): 107–18.

153. **calling itself a "health studio":** Sally E. Bahner. "Marlow's Prostitution Update: Investigation Ongoing; More Arrests Expected," *Branford Eagle* (CT), January 20, 2010.

156. **British psychologists conducted a study:** Munirah Bangee et al. "Loneliness and Attention to Social Threat in Young Adults: Findings from an Eye Tracker Study." *Personality and Individual Differences* 63 (2014): 16–23.

157. **"We do not see things":** Anaïs Nin. *Seduction of the Minotaur.* Chicago: Swallow Press, 1972, 124; *Babylonian Talmud: Tractate Berakoth*, Folio 55b. Translated into English by Maurice Simon, under the editorship of Rabbi Dr. Isidore Epstein, accessed March 8, 2014, halakhah .com.

157. **screening out all the positive:** Kenneth A. Dodge, Roberta R. Murphy, and Kathy Buchsbaum. "The Assessment of Intention-Cue Detection Skills in Children: Implications for Developmental Psychopathology." *Child Development* 55, no. 1 (1984): 163–73; Kenneth A. Dodge and Angela M. Tomlin. "Utilization of Self-Schemas as a Mechanism of Interpretational Bias in Aggressive Children." *Social Cognition* 5, no. 3 (1987): 280; Karen R. Gouze. "Attention and Social Problem Solving as Correlates of Aggression in Preschool Males." *Journal of Abnormal Child Psychology* 15, no. 2 (1987): 181–97.

158. **referred to as "depressive realism":** Michael T. Moore and David M. Fresco. "Depressive Realism: A Meta-analytic Review." *Clinical Psychology Review* 32, no. 6 (2012): 496–509.

159. **better at identifying others' feelings:** Adam D. Galinsky, Joe C. Magee, M. Ena Inesi, and Deborah H. Gruenfeld. "Power and Perspectives Not Taken." *Psychological Science* 17, no. 12 (2006): 1068–74; Michael W. Kraus, Stéphane Côté, and Dacher Keltner. "Social Class, Contextualism, and Empathic Accuracy." *Psychological Science* 21, no. 11 (2010): 1716–23; Keely A. Muscatell et al. "Social Status Modulates Neural Activity in the Mentalizing Network." *Neuroimage* 60, no. 3 (2012): 1771–77.

160. **a box, while three colored circles:** Adapted from: Fritz Heider and Marianne Simmel. "An Experimental Study of Apparent Behavior." *American Journal of Psychology* 57, no. 2 (1944): 243–59.

163. **"rejection sensitivity" bias:** Geraldine Downey and Scott I. Feldman. "Implications of Rejection Sensitivity for Intimate Relationships." *Journal of Personality and Social Psychology* 70, no. 6 (1996): 1327.

163. **a host of related negative outcomes:** Rachel M. Calogero, Lora E. Park, Zara K. Rahemtulla, and Katherine C. D. Williams. "Predicting Excessive Body Image Concerns Among British University Students: The Unique Role of Appearance-Based Rejection Sensitivity." *Body Image* 7, no. 1 (2010): 78–81; Renzo Bianchi, Irvin Sam Schonfeld, and Eric Laurent. "Interpersonal Rejection Sensitivity Predicts Burnout: A Prospective Study." *Personality and Individual Differences* 75 (2015): 216–19; Teresa J. Marin and Gregory E. Miller. "The Interpersonally Sensitive Disposition and Health: An Integrative Review." *Psychological Bulletin* 139, no. 5 (2013): 941; Mattie Tops et al. "Rejection Sensitivity Relates to Hypocortisolism and Depressed Mood State in Young Women." *Psychoneuroendocrinology* 33, no. 5 (2008): 551–59; Katherine A. Pearson, Edward R. Watkins, and Eugene G. Mullan. "Rejection Sensitivity Prospectively Predicts Increased Rumination." *Behaviour Research and Therapy* 49, no. 10 (2011): 597–605; Ozlem Ayduk, Geraldine Downey, and Minji Kim. "Rejection Sensitivity and

Depressive Symptoms in Women." *Personality and Social Psychology Bulletin* 27, no. 7 (2001): 868–77.

164. **neural responses to social evaluation:** Katherine E. Powers, Leah H. Somerville, William M. Kelley, and Todd F. Heatherton. "Rejection Sensitivity Polarizes Striatal-Medial Prefrontal Activity When Anticipating Social Feedback." *Journal of Cognitive Neuroscience* 25, no. 11 (2013): 1887–95.

164. **A person with a hostile attribution bias:** William Nasby, Brian Hayden, and Bella M. DePaulo. "Attributional Bias Among Aggressive Boys to Interpret Unambiguous Social Stimuli as Displays of Hostility." *Journal of Abnormal Psychology* 89, no. 3 (1980): 459; Kenneth A. Dodge. "Social Cognition and Children's Aggressive Behavior." *Child Development* 51, no. 1 (1980): 162–70; Esther Feldman and Kenneth A. Dodge. "Social Information Processing and Sociometric Status: Sex, Age, and Situational Effects." *Journal of Abnormal Child Psychology* 15, no. 2 (1987): 211–27.

165. **some children never outgrow this bias:** Nicole E. Werner. "Do Hostile Attribution Biases in Children and Parents Predict Relationally Aggressive Behavior?" *Journal of Genetic Psychology* 173, no. 3 (2012): 221–45; Zhiqing E. Zhou, Yu Yan, Xin Xuan Che, and Laurenz L. Meier. "Effect of Workplace Incivility on End-of-Work Negative Affect: Examining Individual and Organizational Moderators in a Daily Diary Study." *Journal of Occupational Health Psychology* 20, no. 1 (2015): 117; Christopher I. Eckhardt, Krista A. Barbour, and Gerald C. Davison. "Articulated Thoughts of Maritally Violent and Nonviolent Men During Anger Arousal." *Journal of Consulting and Clinical Psychology* 66, no. 2 (1998): 259.

166. **These "response biases":** Elizabeth A Lemerise et al. "Do Provocateurs' Emotion Displays Influence Children's Social Goals and Problem Solving?" *Journal of Abnormal Child Psychology* 34, no. 4 (2006): 555–67; David A. Nelson and Nicki R. Crick. "Rose-Colored Glasses: Examining the Social Information-Processing of Prosocial Young Adolescents." *Journal of Early Adolescence* 19, no. 1 (1999): 17–38.

167. **very emotional or are intoxicated:** Richard L. Ogle and William R. Miller. "The Effects of Alcohol Intoxication and Gender on the Social Information Processing of Hostile Provocations Involving Male and Female Provocateurs." *Journal of Studies on Alcohol* 65, no. 1 (2004): 54–62; David Schultz, Angela Grodack, and Carroll E. Izard. "State and Trait Anger, Fear, and Social Information Processing." *International Handbook of Anger*. New York: Springer, 2010, 311–25.

CHAPTER 7. Clicks and Cliques: What's Not to "Like"?

169. **It was this conversation:** Alan Farnham. "Hot or Not's Co-Founders: Where Are They Now?" ABC News, June 2, 2014.

170. **four years earlier that Google had:** "Our History in Depth," accessed July 8, 2016, https://www.google.com/about/company/history/.

170. **Zuckerberg's own Harvard-based Facemash:** Katharine A. Kaplan. "Facemash Creator Survives Ad Board." *Harvard Crimson*, November 19, 2003.

172. **social media may have the same:** Lauren E. Sherman et al. "The Power of the Like in Adolescence: Effects of Peer Influence on Neural and Behavioral Responses to Social Media." *Psychological Science* 27 no. 7 (2016); 1027–35.

173. **the Pew Research Center:** Amanda Lenhart. "Teen, Social Media and Technology Overview 2015." Pew Research Center, April 2015; Andrew Perrin. "Social Networking Usage: 2005–2015." Pew Research Center, October 2015, retrieved from http://www.pewinternet.org/2015/10/08/2015/Social-Networking-Usage-2005-2015.

174. **literature as "Facebook depression":** Lauren A. Jelenchick, Jens C. Eickhoff, and Megan A. Moreno. "'Facebook Depression?' Social Networking Site Use and Depression in Older Adolescents." *Journal of Adolescent Health* 52, no. 1 (2013): 128–30.

174. **Excessive use of the internet:** American Psychiatric Association. *Diag-*

nostic and Statistical Manual of Mental Disorders (*DSM-V*). American Psychiatric Pub., 2013; Jerald J. Block. "Issues for *DSM-V*: Internet Addiction." *American Journal of Psychiatry* 165, no. 3 (2008): 306–7.

174. **resolve arguments or express relationship needs:** Jacqueline Nesi, Laura Widman, Sophia Choukas-Bradley, and Mitchell J. Prinstein. "Technology-Based Communication and the Development of Interpersonal Competencies Within Adolescent Romantic Relationships: A Preliminary Investigation." *Journal of Research on Adolescence* (2016), accessed December 14, 2016, http://onlinelibrary.wiley.com/doi/10.1111/jora.12274/abstract.

175. **NPR's *This American Life*:** Ira Glass. "573: Status Update." *This American Life*, November 27, 2015.

175. **"social comparison" and "feedback-seeking":** Jacqueline Nesi and Mitchell J. Prinstein. "Using Social Media for Social Comparison and Feedback-Seeking: Gender and Popularity Moderate Associations with Depressive Symptoms." *Journal of Abnormal Child Psychology* 43, no. 8 (2015): 1427–38.

178. **It began with an article:** "5SOS: How We Bounced Back from Unpopularity." *Tiger Beat* magazine, May 2015; "How to Be Social Media Famous!" *Tiger Beat* magazine, May 2015.

179. **"Blow Up Your Feed":** Julia Kramer. "Blow Up Your Feed: The 10 Commandments of Taking Instagram Food Pics." *Bon Appétit*, March 2016.

179. **use "known hashtags":** Jason DeMers. "50 Free Ways to Increase Your Instagram Followers." *Forbes*, June 18, 2015.

179. **the "selfie stick" market:** Global Selfie Stick Consumption 2016 Market Research Report, accessed July 9, 2016, http://www.einnews.com/pr_news/336345654/selfie-stick-consumption-industry-2016-market-analysis-and-forecast-to-2022.

179. **Russian government has released guidelines:** Payal Uttam. "Death by Selfie? Russian Police Release Brochure After Spate of Fatal Accidents." CNN, July 8, 2015, accessed July 9, 2016, https://mvd.ru/upload/site1/folder_page/006/158/477/Selfie2015.pdf.

179. **Cover Girl cosmetics:** Courtney Rubin. "Makeup for the Selfie Generation." *New York Times*, September 22, 2015.

180. **reduced their prefrontal cortex activity:** Sherman et al. "The Power of the Like in Adolescence." 1027–35.

CHAPTER 8. Parenting for Popularity: Can Mom and Dad Make a Difference, and Should They?

182. **"My Favorite Things":** *The Sound of Music*. Directed by Robert Wise. Los Angeles: Twentieth Century Fox, 1965.

183. **mothers' recollections of their own childhood:** Martha Putallaz, Philip R. Costanzo, and Rebecca B. Smith. "Maternal Recollections of Childhood Peer Relationships: Implications for Their Children's Social Competence." *Journal of Social and Personal Relationships* 8, no. 3 (1991): 403–22; Mitchell J. Prinstein and Annette M. La Greca. "Links Between Mothers' and Children's Social Competence and Associations with Maternal Adjustment." *Journal of Clinical Child Psychology* 28, no. 2 (1999): 197–210.

185. **mothers' recollections as "social frames":** Martha Putallaz, Tovah P. Klein, Philip R. Costanzo, and Lea A. Hedges. "Relating Mothers' Social Framing to Their Children's Entry Competence with Peers." *Social Development* 3, no. 3 (1994): 222–37.

186. **attractiveness is a predictor of likability:** Judith H. Langlois et al. "Maxims or Myths of Beauty? A Meta-analytic and Theoretical Review." *Psychological Bulletin* 126, no. 3 (2000): 390.

186. **Obese children, for example, are more:** Michelle J. Pearce, Julie Boergers, and Mitchell J. Prinstein. "Adolescent Obesity, Overt and Relational Peer Victimization, and Romantic Relationships." *Obesity Research* 10, no. 5 (2002): 386–93.

187. **children rated least attractive are:** Dodge. "Behavioral Antecedents of Peer Social Status." 1386–99; Brian E. Vaughn and Judith H. Langlois. "Physical Attractiveness as a Correlate of Peer Status and Social Compe-

tence in Preschool Children." *Developmental Psychology* 19, no. 4 (1983): 561; Patricia H. Hawley, Sarah E. Johnson, Jennifer A. Mize, and Kelly A. McNamara. "Physical Attractiveness in Preschoolers: Relationships with Power, Status, Aggression and Social Skills. *Journal of School Psychology,* 45, no. 5 (2007): 499–521.

187. **three months old stare longer:** Judith H. Langlois et al. "Infant Preferences for Attractive Faces: Rudiments of a Stereotype?" *Developmental Psychology* 23, no. 3 (1987): 363.

187. **fussy around unattractive strangers:** Judith H. Langlois, Lori A. Roggman, and Loretta A. Rieser-Danner. "Infants' Differential Social Responses to Attractive and Unattractive Faces." *Developmental Psychology* 26, no. 1 (1990): 153.

187. **attractive faces signal good genetic health:** S. Michael Kalick, Leslie A. Zebrowitz, Judith H. Langlois, and Robert M. Johnson. "Does Human Facial Attractiveness Honestly Advertise Health? Longitudinal Data on an Evolutionary Question." *Psychological Science* 9, no. 1 (1998): 8–13; Langlois et al. "Maxims or Myths of Beauty?" 390.

188. **large part on facial "averageness":** Michelle de Haan, Mark H. Johnson, Daphne Maurer, and David I. Perrett. "Recognition of Individual Faces and Average Face Prototypes by 1- and 3-Month-Old Infants." *Cognitive Development* 16, no. 2 (2001): 659–78; Judith H. Langlois and Lori A. Roggman. "Attractive Faces Are Only Average." *Psychological Science* 1, no. 2 (1990): 115–21; Judith H. Langlois, Lori A. Roggman, and Lisa Musselman. "What Is Average and What Is Not Average About Attractive Faces?" *Psychological Science* 5, no. 4 (1994): 214–20.

188. **teachers pay greater attention:** Vicki Ritts, Miles L. Patterson, and Mark E. Tubbs. "Expectations, Impressions, and Judgments of Physically Attractive Students: A Review." *Review of Educational Research* 62, no. 4 (1992): 413–26.

188. **Even parents, in subtle ways:** Judith H. Langlois, Jean M. Ritter, Rita J. Casey, and Douglas B. Sawin. "Infant Attractiveness Predicts Maternal Behaviors and Attitudes." *Developmental Psychology* 31, no. 3 (1995): 464.

188. **referred to as "behavioral inhibition":** Jerome Kagan, J. Steven Reznick, and Nancy Snidman. "The Physiology and Psychology of Behavioral Inhibition in Children." *Annual Progress in Child Psychiatry & Child Development* (1988): 102–27; Nathan A. Fox et al. "Behavioral Inhibition: Linking Biology and Behavior Within a Developmental Framework." *Annual Review of Psychology* 56 (2005): 235–62; Kenneth H. Rubin and Robert J. Coplan, eds. *The Development of Shyness and Social Withdrawal.* New York: Guilford Press, 2010.

190. **kind of parents we become:** Lisa Allison Efron. "Linkages Between Parents' Childhood Relationships with Their Parents and Peers, Parents' Relationships with Their Children, and Children's Peer Relationships." *Dissertation Abstracts International* 56 (1998): 3504.

190. **an aggressive social environment:** Ross D. Parke et al. "Familial Contribution to Peer Competence Among Young Children: The Role of Interactive and Affective Processes." In *Family-Peer Relationships: Modes of Linkage.* Hillsdale, NJ: Lawrence Erlbaum Associates, 1992, 107–34.

190. **persist across generations of a family:** Lisa Serbin and Jennifer Karp. "Intergenerational Studies of Parenting and the Transfer of Risk from Parent to Child." *Current Directions in Psychological Science* 12, no. 4 (2003): 138–42.

190. **a world of differences:** Avshalom Caspi et al. "Maternal Expressed Emotion Predicts Children's Antisocial Behavior Problems: Using Monozygotic-Twin Differences to Identify Environmental Effects on Behavioral Development." *Developmental Psychology* 40, no. 2 (2004): 149; Ana B. Magaña et al. "A Brief Method for Assessing Expressed Emotion in Relatives of Psychiatric Patients." *Psychiatry Research* 17, no. 3 (1986): 203–12.

191. **subsequently grow up to be unpopular:** Tara S. Peris and Stephen P. Hinshaw. "Family Dynamics and Preadolescent Girls with ADHD: The Relationship Between Expressed Emotion, ADHD Symptomatology, and Comorbid Disruptive Behavior." *Journal of Child Psychology and Psychiatry* 44, no. 8 (2003): 1177–90.

192. **depressed mothers may differ:** Carolyn Zahn-Waxler, Susanne Denham, Ronald J. Iannotti, and E. Mark Cummings. "Peer Relations in Children with a Depressed Caregiver." In *Family-Peer Relationships: Modes of Linkage*, 317–44; Geraldine Downey and James C. Coyne. "Children of Depressed Parents: An Integrative Review." *Psychological Bulletin* 108, no. 1 (1990): 50.

192. **biological reaction in the baby's brain:** Tiffany Field. "Touch for Socioemotional and Physical Well-being: A Review." *Developmental Review* 30, no. 4 (2010): 367–83; Miguel A. Diego et al. "Facial Expressions and EEG in Infants of Intrusive and Withdrawn Mothers with Depressive Symptoms." *Depression and Anxiety* 15, no. 1 (2002): 10–17.

192. **the concept of turn taking:** Robert M. Hodapp, Eugene C. Goldfield, and Chris J. Boyatzis. "The Use and Effectiveness of Maternal Scaffolding in Mother-Infant Games." *Child Development* 55, no. 3 (1984): 772–81.

193. **how to regulate them:** Adi Granat, Reuma Gadassi, Eva Gilboa-Schechtman, and Ruth Feldman. "Maternal Depression and Anxiety, Social Synchrony, and Infant Regulation of Negative and Positive Emotions." *Emotion* (2016), accessed December 14, 2016, doi:10.1037/emo000.0204.

194. **experiencing a clinically significant:** Benjamin L. Hankin et al. "Development of Depression from Preadolescence to Young Adulthood: Emerging Gender Differences in a 10-Year Longitudinal Study." *Journal of Abnormal Psychology* 107, no. 1 (1998): 128.

194. **the parent-child "attachment":** Mary D. Salter Ainsworth, Mary C. Blehar, Everett Waters, and Sally Wall. *Patterns of Attachment: A Psychological Study of the Strange Situation.* Oxford, UK: Lawrence Erlbaum Associates, 1978. Reissued by Psychology Press, 2015.

195. **far more interpersonal success:** J. Elicker, Michelle England, and L. Alan Sroufe. "Predicting Peer Competence and Peer Relationships in Childhood from Early Parent-Child Relationships." In *Family-Peer Relationships: Modes of Linkage*. 77–106.

195. **twelve-month-olds who were adopted:** Geert-Jan J. M. Stams, Femmie Juffer, and Marinus H. van IJzendoorn. "Maternal Sensitivity, Infant Attachment, and Temperament in Early Childhood Predict Adjustment in Middle Childhood: The Case of Adopted Children and Their Biologically Unrelated Parents." *Developmental Psychology* 38, no. 5 (2002): 806.

196. **differences that help set the stage:** Kevin MacDonald and Ross D. Parke. "Bridging the Gap: Parent-Child Play Interaction and Peer Interactive Competence." *Child Development* 55, no. 4 (1984): 1265–77; Eric W. Lindsey, Jacquelyn Mize, and Gregory S. Pettit. "Mutuality in Parent-Child Play: Consequences for Children's Peer Competence." *Journal of Social and Personal Relationships* 14, no. 4 (1997): 523–38.

196. **Some dominate, set stern limits:** Kenneth H. Rubin et al. "Intrapersonal and Maternal Correlates of Aggression, Conflict, and Externalizing Problems in Toddlers." *Child Development* 69, no. 6 (1998): 1614–29.

196. **The way that fathers play:** Eric W. Lindsey, Penny R. Cremeens, and Yvonne M. Caldera. "Mother-Child and Father-Child Mutuality in Two Contexts: Consequences for Young Children's Peer Relationships." *Infant and Child Development* 19, no. 2 (2010): 142–60; Gary W. Ladd and Gregory S. Pettit. "Parenting and the Development of Children's Peer Relationships." *Handbook of Parenting Volume 5: Practical Issues in Parenting* (2002): 268.

197. **parents who are hypersensitive:** Regina A. Finnegan, Ernest V. E. Hodges, and David G. Perry. "Victimization by Peers: Associations with Children's Reports of Mother-Child Interaction." *Journal of Personality and Social Psychology* 75, no. 4 (1998): 1076.

197. **directly intervening in their social lives:** Ladd and Pettit. "Parenting and the Development of Children's Peer Relationships." 268.

199. **psychologists call this "scaffolding":** Ibid.; Gary W. Ladd and Craig H. Hart. "Creating Informal Play Opportunities: Are Parents' and Preschoolers' Initiations Related to Children's Competence with Peers?" *Developmental Psychology* 28, no. 6 (1992): 1179; Navaz P. Bhavnagri

and Ross D. Parke. “Parents as Direct Facilitators of Children’s Peer Relationships: Effects of Age of Child and Sex of Parent.” *Journal of Social and Personal Relationships* 8, no. 3 (1991): 423–40.

200. **a play session with other toddlers:** Bhavnagri and Parke. “Parents as Direct Facilitators of Children’s Peer Relationships.” 423–40.

200. **parents monitor from afar:** Gary W. Ladd and Beckie S. Golter. “Parents’ Management of Preschooler’s Peer Relations: Is It Related to Children’s Social Competence?” *Developmental Psychology* 24, no. 1 (1988): 109.

201. **how parents coach their children:** Susan P. Lollis, Hildy S. Ross, and Ellen Tate. “Parents’ Regulation of Children’s Peer Interactions: Direct Influences.” In *Family-Peer Relationships: Modes of Linkage*. 255–281.

201. **intergenerational similarities in popularity:** Martha Putallaz. “Maternal Behavior and Children’s Sociometric Status.” *Child Development* 58, no. 2 (1987): 324–40.

202. **at least once every other day:** Robert D. Laird et al. “Mother-Child Conversations About Peers: Contributions to Competence.” *Family Relations: An Interdisciplinary Journal of Applied Family Studies* 43, no. 4 (1994): 425–32.

202. **and this predicts children’s popularity:** Ibid.; Jacquelyn Mize and Gregory S. Pettit. “Mothers’ Social Coaching, Mother-Child Relationship Style, and Children’s Peer Competence: Is the Medium the Message?” *Child Development* 68, no. 2 (1997): 312–23.

202. **still need their parents to guide:** Eric M. Vernberg, Susan H. Beery, Keith K. Ewell, and David A. Absender. “Parents’ Use of Friendship Facilitation Strategies and the Formation of Friendships in Early Adolescence: A Prospective Study.” *Journal of Family Psychology* 7, no. 3 (1993): 356.

204. **the massacre in Columbine:** James Brooke. “Terror in Littleton: The Overview; 2 Students in Colorado Said to Gun Down as Many as 23 and Kill Themselves in a Siege.” *New York Times*, April 21, 1999; CNN Library, Columbine High School Shootings Fast Facts, May 26, 2016,

http://www.cnn.com/2013/09/18/us/columbine-high-school-shootings-fast-facts/.

204. **federal anti-bullying legislation:** H.R. 4776—To Amend the Safe and Drug-Free Schools and Communities Act to Include Bullying and Harassment Prevention Programs. U.S. Congress, https://www.congress.gov/bill/108th-congress/house-bill/4776.

204. **states enacted their own laws:** Victoria Stuart-Cassel, Ariana Bell, and J. Fred Springer. "Analysis of State Bullying Laws and Policies." Office of Planning, Evaluation and Policy Development, U.S. Department of Education (2011); Policies and laws, https://www.stopbullying.gov/laws/.

204. **attention to the issue have helped:** Mark L. Hatzenbuehler et al. "Associations Between Antibullying Policies and Bullying in 25 States." *JAMA Pediatrics* 169, no. 10 (2015): e152411.

204. **some anti-bullying measures are effective:** Maria M. Ttofi and David P. Farrington. "Effectiveness of School-Based Programs to Reduce Bullying: A Systematic and Meta-analytic Review." *Journal of Experimental Criminology* 7, no. 1 (2011): 27–56; Christina Salmivalli, Antti Kärnä, and Elisa Poskiparta. "Counteracting Bullying in Finland: The KiVa Program and Its Effects on Different Forms of Being Bullied." *International Journal of Behavioral Development* 35, no. 5 (2011): 405–11.

205. **what psychologists call "attributional style":** Lyn Y. Abramson, Martin E. Seligman, and John D. Teasdale. "Learned Helplessness in Humans: Critique and Reformulation." *Journal of Abnormal Psychology* 87, no. 1 (1978): 49; Lyn Y. Abramson, Gerald I. Metalsky, and Lauren B. Alloy. "Hopelessness Depression: A Theory-Based Subtype of Depression." *Psychological Review* 96, no. 2 (1989): 358; Benjamin L. Hankin and Lyn Y. Abramson. "Development of Gender Differences in Depression: An Elaborated Cognitive Vulnerability-Transactional Stress Theory." *Psychological Bulletin* 127, no. 6 (2001): 773.

206. **Sandra Graham and Jaana Juvonen:** Sandra Graham and Jaana Juvonen. "Self-Blame and Peer Victimization in Middle School: An Attributional Analysis." *Developmental Psychology* 34, no. 3 (1998): 587.

206. **attributional style their children develop:** Judy Garber and Cynthia Flynn. "Predictors of Depressive Cognitions in Young Adolescents." *Cognitive Therapy and Research* 25, no. 4 (2001): 353–76.

206. **easy to modify:** Aaron T. Beck, ed. *Cognitive Therapy of Depression.* New York: Guilford Press, 1979; Judith S. Beck. *Cognitive Behavior Therapy: Basics and Beyond.* New York: Guilford Press, 2011.

206. **Bullies often have the harshest upbringings:** Kenneth A. Dodge et al. "Reactive and Proactive Aggression in School Children and Psychiatrically Impaired Chronically Assaultive Youth." *Journal of Abnormal Psychology* 106, no. 1 (1997): 37.

206. **often been victims themselves:** David Schwartz, Kenneth A. Dodge, Gregory S. Pettit, and John E. Bates. "The Early Socialization of Aggressive Victims of Bullying." *Child Development* 68, no. 4 (1997): 665–75; D. Schwartz, L. J. Proctor, and D. H. Chien. "The Aggressive Victim of Bullying." In *Peer Harassment in School: The Plight of the Vulnerable and Victimized.* New York: Guilford Press, 2001, 147–74.

208. **In 1991, Texas mother Wanda Holloway:** Roberto Suro. "Texas Mother Gets 15 Years in Murder Plot." *New York Times*, September 5, 1991.

208. **the story of a race car:** *Cars.* Directed by John Lasseter and Joe Ranft. Los Angeles: Buena Vista Pictures, 2006.

CHAPTER 9. Most Likely to Succeed: Choosing the Type of Popularity We Want

213. **For many, being unpopular:** Penn Medicine. "'Father of Cognitive Behavior' Aaron T. Beck Receives First Ever Kennedy Community Mental Health Award," accessed October 23, 2013, http://www.uphs.upenn.edu/news/News_Releases/2013/10/beck.

214. **Jeff Young discovered that:** Jeffrey E. Young, Janet S. Klosko, and Marjorie E. Weishaar. *Schema Therapy: A Practitioner's Guide.* New York: Guilford Press, 2003; Jeffrey E. Young and Janet S. Klosko. *Reinventing Your Life: The Breakthrough Program to End Negative Behavior . . . and Feel Great Again.* New York: Plume, 1994.

214. **every culture have in common:** Jeffrey E. Young. *Cognitive Therapy for Personality Disorders: A Schema-Focused Approach.* Sarasota, FL: Professional Resource Press/Professional Resource Exchange, 1990; Norman B. Schmidt, Thomas E. Joiner Jr., Jeffrey E. Young, and Michael J. Telch. "The Schema Questionnaire: Investigation of Psychometric Properties and the Hierarchical Structure of a Measure of Maladaptive Schemas." *Cognitive Therapy and Research* 19, no. 3 (1995): 295–321.

215. **wide range of serious life problems:** Allen, Schad, Oudekerk, and Chango. "Whatever Happened to the 'Cool' Kids?" 1866–80; Sheldon, Ryan, Deci, and Kasser. "The Independent Effects of Goal Contents and Motives on Well-being." 475–86.

INDEX